THE MASTER

The Masters of Manton

From Alec Taylor to George Todd

Paul Mathieu

Racing Post

This edition published in 2016 by Racing Post Books
27 Kingfisher Court, Hambridge Road, Newbury, RG14 5SJ

First published in Great Britain in 2010

10 9 8 7 6 5 4 3 2 1

A catalogue record for this book is available from the British Library.

ISBN 978-1-910498-97-2

Cover designed by Nathan Bines

Design, typesetting and image production by
Matt Swann Creative Ltd – MSCdesigner.com

Printed and bound in the UK by CPI Group (UK) Ltd, Croydon, CR0 4YY

www.racingpost.com/shop

To the memory of
Alexander Jean Mathieu
and
Cecilia Mary Mathieu

Contents

Illustrations

Sir Alfred Munnings' *Early Morning on Manton Downs* entranced me when I first saw it in Sotheby's 2001 Munnings exhibition, *An English Idyll*. I thought there and then that if I wrote about Manton, *Early Morning* would be a perfect accompaniment. Establishing the image rights to major works of art isn't necessarily straightforward, but a number of people made the process swift and painless. They were, first, Diane Roe at the Sir Alfred Munnings Museum, which owns copyright to most of Sir Alfred's paintings; then Joanna Ling at Sotheby's, who located the physical image; and Susan Morris at the Richard Green Gallery. A European private collector and Richard Green generously gave the final nod for the reproduction here of *Early Morning*. Sotheby's also sent me the image of the other Munnings painting in this book, *Lord Astor's Horses*.

Dorothy Thomas's father was a paid lad at Manton, and died young. Her widowed mother married another lad, Sandy Lee, and among her effects was Lee's annual salary statement from 1923. It gives an insight into the precarious financial position of manual workers in those days, though mitigated in Lee's case by an owner's present which, at least in the following year, multiplied his net wages several times over. Dorothy has the covering letter, and the photograph of the Manton staff in 1927.

David Hunt lent me Old Alec Taylor's personalised horse brasses: Peter Meakin photographed them. Erica Garratt gave me the Manton issue of *Racing Illustrated*, with its photographs of the old yard in 1895 and the brothers Tom and Alec Taylor. Roy Brennan lent the pictures of Joe Lawson and of the apprentices in the Manton chapel.

John Claydon provided the photograph of George Todd's first yard, Crossways in East Ilsley. Anne Dalgety has the photograph of her grandfather Ben Warner with his confederates. She also lent me Warner's two surviving betting books. John Cherry provided the photographs of Vic Gardner on French Design, Gordon Richards riding to the winner's enclosure on Dramatic, and Radha Sigtia with Sodium.

The front page of *The Sporting Life* from 1950 is copyright Mirrorpix, and the images of Picaroon and of the 'big four' from the years between the wars – Taylor, Astor, Tattersall and Deane – are licensed by the Rouch Wilmot Library. The National Portrait Gallery London gave permission for the use of the images of Stirling Crawfurd and the Duchess of Montrose.

With the old newspaper adage in mind, that a good picture is worth a thousand words, my thanks to them all.

The value of money

A number of reviewers of *The Druid's Lodge Confederacy* commented favourably on its conversion of the value of the pound from the 1890s and 1900s to today's equivalent. It seems to have served its purpose, which was to show that an apparently innocuous £20 bet back then equates to £1,000 now. The same re-calibration has been attempted here, with the contemporary and current values shown as, for example: £100 [*£4,400*].

Three are three caveats. First, not every old-time number is re-calculated. The aim is to avoid passages of the book which look like a store's price stickers at sale time; therefore some values are shown only in their previous or current form. In all cases, the current sterling equivalents are shown in *italics*.

Second, readers may spot sharply different conversion rates, next door to each other. The explanation is that external factors such as wars caused massive swings in the value of the currency. A pound in 1914 was worth *£49* in our money; by 1918, it had lost almost half its value, to just under *£26*.

The third proviso is that over decades, let alone centuries, the retail price index measures shopping baskets as different as a five-furlong sprint and a three-mile steeplechase. In 1914, 60 per cent of a family's budget was spent on food; now, it's only 11 per cent. We buy consumer goods that our grandparents would have thought to be science fiction. The Bank of England makes the point: 'Comparisons of prices over long periods are less accurate than comparisons [in] recent years.' Which may translate as, the RPI isn't a perfect record of changes in money's worth, but it's the only one we've got.

On the Wiltshire Downs

Extract from my sketch-book when staying at Manton

"What a place! What peace! And as I write, behold, coming up from a fold in the Downs, there appear first a row of men's heads, then their figures, then the horses. A long string – over thirty I can count, with trainer and head-lad, and following in their wake a very small boy in knickerbockers on an old cob. The latest apprentice, no doubt.

"Some of the horses I have seen at Epsom and Ascot. There's Tiberius, winner of the Gold Cup and the Goodwood Cup, and so they pass on. I murmur again, 'What a place!' and what a place for the horse. The best in the world for horses, and men too. I watch the string going farther away down, and as they go the voices of the lads die away, and they disappear again in another dip. If we followed them to the big stable yard we should see there the right place for the horse – perfect management, discipline, kindness and quiet."

Sir Alfred Munnings
The Second Burst

Chapter 1

The making of a Master

It began with a gamble, as many a racehorse trainer's career has begun. Often, the coup is in an out-of-the-way selling race, or in a modest maiden, or in a handicap with a strong betting market. What distinguished the plunge on Teddington was that it took place in the merciless scrutiny of the Derby. Teddington was owned by Sir Joseph Hawley and John Stanley, and trained by Alec Taylor at Fyfield near Marlborough.

Teddington gave Alec Taylor his first classic win in 1851, at the age of 28, in only his third season as a trainer. The young man who was to create Manton, and turn it into England's greatest racing stable, had training in his blood. He was born in Kirkby Lonsdale and raised at Murton on the outskirts of York, where his father Tom was stud groom to Robert Ridsdale, a prominent breeder, owner and gambler. Ridsdale had himself begun as a groom, but he soon worked out that there were easier ways to make money from horses than by mucking them out, so he made a book instead. He prospered, even more so when he started buying off jockeys and trainers. Before long, he had an elegantly furnished house and a string of horses. For a time Ridsdale associated with another rags-to-riches figure, John Gully, the prizefighter turned publican, bookmaker and, improbably, Member of Parliament. Together they brought off a big coup with St Giles in the Derby of 1832, but they fell out, as two such characters were always likely to. They even came to blows while out hunting, the result being a court action and damages against Gully.

Ridsdale's wire-pulling didn't always run to plan. There was a St Leger in which he decided to lay one of the fancied horses, Jerry. To protect himself, he nobbled the jockey. The two met in a coaching inn north of Doncaster to arrange matters. By chance, Jerry's trainer was staying in the same inn. He saw them arrive, and overheard their conversation. The trainer bided his time. He took no action until the jockey appeared in Jerry's colours in the Doncaster weighing room. Then he stepped forward, took the colours from the jockey and handed them to another rider. For good measure, he stationed two men at the weighing room door to make sure that no word of the jockey change leaked out. In the betting ring, Ridsdale, oblivious, was laying Jerry. By the time the horse cantered past with its new jockey, he had no hope of hedging his liabilities and, poetic justice, Jerry won the St Leger.

The fates caught up with Ridsdale after he'd taken a few risks too many. His home, his antiques, his fine wine and his horses were all sold to pay his debts. He died penniless. His stud groom Tom Taylor was out of a job, but well regarded in North of England bloodstock circles. He was invited to move to Lord Chesterfield's stud at Bretby Park in Derbyshire, to train as well as to look after the breeding side. It was a second-generation arrangement: Tom Taylor's father George had trained for Chesterfield's own father. Tom's son Alec was 13. Having spent his childhood around horses, he now learned how to train them from his father at Bretby.

Ironically, Ridsdale's dispersal sale included a foal, Bloomsbury, who won a Derby, and a yearling, Don Juan, who was sold to Chesterfield for £140 [*£6,160*] and won him a St Leger. Either colt could have rescued Ridsdale, but by then it was too late. Don Juan was trained at Malton, but increasingly Chesterfield kept his horses at home, with Tom Taylor as his private trainer.

Alec Taylor spent his teens and early twenties as assistant to his father, with a spell as stud groom for his godfather Alec Nowell in Westmoreland. The long-term outlook at Bretby wasn't overly secure: Chesterfield spent money on a heroic scale, and every now and then, a parcel of land was sold to pay for his commitments. In time, that drove Tom Taylor to quit and set himself up in Newmarket, but in the late 1840s Chesterfield gave Taylor's son Alec a wonderful opportunity. He recommended him to two wealthy owners who were on the lookout for a private trainer.

Sir Joseph Hawley and John Stanley met in Italy. Sir Joseph was a man of leisure. Having bought himself out of an Army commission, he devoted himself to sailing around the Mediterranean. When he stopped off to enjoy Florence, he amused himself running a few horses against the locals at the racecourse in the Cascine park. John Stanley introduced himself and persuaded Hawley that the grass of home was greener.

They trained in Newmarket with some success, Sir Joseph's Miami winning the 1847 Oaks, but Hawley disliked the goldfish bowl of a public yard. He and Stanley set off in search of their own stable, and they found it below chalk downs, away from any training centre. The yard was at Fyfield, just off the Bath Road to the west of Marlborough. The owner Tom Parr offered Hawley and Stanley everything they could see: the yard, the tack, the tables and chairs, and two of his horses for luck.

The trio shook hands on a purchase price of £3,000 [*£176,000*]. Parr was a noted eccentric who began peddling tea, wandering the west country, first on foot, then with a pony. He got going as a racehorse trainer with a selling plater called Weathergate which he transformed into a multiple winner, including of the Goodwood Stakes and Cesarewitch, both easily. Parr went on to win two St Legers and two Gold Cups, but somehow he was always broke. Many a time he hid in the hayloft while his head lad told the bailiffs that his master was, 'Away at a race meeting.'

The new owners had two priorities: to find a trainer and to expand. Their first choice of trainer was William Beresford, who'd just won them the Oaks, but he refused to leave Newmarket. Then Lord Chesterfield put forward Alec Taylor. Parr's stable had only eight boxes and Hawley and Stanley had bold plans, so Taylor's first task was to oversee builders who increased the yard's capacity four- or five-fold. It didn't take him long to repay his owners' confidence. The horses that Tom Parr had included in the sale were Sponge and Fernhill. They both won races, most importantly Fernhill in the 1849 renewal of Epsom's Great Metropolitan handicap, in those days one of the richest races in the calendar. On the morning of the race, Epsom was blanketed in snow. Hawley had backed Fernhill to win £20,000 [*£1.17 million*]. If the race was postponed to the next day, all bets stood: if the postponement was for longer, wagers were voided. Sir Joseph hired a host of labourers to clear the downs, the snow was brushed away, Fernhill won, and Fyfield was paid for several times over.

That autumn, Hawley sent Taylor 14 yearlings from his stud near Maidstone. Most were home-bred, but they included Teddington, a colt bought privately. His dam, Miss Twickenham, was a gift to a blacksmith and tollgate operator, Jack Tomlinson. He sent her to a first-season sire, Orlando: the outcome was the chestnut Teddington. Tomlinson liked what he saw, and he sent Miss Twickenham back to Orlando. The mare and her foal were spotted by Sir Joseph Hawley. He bought them for £500

[*£27,000*], with a contingency of £1,000 if the foal should win the Derby.

Teddington was unruly in his first exercise as a yearling. He ran away with his lad, so for a while the heavier Taylor rode the colt himself, to make him more tractable. The following March, Teddington worked with one of Taylor's three-year-olds, getting 21lb. The weight-for-age scale doesn't cater for two- and three-year-olds keeping company until May, when the younger horse's allowance is specified as 31lb, so Teddington was galloped at 10lb higher than weight-for-age, ahead of time. He won the impromptu trial so easily that Taylor worked him again with the older horse, at level weights. Teddington won again.

This is the moment when a trainer's pulse quickens. Taylor, cautious, had another look. He put Teddington in a proper trial with four of Sir Joseph Hawley's other two-year-olds: Storyteller, Confessor, The Ban and the filly Aphrodite. Teddington finished in front, but only by half a length, and to Taylor's and Hawley's consternation, the others, headed by Aphrodite, could have been covered by the proverbial blanket. The implication was that the five, having shown themselves to be much of a muchness, were probably all moderate. It turned out otherwise. The events of the next 12 months showed that, like first-time forty-niners striking a nugget of purest gold, Taylor and his patrons had watched as good a gallop as they could've prayed for. Teddington went on to win the Derby, Aphrodite the 1,000 Guineas, Confessor the Great Yorkshire handicap, and The Ban the Great Metropolitan handicap and the Doncaster Cup.

Teddington took time to perform on the racecourse to the level he showed at home. As a two-year-old, he won at Newmarket and Goodwood, but was beaten in three races, among them the Woodcote Stakes at Epsom, where he was carried wide when finishing two lengths second to Marlborough Buck. The sum of his form didn't seem to make him a serious classic contender, but at the end of the following March, the racing papers noted that Teddington had, "Sprung to 20-1" in the Derby market, "taken freely." A fortnight later when he made a winning seasonal debut in a two-horse race at Newmarket, he was down to 8-1 for Epsom. Aphrodite's 1,000 Guineas win quickened public interest in Teddington for the Derby, and for that matter in her own chance for the Oaks: by mid-May, their respective odds were 3-1 and 4-1.

Normally, winning a match by a length, in receipt of 4lb from the solitary opponent, wouldn't promote a colt to Derby favourite. The market support was based on reports that Teddington had been tried, with sensational results, against a useful five-year-old called Vatican. Taylor set up a searching trial: the 'tackle' comprised Vatican, to whom Teddington gave 6lb – the equivalent of a 26lb handicap for the younger horse; and the three-year-olds The Ban and Gladiote, receiving 21lb and 28lb respectively from Teddington. The filly Gladiote set a fast pace for the first mile of the gallop. Vatican and Teddington passed her going into the last half mile, with Teddington unextended, and at the finish, he beat the older horse easily.

The watching Hawley and Stanley thought the trial was too good to be true. "Let's try him again [tomorrow] morning," said Taylor, and they did, with the same galloping companions and the same result. If it seems outlandish to subject a Derby horse to a severe test two mornings in a row, well, Taylor liked to give his yearlings a rough gallop before Christmas, to sort out the pecking order. The gallop was over two miles.

Taylor knew exactly what Teddington had achieved in the trials with Vatican. At that time there was a champion, The Flying Dutchman, undefeated in nine contested races as a two- and three-year-old, including the Derby and St Leger of 1849. He was still unbeaten on the day that Taylor told the colt's trainer, John Fobert, that the gallop with Vatican showed him that Teddington was, "A second Flying Dutchman." The previous season, Vatican had twice run against The Flying Dutchman at level weights, beaten 10 lengths on one occasion and five lengths in the St Leger. If Teddington was 26lb and more in front of Vatican, then he was, potentially, superior to the best horse in training. Taylor and Teddington's owners could hardly have been more confident had they known that within weeks of the gallop, Vatican would win the Ascot Stakes and The Ban the Doncaster Cup.

Then Sir Joseph Hawley had a surprise. He was at York for the spring meeting and noticed that many bookmakers wanted to lay his horse for the Derby, seemingly with no concern for their liabilities: 11-2 and 6-1 were offered freely. Hawley thought this odd, and perhaps worse than odd. He caught a train south and arrived at Fyfield early the next day. Taylor acted at once. Teddington's box was changed, he was put in the care of a different lad, and a 24-hour watch was posted. The effect was instant: the layers went into hiding, and Teddington hardened again in the betting to 3-1.

From that day to the Epsom winning post, the race seems to have been the simple part. Teddington was intermittently lame in the last few days before the Derby, but won it in a common canter. At one point, he was travelling so strongly that he ran into the back of another runner. His jockey Job Marson shouted an apology: "I can't hold my horse," prompting the envious reply, "I wish I couldn't hold mine!" A furlong from the winning post, Marson took a pull at his mount and allowed his nearest rivals to draw almost alongside. Then, under hands and heels driving, Teddington went away to win easily by two lengths from the second favourite, Marlborough Buck. Sir Joseph Hawley was said to have won over £80,000 [nearly *£4.7 million*] over Teddington's Derby.

The figure is impossible to confirm. Newspapers and bookmakers have a shared interest in inflating the scale of successful gambles. The headline, 'Owner wins small bet' doesn't sell papers or excite punters. Add a few noughts and interest stirs. But Hawley's coup must have been something far out of the ordinary, because Marson said that when he mounted Teddington in the Epsom paddock, "[Hawley] says, 'Marson, you stand a thousand with me and another thousand with friends of the horse.' When I won he says, 'My friends' thousand [is] down to me,' and he gave me a cheque for £2,000 the day after. Nice gent, Sir Joseph."

Marson's windfall of *£117,000* was condemned furiously by Admiral Henry Rous, the leading racing administrator in the second half of the nineteenth century, and the creator of modern handicapping and the weight-for-age scale.

Rous's chief dislikes were tobacco, heavy betting and Sir Joseph Hawley. As Hawley was seldom seen without a cheroot and bet like a kicking horse, he affronted Rous in every possible way. On the face of it, the enmity between the two began with Rous's criticism of the excessive reward lavished on Teddington's jockey. The real sparking point was a manoeuvre by Hawley to protect his bets on Teddington.

The successive big-race wins of Aphrodite and The Ban had accelerated the public gamble on Teddington. The local paper reported years later on the scale of the Derby celebrations: "There were such goings-on at Marlborough as to this day are not forgotten." What had long passed from the memory was that Aphrodite had been a strong favourite for the Oaks. The biggest bookmaker of the day, William Davies, paid out around £100,000 over Teddington without turning a hair. In one bet, he laid

£30,000 to £2,000 [*£1.75 million* to *£117,000*] to an associate of Hawley's. "He took no more notice than of his washing bill," one paper marvelled. Davies' liabilities over a Teddington-Aphrodite double were even larger. Had the filly won the Oaks, even Davies, known as 'the Leviathan' of the betting ring, would've been broken. Davies had no choice but to approach Hawley and make him an offer. The key was Aphrodite. If she didn't run, Davies would win enough dead money over the Oaks and the double bets to guarantee Hawley a full pay-out over Teddington.

Davies began as a carpenter. He was doing some repairs in the Subscription Rooms in Newmarket. Between hammering and sawing, he overheard the members' wagers, and he made notes. When he checked them against race results, he saw that the bookmakers were doing rather better than their clients. There and then, he decided that laying the odds would be more profitable than laying floorboards.

Shortly before the Derby, a friend of Hawley's amazed a dinner gathering by offering to lay Aphrodite over the odds for the Oaks. The other guests queued up. Among them was Admiral Rous, who had £500 [*£27,000*] on Aphrodite. Hardly were the plates cleared and the port passed before Aphrodite drifted in the betting. She was scratched a few hours before the Oaks, which was won by a filly that she'd beaten easily in the Guineas. Rous's feelings can be imagined. Hawley had made safe his winnings on Teddington by sacrificing Aphrodite, and then recouped his own bets on the filly by arranging to lay her. It's unlikely that the dinner party where Rous happened to be a guest was the only venue where Hawley's commissioners plucked a pigeon or two.

Hawley acquired a reputation for double-dealing which he never shrugged off. Some years on, when he no longer trained with Alec Taylor, he had three horses entered for one of the Cup races. He withdrew the favourite and one other, and proceeded to win the race with his presumed third best. The outcome was a sensational attack in *The Sporting Times*, 'the Pink 'Un'. Over a dinner, the editorial staff decided to stir up a few prominent racing personalities. They saw that what tabloids today call a 'monstering' carried the risk of libel costs, but that would be set off by the boost to circulation. A shortlist of targets was drawn up, and Hawley was chosen to start the series. The author of the resulting piece was a wine merchant turned journalist, a perilous combination. His profile referred throughout to 'Sir Joseph Scratch Hawley' of the 'Lame 'Un Grange' stables. Its charge was damning: "Whenever any of his horses have been fairly handicapped, the public have been allowed to get well on them, and they have been scratched." There was plenty more in the same vein. The reaction met all the reporters' expectations of uproar and controversy, but they made a grievous miscalculation. Instead of civil proceedings for libel, Hawley launched a criminal suit against the editor. Ironically, the man hadn't been at the fateful editorial meeting. The first he knew of the attack was when he read it in his own paper. He wrote an open apology to Sir Joseph, but Hawley wasn't for turning, and pressed ahead. The editor was jailed for three months.

The hullaballoo over Hawley's and Stanley's £2,000 gift to their jockey left one question unasked: how much did they give to Alec Taylor? Sir Joseph can't have overlooked Taylor in the post-Derby celebrations. Taylor would leave a huge fortune when he died. Teddington laid its foundation. Only the colt's breeder, the blacksmith Tomlinson, missed out: Hawley never did pay him the full contingency promised for winning the Derby.

Chapter 2

Crawfurd, Payne and Glasgow

No sooner had Alec Taylor arrived at centre stage than Hawley brought down the curtain on the first act. He fell out with Stanley, despite their wonderful 1851 season together, and withdrew from the Fyfield yard. Stanley bought Hawley's half-share in Teddington for £1,500 [*£88,000*], and continued with Taylor as his private trainer. Lady Luck decamped with Hawley, and over the next five years Taylor won nothing significant. Matters worsened at the end of 1856 when Stanley left racing altogether, unable to sustain the cost of a private yard.

Having lost both his employers, Taylor was now a tenant at Fyfield, with no option but to offer his services as a public trainer. His fortunes turned when the Marquis of Ailesbury sent him some horses. Ailesbury seldom had more than a handful in training, but he was a good judge and, living as he did at Savernake, just the other side of Marlborough, he rode over to Fyfield most days to offer Taylor encouragement and advice. The first big winner that Taylor trained for Ailesbury was St Albans, winner of the 1860 Chester Cup and St Leger. The following year he won the City and Suburban with Cantine for the same owner. There were two second-placings in the Derby, with Palmerston in 1864 and Savernake two years later. Victory for Savernake would've been an astonishing training achievement: the colt was running his first race. Taylor was quietly confident, and Savernake was beaten only a head by the 2,000 Guineas winner, Lord Lyon. The two colts, sons of the 1852 Guineas and St Leger winner Stockwell, finished in the same order in the Doncaster classic. Further success for the Ailesbury colours came with Adventuriere in the Cesarewitch and Goodwood Cup, and a fast filly called Cantiniere, winner of six races as a two-year-old.

Taylor's wins for Ailesbury showed that his first years at Fyfield had been no fluke. That began to attract other high-profile owners. Among them were two lifelong friends and Jockey Club stalwarts, Stirling Crawfurd and George Payne. Crawfurd, 'Craw' to his friends, took his horses to Taylor after being double-crossed by a previous trainer, Rogers. In the run-up to a Cesarewitch, the stable's stayers were tried together. Crawfurd's horse Darkie won the trial so easily that Craw bet £700 [*£40,000*] at fancy prices. He then noticed that another in the stable, Mrs Taft, was being backed at even longer odds. Craw asked Rogers about Mrs Taft, and was assured that, 'She wasn't even worth putting in the gallop' that his horse had won. Lo and behold, Mrs Taft was a facile winner: Darkie was never sighted in the race. The blow was more to Crawfurd's pride than to his pocket. He had a vast fortune, derived from Scottish coal mines and property in central Glasgow. For many seasons, he hunted with the Pytchley under the mastership of Lord Chesterfield, and Chesterfield encouraged Craw to have horses with Tom Taylor at Bretby. When Taylor's son Alec became a public trainer, Craw supported him.

Moslem was the first classic winner that Taylor trained for Crawfurd, dead heating for the 1868 2,000 Guineas. It was one of the least distinguished runnings of the race. Moslem was unfancied, had a wind infirmity, and was sold soon after his unexpected win. He ended up in races like a £50-to-the-winner selling handicap at Hendon. Two years later, Taylor came close to winning his second Derby with Craw's Palmerston, but as with Moslem, the result reflected more on the trainer's skills than the horse's talent. Then along came Craw's first good horse with Taylor, the chestnut Gang Forward, by Stockwell out of Lady Mary.

Gang Forward was always well backed and always gave his running, but essentially, he was unlucky. On his two-year-old debut, he was backed at long odds on, but ran green and was just touched off. He won a couple of minor races at Newmarket and was prominent all through the winter in the ante-post markets for the classics. After a home trial at the end of April, the stable commission was launched, and Gang Forward duly won the 2,000 Guineas of 1873, albeit only by a neck from Kaiser. In the Derby, Gang Forward and Kaiser dead-heated for second. The pair clashed again at Ascot in the Prince of Wales's Stakes, when Craw had £3,000 [*£117,000*] on his colt, only to lose it when a stirrup leather broke close home, enabling Kaiser to nose in front in the last stride. Gang Forward was then made a red-hot favourite for the St Leger, but was injured on the journey north. As a four-year-old, he won the Jockey Club Cup. He lost enough races to make him a net loser for Crawfurd, but Craw had well-nigh limitless resources. In absolute terms, he was a large-scale punter: relative to his wealth, not. One of his coal mines brought him an annual income of as much as £30,000 [*£1.2 million*]. He mostly confined himself to backing his own horses, but as there were plenty of them he was never short of betting interest, and every now and then when an unconsidered outsider won in his colours, he could celebrate a nice coup.

Craw's success with Gang Forward encouraged him to spend heavily on broodmares and yearlings. His eye and his chequebook roamed everywhere. *The Sporting Times* wrote that he was, "An irrepressible buyer of yearlings [and] he could not see a first-class broodmare without bidding for her. [In] all probability he bought more costly animals that turned out failures than any man who ever lived."

George Payne was Alec Taylor's third founding owner as a public trainer. Payne came into a gigantic inheritance as a child and spent his adult life dissipating it. His father was killed in a duel by a man whose sister he'd seduced. The agreed venue was Wimbledon Common, and Payne's father arrived there from an all-night card game in St James's. No matter, he told his second, even at 12 paces his opponent wouldn't hit him. Payne senior, who was a crack shot, didn't lift his pistol. It was a fatal misjudgement. His opponent's bullet passed, appropriately enough, through Payne's crotch, and he bled to death in a nearby pub. His son George, aged six, inherited £300,000 [*£10.2 million*] and estates in Northamptonshire that produced £13,000 a year in rent, rising to £17,000 [*£714,000*] a year when he came of age. Payne was besotted with horses. First, it was hunting. As an undergraduate at Oxford, he turned Christ Church into a satellite of the Pytchley, with his horses stabled all round the college. Eventually, the authorities sent him down.

He was master of the Pytchley for nine seasons, and invested so much in the post that when he stood down, local farmers and tradesman clubbed together to present him with a magnificent 600-ounce silver table centrepiece, three-and-a-half feet high. Payne himself featured in its decoration, holding a fox above his hounds. In later life, Payne forsook the hedges and coverts of Northamptonshire in winter for the card tables of Nice, where he stayed between November and February, with regular visits to Crawfurd's house at Cannes. Payne was a skilled whist player. "For upwards of 50 years he spent more nights at play than any man that ever cut a pack of cards," it was said. And though he would moan to friends that he'd, "Hardly won a rubber for weeks, b'God," he had his moments. One long night he took £30,000 off Lord Denison, who headed straight from the card table to his wedding.

Payne's turf career had many troughs and few peaks. Considering that he went racing every day when there was a flat race meeting within reach, he was a chronically bad judge of a horse and a wager. He might have come out ahead, had he stuck to his own horses or to Alec Taylor's, but he liked to bet in every race he watched, and usually two or three runners in each. He was drawn like a moth to flame to the ante-post markets on the big handicaps, sometimes backing a dozen or more without so much as a sniff of the winner. No matter what he knew from his trainer, he was still inclined to follow a tip from the last stranger he spoke to before a race. Yet, however severe the setback, his account was settled without fail the following Monday. Aged 20, he lost the best part of *£1,250,000* over the 1824 St Leger, backing his own horse and another while laying against the winner. After the race, Payne's sympathisers were surprised when he shrugged and told them cheerfully, "It's a pleasure to lose it!"

Not surprisingly, Payne was greeted everywhere with affection and enthusiasm. Wealthy, good-natured men who lose consistently and settle promptly are always likely to be popular. His poor judgement extended to the gallops. He and his friend Charles Greville would watch as their horses were tried by Taylor, and to the delight of the riders, they could seldom even agree which horse had won. They made a fearful mess of one trial when Payne's horse Glauca worked before the Cesarewitch. They thought Glauca disappointed, oblivious to its rider being a young stable lad. With a proper jockey aboard at Newmarket, the horse won, unbacked.

Whenever Payne was asked about his horses, he put on a doleful expression and confided that they'd 'been beaten 100 yards' in their latest work. This became such a routine that wherever he went, Payne was begged to name the mystery horse who was winning all the trials so easily.

As Payne's plots unravelled, Greville became agitated. He had neither Payne's deep pockets, nor his stoical reaction to losses. Greville was unfortunate in having been raised with wealth all around his family, with little of it destined to come his way. For many years, he was Clerk to the Privy Council, the confidant of royalty and prime ministers. If that was the

Dr Jekyll part of his personality, his Mr Hyde was in thrall to gambling. His extensive diaries provide a close-up of early Victorian public life. They also contain frank confessions about racing and betting: "A month since I have written a line [of my diary]: always racing and always idleness... I went to Newmarket and lost £400 – few people, and bad sport." "Jockeys, trainers and blacklegs are my companions and it is like dram-drinking: once having entered upon it, I cannot leave it off, although I am disgusted with the occupation all the time."

One entry sums up his day as, 'Lost £100 at the races; lost £200 at whist; won £500 at hazard'[1]. He exulted over his 'best year but one' when he finished £7,000 [*£390,000*] ahead, revealing that it was better than his previous 'best' because that year, "I lost nearly all of it at play."

For a man whose position in public service called for discretion and high standards, Greville was remarkably at home in what he wrote of as, 'the atmosphere of villainy' of the racecourse. He laid one of his horses before it became public knowledge that it'd gone lame before the Derby. He addressed the resulting fury in his diary:

> "I did [what] according to racing practise I had a perfect right to do, and which nobody on the turf considers the least unfair. But it would have been quite impossible to make a judge, a jury or the public regard it as a proper or an honourable act, to bet against a horse whom I knew to be lame, [when] the person I betted against did not know."

After each new disaster, Greville would take Payne aside and mutter, "Here we are again, George." At that time, the London scene was enlivened by a rare talent for satirical verse, Lord Maidstone. He lampooned the confederates' serial failures:

> "The race is run, the favourite's beat!
> And Greville turns to Payne,
> With face at least a cloth-yard long,
> 'Well, here we are again!'"

Payne's poor luck extended to bloodstock. He was offered all Lord George Bentinck's horses in training and broodmares for *£500,000,* but he was in one of his many losing runs, and declined. He passed up the chance to own the successful sire Bay Middleton and a yearling, Surplice, who went on to win the Derby and St Leger. Payne did, though, benefit from the will of his friend and fellow owner at Fyfield, Lord Glasgow,

[1] dice

who left him £25,000 [*£1.13 million*] and half his horses. The pick of them was the stayer Musket, who sired Carbine, one of the best horses ever to race in Australia. Carbine's wins included the Melbourne Cup of 1890, when he broke both the time and weight-carrying records for the race. Carbine in turn sired Spearmint, winner of the 1906 Derby.

Glasgow stood out in an age of wealthy eccentrics. He was notoriously impatient and short-tempered, prone to arrive in Middleham before Christmas to see his young horses coming into training. He summoned the resident jockeys from their winter rest, to ride in impromptu trials. The animals that disappointed him were shot on the spot. He was lunching alone one day in the first-floor restaurant of a hotel in York when a waiter annoyed him. He pushed the man through a window to the pavement below. The waiter had a broken leg and other injuries. The manager approached Glasgow and asked what was to be done, as 'The man is badly hurt and the matter is very serious.' "Put him on my bill," replied Glasgow.

Another time, he arrived back late at his hotel and called for whisky, only to find that the bar steward had retired for the night. He set fire to the man's bed to wake him up. He was equally prone to humiliate his social equals. One day in Crockfords, Bentinck appeared and asked loudly if anyone would lay him 3 to 1 against his horse Gaper in the Derby. 'Yes,' grunted Glasgow. Bentinck persisted, unwisely: 'I want a proper bet,' to which Glasgow replied, "You can have £90,000 to £30,000" – the best part of *£5 million* to *£1.6 million* today. Bentinck retreated in silence. Gaper lost.

It was a mistake for anyone but his intimates to risk a joke at Glasgow's expense. He changed his trainers as often as his socks. One of the multitude took him round evening stables. Glasgow came across another owner's horse: he thought it, "Damn good looking. I should be proud to own him, and prouder still to have bred him." "It's a remarkable thing, my lord, but the owner has never seen his colt," replied the trainer, deadpan. After Glasgow had voiced his disbelief, the trainer revealed his punch line: the owner was blind. Glasgow turned on his heel, and took away all his horses the following morning. It probably wasn't a great loss. Glasgow seldom had a decent horse, but when anyone called him unlucky, he put them straight by pointing out that, "No one who has an income of £150,000 a year [*£6 million*] can be called unlucky."

One of his many quirks was a dislike of naming his horses. Ordinarily, this might not have mattered much: few of them were likely to cause a re-writing of the Stud Book. But as his horses were similarly, sometimes identically, home bred, he caused much confusion. At times, he had three or four animals in training who shared a sire and dam, all of them unnamed. There were two Brothers to Physalis sharing the form book with an Out of Physalis, not to be mistaken for the one who was Out of Physalis's Dam. A nadir was reached when he had a Derby runner who appears in the *Racing Calendar* as, "By brother to Bird on the Wing (foaled in 1853) – Rapid Rhone's dam." Payne, Rous and a handful of others whom Glasgow tolerated used to tease him about his runners' anonymity. Eventually and crossly, he gave in, up to a point. He then ran horses called He Has A Name, He Hasn't Got A Name, Give Him A New Name and Isn't Worth A Name.

Nowadays, George Payne would be condemned as a wastrel, for all his good nature and sportsmanship. Some in his own time took that view. The trade-off for great wealth was a contribution to the common good. Many in Payne's enviable position agreed to serve as Members of Parliament. It was a far less featherbedded role than today, since it involved no pay, no expenses, and exposure to the changeable moods of constituents at public meetings. Payne was a good speaker, including when proposing other candidates at the hustings, but he turned down every attempt to get him to stand for Parliament himself.

He made no bones about it: if he were to look after constituents' interests, it would interfere with his racing. After Payne's death, a Pytchley historian gave this biting verdict: "To what a sorry use he put all the gifts the gods had so lavishly bestowed on him. [He lost] three separate fortunes, gambled away at cards and betting. He was a man who might have done anything and did nothing." The writer continued that to take on the mastership of a fashionable hunt might seem a strange form of economy, but in Payne's case anything that kept him away from London was a saving, "For he often lost in one night at Crockford's or the Portland more than would keep the hunt for a year."

The frivolity of Payne's lifestyle was exposed as early as his mid-30s, when he was a witness in a libel trial. The plaintiff was Lord de Ros, who won so consistently at card games that he was closely watched. Amid whispers of card marking and sleight-of-hand, de Ros sued one of his accusers. Payne was the last defence witness. His cross-examiner raised doubts about his character:

"You have been a good deal connected with gambling transactions, have you not?"
"Yes, I have"
"[You have] spent a great deal of money on the racecourse, and also been connected with racing proceedings, and with cards?"
"Yes"
"In the early part of your career, Mr Payne, you were very unfortunate, I think?"
"Very much so"
"And lost a considerable fortune?"
"I lost a considerable sum of money, certainly"
"You lost, I believe, the whole of your [inheritance]?"
"Yes, sir, I lost a considerable part of it"
"You have been more fortunate since, though?"
"No, my old luck has continued pretty much throughout."

Worse followed when de Ros's counsel tore into Payne in his closing address to the jury. He mocked, "Payne, the professional gamester," and sneered that Payne, "Having started as a dupe, soon crystallised into something worse." Payne was so outraged that, even though the jury found against de Ros, he lurked outside the court for the next couple of days, gripping a horse whip, with every intention of giving the QC a good hiding. Payne was rather conspicuous, and the lawyer slipped in and out of a side door until an intermediary could pass on a, *'Sorry, it was business, not personal'* message to Payne, who reverted at once to his normal good humour.

Payne and Crawfurd were long-standing and prominent members of the Jockey Club, where they gave unquestioning support to Admiral Rous. Craw was never heard to contribute anything to the Club's deliberations, other than to follow Rous with, "Ditto," to which Payne would add, "I agree." Their backing was precious to Rous when he fought a series of battles with Sir Joseph Hawley over Turf reform. Hawley had reinvented himself after his sharp practice over Aphrodite's scratching in the 1851 Oaks. He was now a critic of 'plunging' and an advocate of various reforms. Those who knew about his past listened with disbelief to his strictures about heavy betting. Rous sensed hypocrisy, and a chance for revenge. At a meeting of the Jockey Club in May 1869, Sir Joseph tabled what became known as his Reform Bill. It included proposals to limit opportunities for two-year-olds. These included that, 'No two-year-old shall run earlier in the year than the first of July,' and, 'No two-year-old shall start for any handicap.' Thus, no two-year-olds at Royal Ascot and no nursery handicaps. Most of the proposals were thrown out, but Hawley did win a compromise motion that no two-year-old was to run before May.

Over the next few years, Hawley submitted various new ideas. All were rejected or watered down. At one meeting, he petitioned for the membership of the Jockey Club itself to be broadened, and then told the members present some home truths, to their faces. Not surprisingly, the vote was lost. At a Jockey Club meeting at the last November fixture of 1873, Rous sprang his final trap. One of his proxies moved that the May restriction on the running of two-year-olds be lifted. Crawfurd seconded the motion, Payne was unusually vocal in supporting it, and the *status quo ante* was restored. That was the end of Sir Joseph Hawley's reform plan, and he didn't outlive it by long.

Chapter 3

The creation of Manton

The patronage of Ailesbury, Crawfurd and Payne meant that by the middle of the 1860s, Alec Taylor's Fyfield yard was bursting at the seams. With the encouragement of his owners, Taylor began to think of creating his own purpose-built yard up on the downs the other side of the Bath road. He was there most days, working his horses: why not base himself in the middle of his gallops, far from prying eyes? Taylor's second son and successor, also Alec, would recall that the day when his father took him to the site chosen for his stable, "Where Manton now stands [was] a bare down without a house or even a road to it."

The yard that Alec Taylor created, with financial backing from Stirling Crawfurd, was called by a contemporary, "One of the most perfect training establishments in England." *The Sporting Life* wrote that, "Those fortunate enough to visit the Manton establishment cannot fail to be impressed by the completeness of every detail. The buildings possess a singularly attractive and quiet beauty. [There are] spacious paddocks, splendid stables, and boxes unsurpassed for size and abundance of light and air."

Taylor arranged the stables around a square courtyard, 55 yards along each side. Outside and a little below the yard was a second, smaller stable, the Lower Yard[1], housing 20 boxes. Inside the main yard, one side of the square, facing the entrance, was Taylor's own house. The other three sides of the square contained 44 boxes at ground level. The loft space above housed feed and the lads' dormitories. Immediately to the right of the gate as Taylor looked out was the blacksmith's workshop. Apart from his own house, the yard didn't have a single window facing outwards: "At night when the great doors were closed it was impossible to hold communications with anyone outside the walls." If the original impulse to

[1] The Lower Yard was demolished in the 1970s

build Manton had been to create more space and provide every facility, its location and design spoke of an additional motive: secrecy.

George Payne and Stirling Crawfurd bet in a predictable and often naïve way. They dreamed of plots with 'dark 'uns', but generally they backed their own horses whenever they ran, irrespective of the competition and to serious money. In the circumstances, one might think that it hardly mattered if third parties knew about their horses' gallops, but nothing could be further from the owners' thoughts. They detested touts, and fortress Manton was intended to put their trainer and their horses out of the reach of the touts' spies. To that end, Taylor built the yard at the foot of a deep cleft in the downs, along which he could work his horses with little or no prospect of them being watched. It was known as the Valley gallop. On the open downs, though, determined touts might be able to camouflage themselves, and Taylor went to extreme lengths to frustrate them. Within sight of one gallop, there was a tree that he thought could hide a tout. He whitewashed its trunk, to silhouette any intruder.

Taylor began training at Manton in 1870, and three years later, there was a glorious scandal when a tout issued a summons for assault. The writ wasn't in itself unusual: back in the Fyfield days, a man called Albert Smith, who'd been employed as a private schoolmaster for the Manton apprentices, was suspected of passing information to *The Sportsman*. He was sacked, after which he outed himself as a tout and, "[Incited] the lads, by drink and offers of money, to betray their master's secrets." When Smith was spotted on a footpath near the gallops, Taylor's foreman Mossum rode his pony at Smith and beat him over the head and shoulders. Mossum was fined five shillings.

Now, though, it was Stirling Crawfurd on the receiving end of the summons, and the complainant wasn't just any tout, but Thomas Fordham, brother of the champion jockey and regular big-race rider for Taylor, George Fordham. Craw spent much of his time at Manton, and seldom missed a morning on the gallops. He and Lord Ailesbury were with Taylor when they spotted a group of men lurking by some firs planted at the top of a gallop. Craw rode at them and they ran off, only to be found hiding in a nearby chalk pit. Craw belaboured the first man he caught. It was Fordham. Once the law had been called in, two quite different accounts emerged. Fordham's side wrote to Taylor's solicitors, Messrs Merriman of Marlborough, claiming that their client had been hit on the head with a heavy stick, scarcely protected by his cap. "The injuries which [he has] sustained are of a most serious character [and] will compel him to abstain from work of any description for a considerable time." Nonsense, replied Edward Merriman, and he told the magistrates, "Mr Crawfurd struck Fordham on the hat with a cane he carried in his hand, which was of a very light make, while the hat was a large and stout one. Therefore, while Fordham was undoubtedly trespassing, he could not have sustained any personal injury." The case was referred to the Berkshire Assizes. To the disappointment of the racing community and press, Fordham failed to put in an appearance and the case was 'indefinitely postponed.'

The yard's aggressive attitude towards intruders was routine at the time. The Jockey Club and *The Sportsman* were at daggers drawn for some time over the paper's publication of the results of Newmarket trials. The reports of its 'men of observation' so annoyed the stewards that most of the editorial staff were warned off the Heath. One cynic took the view that there was a safer way to get information than by lying under a damp bush or hiding in a ditch.

> "The easiest way to arrive at stable secrets, no matter how carefully they are guarded, is to establish a small book in places where horses are trained. That beats touting. By hook or by crook, some of the lads and boys *will* bet. They talk from one stable to another and [you will] be told all you need to know."

Harsh handling of touts was matched by Taylor's treatment of his employees. At Fyfield and then at Manton, he seems to have spent as much time with his solicitor as with his horses. A procession of delinquents were dragged through the Marlborough county and petty sessions. A maid and an odd-job man were charged with stealing bread and cooked meat from Taylor. He spied on them 'from information received' and saw her giving him the stolen food. She was jailed for three days, he for one day. Along with the sentences, they lost their livelihoods and their shelter, they would've been tainted for a future employer, and there was no welfare safety net. One of the few options available to people in their situation was the mop fair, an open-air recruitment market where few references were asked for, or given.

In one hearing, Taylor said that it was unpleasant to take his staff to court. "Personally I would rather give a boy a sound flogging than damage his character permanently by sending him to gaol." He often set his preference aside. Two lads vanished one night after one of them was in trouble over expenses. James Joplin had travelled Manton runners to Goodwood and Salisbury. When he arrived back his cash float was 10d [*£3.70*] short. That night Joplin and the other lads were locked up in their dormitories as usual. In the morning, he and another lad, a malcontent called John Humphreys, were missing. Two towels knotted together were hanging down into the yard. A fortnight later, Joplin and Humphreys were traced to an ironworks on Teesside. Taylor might've been expected to be glad to be rid of the pair, but no, they were hauled back to Marlborough to face the beaks, and sentenced to four and six weeks' hard labour.

Sometimes Taylor himself was on the receiving end of a summons. An apprentice, George Cole, accused him of assault. He claimed that he was hard at work grooming a horse, the sweat running down him, when Taylor hit him several times with a stick. "I was very much hurt and could hardly get any sleep at night." Taylor's ever-present solicitor Merriman cross-examined Cole. It emerged that Crawfurd was visiting the yard, and Taylor had given orders that all Craw's horses be readied for inspection. Cole was slow to respond, whereupon Taylor hurried him up with a cut from his cane. Cole then stuck out his tongue and his bottom, provoking 'another stroke or two.' His summons was thrown out, on the grounds that, "A master has a legal authority to correct his apprentice, and there did not appear to have been any great or improper violence used." The ruling was made under the Master and Servant Act, a law which by its name alone is a reminder that nothing in Alec Taylor's actions was out of the ordinary, or any harsher than the norm.

One court case suggests that in some respects Taylor could be generous, though self-interest was involved. It was a sorry tale of vandalism, assault and touting. The principal defendants were an apprentice, James Alexander, and two other boys. It was shortly after Taylor had settled the year's wages with his staff. He'd paid two of the defendants and some other boys an extra £2 to £3 [*£80 to £120*] for riding in trials - a bonus of 50 per cent on their salaries. Merriman told the Bench that, "Mr Taylor as a matter of pure generosity did give these boys [an extra] half of their earnings as an encouragement to keep their mouths shut." But it had, "Come to Mr Taylor's knowledge that [James Alexander] had been tampered with by a person in the town [and] had communicated the results of trials."

Taylor discussed the breach of security with Crawfurd, who told him on no account should he pay Alexander the same bonus as the other boys.

The sequel was that the trio took their wages down to the Lord's Arms on the Bath road, where they became 'disgustingly' drunk. As they lurched back to the yard, they damaged some young trees that Taylor had planted. They were seen by the head lad's young maidservant, who reported them. A few nights later, the boys lay in wait and beat her. While they were on remand, Alexander and the others were brought food and comfort by a man who took 'every interest in their well-being.' It was Alexander's punter, named in court as Mr Atkinson, a cricket master at Marlborough College. In those days, Marlborough and the other public schools had no provision for sports teaching. The captains of the school teams had to hire their own coaches. Atkinson was a part-time professional for the summer, or just the start of the season. He needed another income, and that came from betting on the apprentices' inside information. "The lads were unquestionably led away [by Atkinson]," charged Taylor's solicitor. They were fined 10 shillings and costs for the damage to the trees, and sentenced to two months' hard labour for assault.

Alec Taylor's determination to impose discipline on his staff was, to a degree, warranted by their local reputation. On the rare days when they were let out of Manton, they were liable to wreak havoc in Marlborough. Hatches were battened, daughters locked up. There's a hint of what was expected in the local paper's coverage of an afternoon when Lord Ailesbury lent a meadow at Fyfield to the Wiltshire Friendly Society, for its Whitsun festival. The Society organised dancing and sports, 'entered into most heartily.' Taylor allowed the stable lads out until 9 pm, and Ailesbury laid on a dinner for them. He and Taylor were both three-cheered for the day out. Plainly, it was a surprise that the day passed off peacefully, because the newspaper report ended, "The behaviour of the lads was all that could be desired."

Taylor's readiness to make an example of troublemakers can also be seen as part of a drive to establish himself as a man of standing. Like his father, he started at the bottom of the ladder, as a stud groom. Now, he was a racehorse trainer of independent means. He wanted to be recognised for that, and perhaps more generally he meant to enhance the status of his profession. Until the nineteenth century was almost ended, trainers were the junior partner in the triangle of owner, trainer and jockey. In part, this was because owners like Sir Joseph Hawley were well versed in breeding, riding and racing. They laid the plans for their horses and they made the entries. Their trainers were more akin to head lads or 'conditioners', expected only to produce a horse sound and fit at the races on the day requested. It wasn't until the 1920s that a race's winning trainer was named in the *Racing Calendar*, and it's been said that training wasn't regarded as a reputable calling until the aristocratic George Lambton made it so. That claim ignores substantial figures in the generation before Lambton: men like Mat Dawson at Newmarket, John Scott in Malton, Sam Darling at Beckhampton, John Porter at Kingsclere, and Taylor himself. But before them, trainers were usually ex-jockeys or grooms, working as tenants, bossed about by their owners and outshone by the jockeys.

Alec Taylor was emphatically not for bossing about. He was his own man, in his own stable, on his own land. Sir Joseph Hawley appeared soon after Manton had been completed, 20 years on from the little yard at Fyfield and Teddington's Derby. He liked what he saw of Manton and invited Taylor to be his private trainer again. Taylor no longer needed Hawley's patronage, and he told the baronet that life as a public trainer suited him well enough. Taylor was also gratified by a visit from Captain James Machell, the best-known owner and racehorse manager of the time. Machell was shown round. He was impressed; as he left, he handed Taylor an open cheque, limited only by the words, "Under £50,000" [*£2.62 million*]. The cheque was never presented, but it would have pleased Taylor more than any praise or recognition, because he was inordinately fond of money. In his will, he made cash bequests of *£685,000* and *£570,000* to his two daughters, yet there was far more for his wife and sons.

Along the path from groom to great wealth, he passed up few opportunities to make a profit. One day, he asked an acquaintance, the editor of the *Sporting Gazette*, how well did he know Richard Naylor, the owner of the fashionable stallion Stockwell? As Naylor was a director of the *Gazette*, the editor knew him very well. 'Can you ask Naylor for a free nomination to Stockwell?' Taylor continued: he said Stockwell's intended mate was Lady Mary, an Orlando mare. Taylor promised that Naylor, "[Wouldn't] be forgotten if anything comes of it."

The answer from Stockwell's owner was yes, "Out of consideration for Taylor's good offices in obtaining Lord Ailesbury's and other [owners' support for] Stockwell for so many years." Stockwell's fee was 200 guineas [*£10,000*]. The outcome of the 'free jump' that Taylor had negotiated was Gang Forward. The day came when he was winter favourite for the

2,000 Guineas. Stockwell's owner asked the *Gazette* editor if, "Taylor has put me on Gang Forward for the Guineas?" The question was relayed to Alec Taylor, who replied that it was now Stirling Crawfurd's business, since he'd bought Lady Mary and her foal. The editor wrote at once to Crawfurd, explaining the circumstances and asking, had it been overlooked that Stockwell's owner 'wouldn't be forgotten'? "To my utter astonishment," he said, "[Crawfurd] stated that he [had] never heard of Taylor's promise, and had actually paid Taylor the amount of Stockwell's fee when he purchased Lady Mary and Gang Forward."

Some treble: Taylor received a free stallion service worth *£10,000*, billed the full amount to Craw, and reneged on a commitment to look after Stockwell's connections. The episode left them with a reduced regard for Taylor, but didn't seem to concern Craw at all. Taylor had bred and trained him a classic winner, and 200 guineas was a drop in the ocean of Craw's millions.

Taylor's creation of his own persona had little to do with gentrification. Even a friendly observer described him as, "Rough, rugged [and] surly in demeanour to strangers, and as taciturn as his father." During his triumphant year of 1851, his mentor Lord Chesterfield complimented him after The Ban had won the Doncaster Cup. "Alec's only answer, in his usual gruff voice, was 'Good horses make good trainers, my Lord.' [His 1851 season], which would have intoxicated most young trainers of 28, left him as undemonstrative as he was at all other times." Taylor was, though, conscious of his position. It showed in the details. His farm horses' harness brasses carried his initials, or his name in full. Up on the downs, 'AT' was chiselled into the boundary stones that marked the limits of his land. As if he'd worn monogrammed shirts, he gave himself daily reminders of how far he'd climbed, how much he'd achieved.

Socialising had little appeal. The *Marlborough Times* wrote: "Locally Mr Taylor never took an active part in public affairs, even when at home. [He] was seldom seen at Marlborough, and much better known on the great racecourses of England." It wouldn't have lost him a moment's sleep. He hadn't built Manton in its isolated perch in order to mingle with his fellow men. He built it for privacy. Whatever there was to know was for himself and his owners, and for others to find out for themselves if they could. Taylor was the inspiration for the trainer Mr Nobbler in Whyte Neville's novel *Digby Grand*. Grand reflects on a visit to Nobbler's yard:

> "We stepped into Mr Nobbler's well-filled and well-arranged training stables. He proceeded to show us through his long range of stabling, answering our questions and supplying us with information in a manner so affable and communicative as to fill me with astonishment. Talk of the secrets of a racing stable, and the mysteries of the turf; everything here was as open as the day. Animals of priceless value were stripped for my inspection...
>
> "Engagements were anticipated, performances [recalled] and capabilities discussed, with a candour and openness which left nothing to be asked or surmised. Though when I came to arrange in my own mind, and to reflect [on] the miscellaneous information I had gathered from Mr Nobbler, I could not [recall] his having supplied me with a single fact by which I could put a shilling into my pocket on the race-course or in the ring."

Taylor's business was training horses, not chatting to visitors, and his first four years at Manton continued his successes at Fyfield. In 1872, he came close to a fabulous coup in the Derby with an unnamed debutant, 'Brother to Flurry', later named Pell Mell. This would've been a stroke to equal Teddington, but Pell Mell, owned by John Astley, finished inches second behind Cremorne. There was no hard luck story: Pell Mell's jockey, Thomas Chaloner, was seen to better effect than the winner's, and Cremorne had a little in hand.

But what might have been. Manton housed a colt of Craw's called Wellingtonia, who'd run well when backward in the 2,000 Guineas, and had each-way claims in the Derby. In the run-up to the race, no one had heard of Brother to Flurry. Then he worked all over Wellingtonia on the Manton trial grounds. Nowadays, to many a trainer's chagrin, mobile phones broadcast the emergence of a new star almost before the horse is back in its box. In 1872, Astley, Craw and the Manton insiders had a day or two to plan their coup. They did what many a clever man has done before and since, and sent a mug punter to work the commission. A man whose bets every bookmaker welcomed with open arms: George Payne.

He went to Tattersalls, beamed at the layers and asked them, 'What price the Brother to Flurry?' He was quoted 200-1, and had £1,000 to £5 [*£40,000 to £200*] several times. The pencillers crowded round him, and he obliged them all, through every rate to 50-1. When he left off, *The Sporting Life* reported that, "'Brother to Flurry' [was] backed at an average £1,000 to £7 to win something [like] *£1.63 million*. [He has] 'come' with quite a rush at the last moment and has been backed at long shots to win enough money to sink a ship."

Chapter 4

Carrie Red

Many a trainer has rued that it's easier to manage horses than their owners. At the start of 1876, Taylor's supporter and friend Stirling Crawfurd married Caroline, the dowager Duchess of Montrose. She was 58. He was a bachelor of 57. Taylor involuntarily acquired the owner from Hell. The Duchess of Montrose meddled, she bet, she was a bad loser, she changed her mind constantly and she tossed blame about like loose change. A few well-worn stories have attached themselves to her. Most of them trace to a passage in George Lambton's 1924 memoir, *Men and Horses I Have Known:*

> "She was blessed with a soft and most charming voice, and when things were going right was the best company in the world; but she was hot-tempered and changeable, and was easily put out if she did not get her own way. When at Newmarket she lived at Sefton Lodge, and just the opposite side of the road was the great Captain Machell, of Bedford Lodge.
>
> "Two such strong personalities at such close quarters were bound to clash. At times, they were devoted friends, at times most bitter enemies. The Duchess used to tell the most amusing stories about her friends, and had a very lively imagination. Once she had told a story she was then firmly persuaded it was true.
>
> "One night, coming home from dinner, Captain Machell, in his fly[1] unfortunately drove over and killed her favourite dog. At the moment they happened to be enemies, and the Duchess, when she told the story, declared that the Captain lifted himself up and came down with a heavy bump on the seat of the fly, so as to make certain of killing her dog.
>
> "At that time Reggie Mainwaring was one of the handicappers, and the Duchess, like many owners, always thought her horses were unfairly treated. She took a great dislike to Mainwaring, who was one of the kindest and most

[1] a small carriage

amiable of men. He was a tall, dark man, rather like Othello, with an habitual scowl on his face. The Duchess used to refer to him as 'the man who murdered his mother.' So far from this being the case, he had an old mother in Wales to whom he was absolutely devoted, and when I told her of this she said, 'Well, I can't help it, he ought not to look like that.'

"The Duchess built and endowed the little church of St Agnes at Newmarket, next door to her house. One very wet summer, when the prospects of the harvest were very bad all over the country, she had a horse in the St Leger particularly suited to the heavy going. One Sunday, the Rev. Colville Wallis put up a special prayer for fine weather. The Duchess rose from her pew and walked out of church. She sent for Wallis and said, 'How dare you pray for fine weather in my church when you know perfectly well it will ruin my horse's chance, and I shall not allow you to preach in my church again.' Mr Wallis, who knew the old lady well and had a great affection for her, did not argue the matter, and holds the living to this day.

"The Duchess owned some of the best blood[stock] in England, and she bred and raced many good horses, but their management left much to be desired, and her success was not what it should have been. She led her trainers an anxious life, with the exception of Alec Taylor, and he was supposed to be the only man she was afraid of. She was very capricious and changeable with regard to her jockeys. Huxtable used to ride for her when the weights were light. On one occasion, when he was beaten, she was furious, and said to him, 'Why on earth didn't you do as you were told and come along[2] with the horse?' 'I am sorry, Your Grace, but I should have had to come along without the horse,' was the reply.

"With all her peculiarities, the Duchess was a great lady, and a good sportswoman. She loved her horses and was a good judge of racing and a great figure on the Turf. She was always wonderfully kind to me and I was very fond of her."

Lambton's kindly assessment can be attributed both to his own gallant good manners, for he was a considerable appreciator of female charms, and to the fact that he wrote 30 years after the Duchess' death. Distance may have lent enchantment. Some of the verdicts of the time were less forgiving.

The *Sporting Mirror* asserted that, "She could never endure defeat with even a semblance of patience. The fault was never her judgement, or lack of merit on [the] part of her horse. It rested either with trainer,

[2] make the running

jockey, or judge. She was a strange figure on a racecourse, and though the late Earl of Malmesbury [said] that in the days of her youth she had as fine a figure and as stately a [bearing] as his eye had ever rested on, it cannot be said that she maintained these distinctions to the end. In fact, Her Grace did not strike the casual observer as being the true type of the high-born dame, and there is little sense in saying that she did. As she advanced in life she became more and more difficult to please, and those who fell under the lash of her tongue were not usually credited with forgetfulness."

The blue-eyed, fair-haired Caroline was hailed in her youth by a British diplomat as, "The most perfect type of English beauty." Yet the Duchess became a stout, florid woman with her hair died a vivid shade: hence her nickname, 'Carrie Red'. She dressed like a much younger woman, and when racing she wore a man's hat. She swore like a barrow boy, and into old age she kept a sharp eye out for a good-looking young man.

Caroline was the youngest daughter of John Beresford, Baron Decies. She grew up at Bolam in Northumberland and it was there in 1836 after a 'hardy but eccentric' upbringing that she was married to James Graham, the fourth Duke of Montrose. At 37, he was twice her age. They had three sons and three daughters. Montrose died in 1874. In January 1876, Caroline married Stirling Crawfurd. Their marriage joined two of the smartest addresses in London. Craw owned the leasehold of a house in Eaton Square. The Duchess lived in Belgrave Square. Craw sold up, paid off the Duchess' mortgage and moved himself and his furniture the few hundred yards across Belgravia.

At least one incident in her past should have served as a health warning: not long after her first marriage, and barely 20, she and another titled lady disgraced themselves by hissing the Queen's procession at Ascot. The Queen had been widely criticised over the shabby treatment of one of her ladies-in-waiting. The episode led to Montrose and her friend being condemned on all sides as, 'foolish, vulgar women.'

Until the Duchess burst into his life, Craw's racing affairs had been open and straightforward. His four classic successes at Manton had established his 'all scarlet' as one of the best-known colours on the racecourse. When Caroline Montrose married Craw, it might've been assumed that the management of his horses would continue as before, but what transpired was seven years of upheaval. In a will that he confirmed on his wedding day, Craw left all his racehorses, brood mares and foals to his brother-in-law. From that date, his wife's growing influence can be precisely timed: it took only 18 months for Craw to revoke his bequest. In its place, he now directed that his bloodstock be left jointly to Caroline and to George Payne. A few months more, and the Duchess persuaded Craw to buy Belle Vue Lodge in Newmarket. It was followed by the acquisition of some land at Exning that was mortgaged for £20,000. In yet another amendment to his will - there were to be 13 in seven years - Craw specified that the land should pass 'free and discharged of the mortgage debt' to Caroline if he should die first.

Before marrying, Craw devoted much legal effort to altering the terms of his legacy. It was common in those days for estates to be left 'entail' in the male line, meaning that no matter how many deserving daughters there might be, everything passed to the nearest male heir. Craw's inheritance was entail, but he changed it in such a way that while his beneficiary was his brother, his sister would inherit if his brother was childless and died before him. With prompting from the Duchess, Craw then amended his earlier change.

The new beneficiary was her eldest son, the fifth Duke of Montrose. The upset this must have caused to his brother was set off to a degree, because Craw's rent-rich Milton estate in central Glasgow remained entail. There things rested until the purchase of Belle Vue Lodge, when Craw yet again rewrote his will, this time to stipulate that the cost of paying off its mortgage should come from Milton. His last significant change directed his trustees to pay Caroline £120,000 [*£5.55 million*] if his was the first death. Crucially, this sum too was to be paid from the Milton estate. Small wonder that his brother's lawyers were busy litigating with the Duchess as soon as he died.

But thoughts of death and legal strife were far from the Duchess' and Crawfurd's minds as they set out on married life, and in her case on making pleasurable inroads into Craw's fortune. The first good horse they had together was Sefton. He was by Seculum, a Derby third who later won a Goodwood Cup, out of a daughter of West Australian, the triple crown winner of 1852. Crawfurd bought Sefton as a yearling at Doncaster for 1,000 guineas. The colt was hailed as, "The crack of the sale. [He has] great size, length and power and shows grand symmetry on the best of legs and feet." As for the purchase price, it was a given that Craw would have paid far more: "Money is no object to him when he really likes a yearling."

There was little in Sefton's two-year-old campaign for Taylor to hint at classic glory. He ran four times without winning. His best effort was on his debut, when he ran a close second in a valuable stakes race at Stockbridge, with Ascot winners back in third and fourth. Still, his breeding held out the promise of better to come over middle distances. His seasonal bow in late April 1878 saw him step up on his past form when running a half-length second in the Craven Stakes. Sefton held a mish-mash of entries. He was in all three colt's classics, but also in Epsom's 10-furlong City and Suburban handicap, which in those days was a valuable and coveted prize. On his first-season form, Sefton had been assigned just 5st 7lb.

From mid-April, Sefton had been quoted at 33-1 and 40-1 for the City and Suburban. The Craven result advanced Sefton within hours to 11-1 for the big handicap, while bets of £2,000 to £70 and £1,000 to £40 for the Derby were struck in the Subscription Rooms. There was just a doubt about Sefton's light weight. Could the stable find a strong enough jockey to ride at 5st 7lb? Gallon was the regular Manton lightweight, and he normally rode at a little over 6st. Taylor had him down to the yard for a few days, starved him to perfection, and legged him up at Epsom just a pound overweight.

The City and Suburban had 28 runners that year. They set off at a headlong gallop, Sefton always prominent. Gallon edged him ahead at the top of the hill. In the straight, he was briefly joined and headed, but he stayed on to win by a head from Lord Lonsdale's Advance. Lonsdale's other runner in the race was Petrarch; his presence showed how seriously owners and trainers took races like the City and Suburban in those days. He was the winner, over three seasons, of the Middle Park, 2,000 Guineas, St Leger and Gold Cup. Now here he was, a six-year-old entire, being asked to carry 9st 4lb against a large field of mostly lightly weighted handicappers. Another quality horse unplaced in the race was Verneuil, a four-year-old carrying 8st 4lb. Verneuil had been placed in the French 2,000 Guineas and Derby. After the Epsom handicap he went on to Ascot in June to win the Gold Cup, the Gold Vase and the Queen Alexandra - leading all the way in each race, not seeing another horse over seven miles in four days.

It was Alec Taylor's first win in the City and Suburban, and there was widespread pleasure at Crawfurd's success. He and the Duchess were showered with congratulations. After the race, Sefton was made 10-1 for the 2,000 Guineas and 25-1 for the Derby. Nine days later, he ran a creditable third at Newmarket, beaten half a length and one and a half lengths by the favourite Pilgrimage, a filly in receipt of 5lb, and the French-owned second favourite Insulaire. Sefton started slowly, recovered the ground to lead at the Bushes, but then wandered under pressure and was outpaced by the first and second.

After three hard races in a fortnight, Sefton was put aside for the Derby. In the middle of May, he was a 20-1 outsider. But then something stirred on Taylor's gallops, because on May 20 *The Sportsman* reported 'a connection of the Manton stable' taking £1,000 to £60 four times for the Derby, after £1,000 to £50 and £950 to £50. On the same day in the City, 'a commissioner identified with Manton' took £3,000 to £180. In our money, the day's work represented an outlay of *£22,800* to win *£393,000.* Three days later Sefton was backed to win another £2,000; then £1,000 to £70 was laid three times. At the end of the month, there was 'No end of money' in £25 and £50 bets at 14-1, and Sefton's place-only odds of 7-4 were taken wherever offered: "For a big race, the money that has been laid out for him to place is something wonderful." On the eve of the race, three more single win bets of £1,000 to £100 were noted.

When the horse and the price were right, Taylor's Manton seldom made mistakes. Besides his owners, Old Alec used some shrewd punters to get his money down. One was an owner of George Lambton's, Frankie Murrietta, described by Captain Machell as, "A clever fellow and a bit of a rogue." According to Lambton, "Taylor took a fancy to Frankie, who worked several good commissions for him, and so quiet was he that no one suspected that he was the agent of that powerful stable." On several occasions, Taylor handed Lambton himself a £100 [*£6,000*] cheque, saying, "Put this on my horse." He went to great lengths to obscure the source of his runners' support, and he usually succeeded. Even when he was having a real 'go', he managed to protect the price, never more than when Buchanan, at 100-8, ran away from 35 rivals in the 1881 Lincoln.

Sefton faced 21 opponents at Epsom. Among them were familiar rivals who provided clear form lines. Favourite for the race was Insulaire, who'd finished a place in front of Sefton in the 2000 Guineas. Remarkably, Insulaire had run in, and won, the French Derby at Chantilly on the preceding Sunday. Here he was three days later, after two cross-Channel journeys, being asked to do it all again. The form gave Sefton solid place claims, but 8-1 didn't appear a generous price against him winning.

Win he did, though. His jockey was Harry Constable, a dependable rider who followed the script from the City and Suburban. Sefton was prominent all the way, led before the descent to Tattenham Corner, kicked clear at the entrance to the straight, and was rousted up in the last furlong to hold off Insulaire by one and a half lengths, with the Fred Archer-ridden Childeric the same distance away in third. Crawfurd threw a lavish party to celebrate his win: 'No yearling in the paddocks cavorted as gaily as Mr Payne.' Alec Taylor went directly to Marlborough. When he arrived that evening, a crowd cheered him. Sefton had a similar reception the following day, when he was led from the station to Manton. The day ended with the Marlborough handbell ringers calling at the yard, to serenade Taylor's and Sefton's success.

Sefton had only three more races after the Derby. He finished third, conceding plenty of weight, in the Prince of Wales's Stakes at Royal Ascot. Then he put up a smashing performance in the Newmarket St Leger, beating Insulaire by six lengths with Childeric far behind. It was a clear step up on all his previous form. Finally, he ran in the Cesarewitch, but broke down and was retired. He was a failure at stud, and short-lived.

Chapter 5

A Plunger visits

Sefton's win was popular. *Truth* reflected racing society's reaction: "[We] congratulate Mr Crawfurd and the Duchess of Montrose on the victory of Sefton [who was] heavily backed." The paper claimed that the connections had won £25,000 [nearly *£1.5 million*] over the race. Meanwhile, the Duchess had become attached to Newmarket. Belle Vue Lodge was renamed after Sefton.

The Duchess spent lavishly on orchid and palm houses in its grounds. She enjoyed the social scene, and she disliked the remoteness of Manton. Before long, she was scheming to set up her own racing operation in Newmarket. When she first raised the subject with Craw, it was couched in terms of how nice it would be to have their horses trained within walking distance. Craw nipped her proposal in the bud: "No. When my horses leave Manton, they go to Tattersalls [sales]," he told her.

Not for the last time in their marriage, the Duchess prevailed. The trainer at Newmarket's Bedford Lodge, Joseph Dawson, died. The Duchess negotiated with his widow: they agreed a rent of £1,850 [*£88,500*] a year and that Bedford Lodge would continue as a public yard, with Dawson's head lad Richard Sherrard taking over as trainer. The 'turf editor' of the *Morning Post* heard about the Duchess' interest in Bedford Lodge, and wrote a short piece. This provoked an immediate complaint, delivered to the man's London club:

> *"Sir, you have taken an unjustifiable course in bringing my wife's name forward in your Newmarket article. No one has a right to mention any lady's name in public print unless what he states is the fact. Now, in the statement you have made there is not one word of truth. My wife has not taken Bedford Lodge, nor has she one single racehorse."*

The letter was signed, *"I am, sir, your most obedient servant, W S Stirling*

Crawfurd." It was ridiculed, in part because the Duchess could be seen bustling in and out of Bedford Lodge, even more so when the *Post* writer revealed that the letter was in her handwriting.

She could never leave well alone. During one of the racing libel cases to which the Victorians were so addicted, a witness mentioned the Duchess. Her name was greeted with mirth in the courtroom. The Duchess sent a message to the judge, asking to be heard. During respectful questioning, she made claims so obviously untrue that, again, there was loud laughter.

The Duchess was soon in charge at Bedford Lodge, for all her denials. Her horses ran under the name 'Mr Manton,' those being the days when only men's colours could be registered. So began a tug-of-war that continued for years, with Crawfurd doing his best to maintain his string at Manton, while his wife bought horses for Sherrard to train at Bedford Lodge.

Craw even persuaded Taylor to bring some of his horses to Newmarket, with the result that Taylor's name appears alongside the local trainers in the gallops reports. But Old Alec had worked for over 20 years to realise the dream of his own purpose-built yard. He didn't much care to leave Manton, even to go racing. He only operated a satellite yard in Newmarket because Crawfurd begged him.

Craw hoped that somehow the Duchess would become reconciled to Taylor, and revert to having all their horses at Manton. He was dreaming. Although, as George Lambton said, Taylor was the only man who ever made the Duchess nervous, that made her more determined to control her own stable. Craw tried to make sure that the best yearlings went to Taylor, but one that slipped through his hands was a colt called St Louis, bought by the Duchess for 2,200 guineas.

St Louis made his debut in the Middle Park Stakes. The Duchess was clad in Craw's scarlet racing colours, even including her veil. Craw wore a scarlet buttonhole. A 'Big commission was thrown into the market' for St Louis, who led out of the Dip and won easily by three lengths. The Duchess' choice of trainer was applauded in the racing press:

"It is plain that [Joseph Dawson left to] his right-hand man Sherrard a grand example in the delicate art of training the thoroughbred. If Mr Crawfurd required a sweetener by way of inducement to a still stronger patronage of Bedford Lodge, he must have received it by the victory of St Louis, who was sent to the post a perfectly trained colt."

Alec Taylor could be forgiven a twinge of resentment as he read this and similar gushings. More likely, he was philosophical. He wasn't inclined to have his routine or judgement challenged. Whatever upset he felt at seeing his long link with Craw reduced, he must have thanked his stars whenever stories about the Duchess' antics reached him. If she appeared at Manton, friction was inevitable.

She heard rumours about the sparkling work of another owner's horse. She was sniffing around for information when Taylor appeared. He refused to be drawn. The Duchess blew her top, accusing, "Never in my life did I see such a filthy yard, and I shall make it my business to tell Mr Crawfurd." Taylor replied: "Your Grace, I have known two really clever women in my time. The first was my mother, who could train horses as well as my father. The second is my wife, who knows how to mind her own business."

Once in a while, the two managed to put their differences aside, as on the day when Taylor had laid out her horse Loved One for Ascot. She was having a good bet, and didn't want the Manton lads spoiling the price. Before racing, Taylor called all his travelling boys together in a saddling box on the course. Then he locked them in. After Loved One had won, the lads were set free, with a guinea each from the Duchess in recompense.

Fortunately for Taylor, he had other horses and owners to occupy him. Early in 1880, Lord Beaufort had transferred his horses to Manton. One of them was Petronel, a son of George Payne's Musket. Shortly after he arrived at Manton, Petronel won the 2,000 Guineas in the hands of George Fordham.

It's an anomaly that in most published records, Petronel is missing from the Manton honours board. Taylor also had a promising filly in the yard that year: the chestnut Thebais, home-bred by Crawfurd. Taylor started her off in the same race at Stockbridge as Sefton; she finished third. She was unplaced at Newmarket, and then went through the rest of the season unbeaten.

When Thebais made her reappearance in the 1,000 Guineas the following May, the best of the previous season's fillies were there ranged against her. Nevertheless, the betting was a shade of odds on Thebais. The racing press reported that, "The confidence reposed in [Thebais] was shown by the extensive nature of the commission executed in her favour, indeed the agent never left off supporting her."

An outsider made first run and seemed to have stolen a winning lead, but Thebais challenged from the Dip and outstayed her to win by a neck. Thebais was greeted with 'loud shouting' and hailed as the best filly Craw had ever bred. When she was unsaddled, 'Cheers were called for on behalf of the Duchess and Mr Crawfurd.' Thebais's win struck every onlooker as a triumph for stamina. As a result, she was made favourite for the Oaks, and a month later, she completed the classic double. Enthusiastic cheering greeted the victory, as it had after the 1,000 Guineas. The Duchess beamed at Crawfurd's side.

Thebais's Oaks was the zenith of the Duchess' standing in the racing community. The irritation that she was starting to create took a little longer to be reflected among racing regulars and in the press. There were already signs that the Duchess didn't conform to a consort's role at a Victorian race meeting, which was to be seen but not heard.

It was unusual to couple 'Mr Crawfurd and the Duchess of Montrose,' as *Truth* did after Sefton's Derby. It showed that her place in Craw's racing affairs was far more than that of the gentle helpmeet, dressed prettily in her husband's racing colours. The brash Duchess created much unease, particularly as Craw's wealth allowed her to indulge herself without restraint. Diluting his patronage of Manton was the first instance of her imposing herself. The next was the Fordham affair.

George Fordham rode his first winner at 14 as a tiny boy, and weighed just 3st 10lb when winning the 1852 Cambridgeshire. Over the next 20 years, he was champion jockey 14 times, earning the nickname 'The Demon.' He had a number of attributes that made him stand out. He rode almost as short as a modern day jockey, and he realised before most of his contemporaries the importance of finding the best ground.

He wasn't inclined to use the whip much, and often not until within the shadow of the post. He was a master of the hold-up ride. He liked to pretend to be applying pressure in a race - pushing, shoving and what most irritated Fred Archer, 'cluck-clucking' - when he really wasn't doing much at all. Then, right at the death, he would pounce.

Fordham rarely bet, which put him in a minority of one in most of the races he rode in. He was also scrupulously honest. However, he had two faults. He was incoherent when it came to the post-race briefings to his owners and trainers. It was all he could do to stammer that he'd won. And he drank heavily.

Sir George Chetwynd told how Fordham was waiting to mount an ungenuine horse when the trainer arrived with a bottle of port. The plan was to give the animal some Dutch courage. The trainer drank a little of the port and the jockey all the rest, but Fordham won the race anyway. In 1876, he decided that he'd saved enough money to retire and make some investments. The gin flowed, the dividends didn't. Chetwynd persuaded Fordham to make a comeback at the start of the 1878 flat season. He showed that none of his powers had diminished, and Taylor renewed his retainer for Manton. Fordham repaid him with the 2,000 Guineas on Petronel and the 1,000 Guineas and Oaks on Thebais. But for whatever reason, the Duchess had taken a scunner to Demon George.

After watching Archer win a race on a rogue, she told all in earshot, "There's the coming Fordham, and he'll teach George a bit before he's much older." She used to call Fordham 'The old man' and she questioned his integrity. In public, she announced that, "He can no longer ride."

It was unpopular on the racecourse and in the press room. Fordham was liked and respected, the more so after his return from retirement. His first winner back was greeted with prolonged cheers. Alec Taylor and Craw showed every confidence in him. It was wretched judgement on her part to contradict them both publicly.

Truth fired a broadside:

> "[An] increasing and reprehensible innovation at Newmarket is the incursion of ladies. Formerly they were content to remain in the stand or in their carriages, but now it is the fashion, and a very bad fashion, for them to take an active personal interest in the horses of their husbands and friends, and to chatter volubly in the detestable paddock and ring jargon. Anyone who has heard a 'racing woman' cross-examine [trainers and jockeys will think] the heckling of a Scottish political meeting is mild in comparison."

The *Sporting Times* added:

> "Few owners of horses take such an active part in the management of their studs as does the Duchess of Montrose in that of Mr Crawfurd's. [The] horses are trained almost under her own eye. She bids for yearlings at public sales, she gives orders to the trainer, she gives orders to the jockeys, and [now we see] her, in not the most seemly manner, very soundly reprimanding them."

Craw tried in vain to be peacemaker. He told Fordham that he could choose which horses he rode, without consulting himself or Taylor. He suggested that Fordham should avoid riding in bad weather, to conserve his health. All this was reported with glee in *The World*: "The deserved rebuff to those who have [tried] to create ill-blood between master and servant will be thoroughly relished in racing circles." *Truth* was much sharper, saying it was, "Full time for Mr Crawfurd to assert himself. The Duchess of Montrose by her wayward interference in racing matters [is] rendering his position impossible." Once again, Craw backed down.

The day came when the Duchess gave Fordham a savage public dressing-down. He tore off the scarlet cap and jacket. The Duchess ordered them to be sent back to Bedford Lodge, which he did as quickly as he could, for fear that she might change her mind.

Craw's humiliation was completed by another report in *The World*: "The lady has conquered and Fordham's connection with Mr Crawfurd is severed. It is expected that the next split will be between Mr Crawfurd and [Alec Taylor]. All the horses will sooner or later be trained at Bedford Lodge, under the Duchess of Montrose's personal superintendence."

The Duchess wanted to replace Fordham with Fred Archer, but he was retained by Lord Falmouth. Her next choice was Sherrard's stable jockey, Charles Wood. Not long after, Wood was riding an odds on favourite for the Duchess in a valuable four-runner race at Newmarket. He led a furlong out. Last of the quartet was Fordham: less than 50 yards from the post, he made his move and won by a head. As he walked past the Duchess to the weighing room, they exchanged looks to freeze the fens.

Jack Robinson was another jockey to feel the lash of Carrie Red's tongue. At Newmarket one afternoon, the judge was another, unrelated Robinson. Two of the Duchess' horses lost in close finishes, after which she broadcast her opinion that, "What with Robinson who cannot ride and Robinson who is apparently colour blind, I seem unlikely to win any races this year." The jockey decided to jump before he was pushed. He won few campaign medals by sending his wife to serve his notice. The scene was described in *The Gentlewoman*:

> "She went to [see] the Duchess at Newmarket, and was most kindly received. Tea was brought in, and at first, the conversation ran only upon general topics, the Duchess conversing with her usual incisive wit and humour. But at length the jockey's wife, with fear and trembling, let out the fatal secret which had led to her visit. She [said] that the change from geniality to wrath promptly effected by her hostess was positively awe-inspiring. The Duchess sat for a moment in complete silence and her visitor got up to go. Then the storm burst

and a devastating storm it was, through which the strongest language hurtled, while bomb-like epithets burst in every direction. It raged with such fury that the visitor quickly sought refuge in flight."

In a remarkably short time, the Duchess had crossed swords with senior jockeys, her husband's long-serving trainer and the racing press. She also believed that the handicappers were united in league against her. She accused one of them, the portly Major Egerton, of piling weight on her horses so that he could ride them. One afternoon at Ascot, she broke a long losing run. Egerton congratulated her, saying he was glad her luck had turned. The Duchess was scornful: "No thanks to you, Major: it wasn't a handicap."

It took a couple of seasons more for her to alienate the racing public and the Stewards of the Jockey Club. Not surprisingly, betting was the cause. The horses involved were two racemares: Corrie Roy and the dual classic winner Thebais. It all began quietly enough in a nursery handicap at Worcester in 1880 where Manton was represented by an unnamed filly, home bred by Crawfurd. She was by a Derby winner, Galopin, out of Corrie. She ran unplaced. That was followed by a half-length defeat in a match at Shrewsbury and another unplaced run in a nursery.

She started her three-year-old season by placing second in a four-runner race at Newmarket. Then she ran twice at the Houghton meeting, still unnamed, 'the Corrie filly'. She wasn't sighted in the Cambridgeshire, but won the Jockey Club Cup, over two miles. That was a potent trial for the Cesarewitch; it at once brought her into the betting, and she was registered as Corrie Roy.

Manton already had a well-backed horse in the 'long race', Fred Gretton's Geologist, but at the time that Corrie Roy was first supported, Geologist's odds drifted. Rumours spread about his well-being. Gretton denied them. Geologist had bruised a leg, he admitted, but a dose of physic had sorted out the problem, and the colt was back at exercise. 'No cause for alarm,' added Gretton. He told the press he'd backed his horse to win £20,000 [*£985,000*] and, "He will run and he will win."

Despite Gretton's protestations, Geologist drifted further in the betting. Five days later, he was scratched. Meanwhile, according to *The Sportsman*, Corrie Roy, "Has been backed to win a very large stake by those who should be best informed as to her merits. The followers of Manton have not been afraid to back their opinion." From another quarter came rumour that, "She is little inferior to the Oaks winner Thebais." The published bets on her came to over £32,000 [*£1.48 million*]. They were struck in a range between 16-1 and 8-1, which suggests a potential take-out of getting on for *£18 million* in our reckoning.

A crystal-ball gazer might reflect on these preliminaries and foretell Corrie Roy winning easily, cheered on by ecstatic connections. To the horror of her backers, what transpired was that she was taken out of the Cesarewitch on the morning of the race. Taylor was appalled. Crawfurd was laid up in bed at Sefton Lodge, his ribs broken in a fall from his hack. The smoking gun was in the Duchess' hand. She'd decided to teach Corrie Roy's punters a lesson. She told her intimates that it was 'because Mr Gretton has got all the money.'

Imagine Gretton's rage. First, he lost a fortune on his own horse through injury. Then when he backed Corrie Roy to cover his losses – just one of his bets on her was £500 at 3-1 to place [*£69,000 to £23,000*], he was cut adrift by his own stable.

Whatever the Duchess claimed, Gretton and the others who lost their money were friendly-fire victims of her obsession with Theodore 'Plunger' Walton, a hotelkeeper from Philadelphia. Walton had arrived in England that June to back the American horse Iroquois for the Derby. Walton won a vast sum: tens of thousands, even in 1881 money, and reinvested it on Iroquois in the St Leger. In between, he scattered money round lesser race meetings like confetti. Unlike other plungers of the time, he won handsomely.

His secret was simple. He paid jockeys for information and tipped them extravagantly when it turned out well. Walton held court outside the weighing room at Newmarket and elsewhere, conferring openly with his informants, right under the noses of the stewards. No one knew what to do. Leopold de Rothschild's jockey was a boy called Barrett, much in demand as a lightweight. Walton won *half a million* in our money on one of Barrett's mounts. He then gave £400 [*£20,000*] to Barrett. Clearly, information that by rights belonged to owners and trainers was being solicited by Walton. The concerns went further. If a rider knows that a large present is coming to him if he wins, then he has a fund available to coerce other jockeys in the race.

"The sight of a turf gambler holding a sort of levee of jockeys and touts between [races] is a flagrant scandal, and when it is announced that a plunger has given £1,000 to the rider of one of his winners, and £400 to another, one knows well enough that this lavish distribution is simply 'bread cast upon the waters'."

With her usual disregard for the facts, the Duchess called Walton, 'The Black Man.' She was convinced that he was targeting Bedford Lodge. She gave an order that he wasn't to be allowed near the yard. Sir John Astley backed his horse Medicus in a Newmarket nursery. It finished nowhere. After racing, he was told that the jockey had stopped it. He ran it in another nursery the following day, with a different jockey.

As the horse went down to the start, he strode into the Ring on his recovery mission, whiskers bristling. He found Medicus was almost favourite. The nest had been robbed. Sir John backed the horse for 'a mere trifle' to win, which it did, and cast about for the villain, who at once showed himself.

A cheerful Walton, betting book in hand, sauntered up and said, "I won four thousand on your horse." The irate Sir John told the Plunger to take his book and himself back to America, adding, fists clenched, "Take care I don't punch your damned head." When the fracas subsided, Walton said he hadn't worried about Astley's threat, "Because it was in business hours." He could afford to be chippy: on the same afternoon, he won another £4,000 on a filly of Crawfurd's, to the visible fury of the Duchess. For the Plunger to stage a *£400,000* coup on two Bedford Lodge horses suggested that he had fingers deep in the Duchess' pie. Not long after, he took himself and his winnings back to America, promising to return.

Over the winter, Corrie Roy was transferred from Manton to Sherrard's care at Bedford Lodge. She wasn't seen out in the following season until the Goodwood Cup. She was backward, drifted out to 50-1 in the betting and ran as the market suggested, tailed off. She was so blatantly not 'off' that some of the jockeys who rode in the race sent immediate instructions to their commission agents to back her for the Cesarewitch.

The year had begun well for Bedford Lodge, with victory for another of Stirling Crawfurd's home-breds, St Marguerite, in the 1,000 Guineas. Oddly, although Taylor isn't properly recognised as the handler of Petronel for the 1880 2,000 Guineas, in the case of St Marguerite he's credited with a classic winner that he didn't train. She won the 1,000 all out by a neck from Shotover, a long odds-on favourite who came into the race from success two days earlier in the 2,000 Guineas. Sherrard's stable jockey Wood was in the saddle and the next day's report in *The Sportsman* was clear: "St Marguerite is trained for Mr Crawfurd by Sherrard at Bedford Lodge."

Chapter 6

A greater storm

Sir George Chetwynd wrote that Corrie Roy, "Required very little long work [and] before the Cesarewitch, she had never been the distance at home. [She] wanted so little training that she only did mile-and-a-half work." Chetwynd was a substantial owner at Bedford Lodge. If the yard had a fancied runner for a big race, it might be supposed that he'd know about her home work. Yet he clearly didn't. So far from 'requiring little work,' her schedule before the marathon handicap was astonishing. The race was run on October 10. Eight days before, she was sent 'a rattling two-mile gallop,' partnered by her big-race jockey Wood. The next day she went 'a capital gallop' over a mile. The day after came 'a good striding gallop' over two miles. On each of the next two mornings, she worked 10 furlongs with Thebais. On the eve of her race, she covered the full Cesarewitch course with a stablemate called Edelweiss who'd just won the Cesarewitch Trial handicap.

Corrie Roy was available at 25-1 a week before the race. Then, according to the *Pink 'Un*, "Corrie Roy, who had been nibbled at for a fortnight, was introduced in downright earnest. At £1,000 to £40 and £1,000 to £50 the stable commission was very actively engaged and from 20-1 she has been supported for a load of money," with several bets of £1,000 to £60 noted before she settled at 100-8. She was all the rage in Newmarket the day before the race, shortening to 9-2 on the day itself. In the race, Corrie Roy faced only 13 opponents. She was held up last to halfway, made rapid headway into mid-field half a mile from home, and was still held hard by Wood past the Bushes and into the Dip. The moment he asked her for an effort, she went three lengths clear and won easily.

As Craw patted one side of her neck and the Duchess the other, the mood on the racecourse was genial. As soon as Corrie Roy's number was hoisted in the runners' frame, there was a public gamble. At least among racegoers, her previous year's last-minute scratching seemed forgiven and forgotten. The tone was reflected in the racing press: "Corrie Roy has grown into one of the grandest mares that ever trod the turf. A grand coup has been landed. [The] victory was very popular."

Corrie Roy's success was the centrepiece of a Newmarket meeting in which Crawfurd and his two trainers won eight races. Among their other wins were the Middle Park Stakes with the highly-touted Manton colt Macheath and a dead-heat in the Champion Stakes with Thebais. Macheath was the medium of a nice touch. Crawfurd had another runner in the same race. The Duchess sailed up to one of the biggest bookmakers and took £1,000 to £100 about the second string, helping to make the market for when 'a huge commission' was sent out for Macheath.

The celebrations at Bedford Lodge were muted. Sherrard had been seen looking at other training yards. There were insistent reports that Craw was going to cut back his racing interests because of poor health. Worse, although he'd had a betting week to make any owner drool - his winnings were reckoned by the *Sporting Times* at close to *£2 million* - he missed out over one of his stable's winners, Energy.

On the eve of the meeting, who should arrive off a liner from New York but Plunger Walton, with, "A cocky air about him. [He] was evidently bent on a good gambling week." His biggest message of the week was for Energy, and he backed the colt for £8,000. Crawfurd's commissioner arrived in the Ring to find, as others had done before him, that the bird had flown. Walton had almost *£400,000* to come, Craw nothing. The report in *The World* read, "The Plunger skimmed the market of all the cream [and he] evidently receives inspiration 'direct from the wood,' as the wine growers say." It was a transparent reference to the jockey, Charles Wood. The Duchess spoke her mind freely to Sherrard.

None of the Bedford Lodge connections had won anything to speak of over Corrie Roy's Cesarewitch. The mare had been messed around so much that even those close to the yard didn't believe she was a certain runner. Some backers took the view that the Duchess' erratic stable management was in the price, but they didn't include many of those who paid the stable's bills. Sir John Astley won just £500 and was so disgusted that he didn't turn up for settlement. Sir George Chetwynd barely broke even on the race.

With reports rife about chaos and low morale at Bedford Lodge, there were nonetheless hopes that the yard could bring off the autumn double. Corrie Roy's win wasn't well received by the Duchess' fellow owners, but it promoted her galloping companion Thebais to favouritism for the Cambridgeshire. Bets of £1,000 to £40 three times and £1,000 to £45 six times were noted. Most of this was bookmakers laying off. One of their number, Myers, had laid £10,000 to £10 against the Corrie Roy and Thebais double. Similar liabilities meant that well over *£1 million* was circulating to hedge against Thebais. The strength of the market in those days meant that three days later the mare was still generally 20-1 for the Cambridgeshire. That changed when she ran a dead-heat in the Champion Stakes. She shared first place with Tristan, whose nine seasonal wins had included the Hardwicke Stakes, the July Cup and the Grand Prix de Deauville. The recent St Leger winner Dutch Oven was third.

On the racecourse and in the Subscription Rooms that night, noted bets on Thebais came to *£54,200* to win over *£850,000*. Then, as the days ticked by towards the Cambridgeshire, Thebais was notable, like the dog that didn't bark in the night, for not shortening any further in the betting. Meanwhile, the *Sporting Times* said that, "Mr Crawfurd [may try to] win the race with St Marguerite, who, there can be no doubt, has been backed by the stable." The favourite was Shrewsbury, the medium of a big move after placing third to Corrie Roy in the Cesarewitch. Next in the betting were Thebais at 11-1 and St Marguerite 16-1. Among the outsiders was the one-time crack two-year-old, St Louis.

On the day before the race, the supporters of Thebais would've been aghast had they been privy to a scene at Sefton Lodge. The Duchess had backed St Louis and St Marguerite for the Cambridgeshire. She learned that, not for the first time, St Louis had broken down. She sent a telegram to Brighton races summoning Sherrard to Newmarket to explain himself.

When he arrived, she locked the door behind him. There was a furious set-to. She blamed Sherrard for encouraging her to back Craw's other runners when all along the true 'lady' in the three cards was Thebais. What's more, she shouted, she had reason to believe that he, Sherrard, stood to win £50,000 over Thebais - nigh on *£2.5 million*. The names Walton and Sir George Chetwynd were prominent in her tantrum. The Duchess accused Sherrard of passing information to Chetwynd as well as to The Plunger.

The Newmarket special commissioner of *The Sporting Life* wired a report to his newspaper: "Ugly rumours reach me about Thebais, upon which I may be better informed before I close my telegram tonight."

A secondary market on the Cambridgeshire formed at the Subscription Rooms. It concerned one horse: Thebais, offered at 5-2 against a run. The 'Monday night update' to *The Sporting Life* spoke of, "Many disquieting rumours on the racecourse. An air of mystery still pervades the Bedford Lodge team."

The Prince of Wales was the Crawfurds' guest at Sefton Lodge that evening. 'Teddy' had his share of scandals, in the bedroom and at the card table. That night, dining with the Duchess, he found himself in the eye of two separate tempests. One of them battered the windows: Tuesday dawned on a scene of devastation on Newmarket Heath.

A howling gale blew. Rain, sleet and hail raged into the afternoon. A carriage blew over, as did the numbers board and the auctioneer's rostrum. Railings were scattered. Then, just before noon, the news spread that Thebais had been taken out of the Cambridgeshire. Somehow or other, the first three races were run despite the ferocity of the weather.

In one of them, Crawfurd had an odds-on favourite, Melioe. It was hissed to post. As the runners came back into view in the downpour, the scarlet colours were in second place behind Nautilus, a horse owned by General Owen Williams. Cheering broke out all over the racecourse. The *Morning Post* called it, "The most significant outburst both from the Ring and the general public that was ever heard on Newmarket Heath." There was another howl of delight when Nautilus's number was put up, and more cheers when the horse came into the winner's enclosure. The Duchess seemed oblivious: she said to a friend, "I had no idea that General Williams was so popular."

The runners for the Cambridgeshire set off into the storm: "Anything more vile, fearful and horrible will be impossible to imagine. It was not simply a visitation of heavy rain, or a fall of snow, a downpour of sleet, or a gale that would make the teeth chatter in the head. It was a combination of everything." Racegoers were spun round and knocked over. Down at the start was, 'a scene of wild disorder'.

After much dithering, the stewards sent Mr Weatherby to recall the runners and postpone the race. He was by no means a small man, but he was blown clean off his horse. Eventually a policeman rode down the course, returning with the shivering, bedraggled field in dribs and drabs. "It was pitiable to see the helpless condition of the light-weights, the little lads, as they returned drenched to the skin and starved with the cold."

The next day's racing pages were dominated by two stories: the great gale and what *The Sportsman* headlined as, 'A Greater Storm'. The paper's reporter James Smith penned a savage assault on the scratching of Thebais. Its theme echoed all round Fleet Street:

> "There occurred during the day [an] outbreak of other than elemental wrath. The scratching [of] Thebais only an hour or two before the race of the day evoked the popular resentment. Those who remember the conduct of Mr WS Crawfurd's racing affairs a few years ago may well marvel at the tactics pursued recently under a new *regime*.
>
> "Let us glance back at the policy which has been adopted of late. Who does not remember the scratching of Corrie Roy at the eleventh hour for the Cesarewitch of last year, and the widespread astonishment, and something worse, to which it gave rise? Again, who cannot readily call to mind the curious course chosen in running the same mare for the Goodwood Stakes, when she was so notoriously unfit that she started [at] 50-1?
>
> "Coming to Thebais, it is well known that a certain amount of uneasiness has prevailed for days. At first vague rumours gained circulation. [Still] the mare was reported as going so exceedingly well and as being so thoroughly prepared to hold her own [in the Cambridgeshire] that the more thoughtful of the racing fraternity could not see how Thebais could be eliminated. On Monday [it] was remarked that 'someone' expressed disgust that the mare had come to be so short a price and that the said 'someone' [had] an inclination to checkmate those who had been audacious enough to [back Thebais].
>
> "[Yesterday morning] the pen was put through the name of Thebais, and thousands of people who had ventured their money upon the mare found that they might with equal profit have thrown it into the gutter. We lament bitterly that conduct so unsportsmanlike should have been pursued with regard to Thebais.
>
> "It is a direct violation of the traditions connected with the 'all scarlet' jacket of Mr Crawfurd. And assuredly, [he] is more pitied than blamed. There can be no doubt that he felt deeply grieved and humiliated as he heard of the applause when Melioe, his filly [and] favourite for the Maiden Plate was defeated. Even those who had lost cheered the [result] and regard it as a kind of retaliation."

Another writer said that, "An evil genius seems recently to hover over the manipulation of Mr Crawfurd's animals. The Press [acquit him] of any double dealing and even write about in terms of pity, as if he were some imbecile old man allowing horses to run in his name over which he has no control."

The Sportsman also drew a line between the Duchess and Craw:

> "Despite the commonly accepted threat on the part of the Duchess of Montrose that Thebais should not run, it was generally thought that Mr Crawfurd would not submit to be a party to any such action. It is no exaggeration to say that the fair fame once associated with Mr Crawfurd's name and colours has within the last four or five years been dimmed to such an extent that at the present moment there is absolutely not a more unpopular racing jacket on the turf than the 'all scarlet'."

One paper called for a change of colours: Craw should keep the scarlet for his horses with Taylor at Manton, and run his Bedford Lodge string in black. The *Pink 'Un* had a sarcastic promise: "If the Duchess of Montrose does not alter the colours of her racing jacket we shall alter the colour of this paper. As matters stand they are too much alike."

The act of an owner scratching his horse from a race because he's been beaten to the best odds has a long pedigree. Back in the 1830s, a colt called Elis won stayers' races at Lewes and Goodwood and was backed to favourite for the St Leger. A few days before the race, a warning was pinned up in Tattersalls:

"Elis will not go north unless the stable
obtain the odds of £1,200 at 12-1"

The equivalent message today would be an advertisement in the trade press: *'If we don't get £720,000 to £60,000 about our horse, we'll scratch him and you can all go and whistle for your money'*. In 1836, the punters with the big prices about Elis clubbed together and laid the bet the stable wanted, whereupon the colt left for Doncaster and won the St Leger easily.

Fred Gretton was a 'biter bit'. When Corrie Roy was struck out he lost twice over, but he didn't get much sympathy. In times past, he hadn't hesitated to scratch one of his horses if he missed the market. So while some asked, 'What did you expect?' the public's puzzled fury centred on the dog-in-a-manger question: why on earth hadn't the Duchess backed Thebais herself?

One bookmaker said that earlier in the season he'd offered Crawfurd

£5,000 to £100 Thebais for the Cambridgeshire, without response. The mare was available at 25-1 before her dead heat in the Champion Stakes. Even after that potent trial, she was never less than 10-1.

The full scope for mishap at Bedford Lodge wasn't fully appreciated. Take an unwell, perhaps not terribly bright, principal owner, Stirling Crawfurd; the erratic and wilful Duchess; and a trainer and jockey, Sherrard and Wood, whose interests weren't always aligned with those of their patrons. Add strong-willed confederates like Chetwynd and a wolf pack of wily punters like Walton, and it was little wonder that this witch's broth produced indecision and paranoia.

The Crawfurds could've backed Thebais to win a big stake in the Cambridgeshire. Because of a breakdown in communication with their trainer, they didn't. Some of their friends did back her: the mare was struck out regardless. It was the last straw for Sir George. Sherrard left Bedford Lodge and opened his own stable in Newmarket, as had been predicted. Chetwynd's horses went with Sherrard. In his memoirs, Chetwynd referred icily to, "A lady to whom I have not spoken for several years."

Back on the Rowley Mile, the Newmarket crowd, encouraged by *The Sportsman* and similar articles, reacted to Crawfurd's runners as it had the day before to Melioe. Every horse in the all scarlet was booed on its way to the start, every loser was cheered. There was a rumour that the Duchess would be burned in effigy in Newmarket that night.

Singed but not scorched, the Duchess marched up to the stewards the following day and demanded that *The Sportsman* should be made to apologise. The stewards said they weren't inclined to interfere with the freedom of the press. The Duchess retorted that if they didn't act, she wouldn't run any more horses at the meeting.

At that moment, the number of one of Craw's entries appeared on the board for the next race. The Duchess gave orders for it to be taken down. The Earl of Cadogan decided enough was enough. He told her that if the horse was withdrawn, the stewards would have no option but to fine Crawfurd. The Duchess burst into what an observer called a wild, hysterical fit. He added that her tears weren't regret, but 'baffled rage'.

A packed crowd in front of the weighing room watched the undignified scene. The tired, ill-looking Crawfurd told the Duchess, "We don't seem to be popular here. Let us go home." Not long afterwards, they left England to spend the winter in Cannes.

Lord Maidstone wrote the epitaph for that dramatic October at Newmarket:

"Corrie Roy and Carrie Red
Carrie Red and Corrie Roy
One for the course and one for the bed:
Isn't Craw a lucky boy?"

Chapter 7

Father to sons

Stirling Crawfurd wasn't lucky at the end, for all his money and privilege. He died in Cannes early the following year, wearied by forever defending his wife and picking up the pieces from her tantrums. He was the last of Manton's founder owners. Ailesbury had passed first, then George Payne. Craw's death voided almost 400 nominations for his horses, notably the classic entries for his colt Macheath, who was winter favourite for the 2,000 Guineas and second favourite for the Derby. The entry money lost was bad enough; there was also the opportunity cost, and the reduction in value of the Middle Park winner Macheath and the other good colts in Craw's ownership.

The Duke of Beaufort increased his presence after Petronel's 1880 Guineas win, and there were one or two new owners at Manton, among them Hamar Bass, the heir to brewery millions. But overall, Alec Taylor's last years were marked by a steady decline in horse numbers. Beaufort was an owner in the Payne and Crawfurd mould, including in his dislike of touts, though he handled them with a degree of civility. Rumour spread about a trial planned for his horses. Every tout for miles headed to the downs, to find that Beaufort had arranged a welcoming party of armed gamekeepers. The touts were rounded up and put into closed coaches. Beaufort spoke to them: "You gentlemen have had the use of these downs for the whole of the year, and I must now ask you to let me have them to myself for a few hours. You will be good enough to be my guests [at an] excellent dinner. You will understand that my invitation is very pressing." So off went the touts. Threats of actions for false imprisonment fell silent as they tucked into his Lordship's meal.

Beaufort was equally polite when the Duchess of Montrose tried him sorely. It was at Ascot, and Taylor had entered one of each owner's horses in each of the first two races. The Duchess said it would be a shame if her horse were to run against Beaufort's, and that she preferred to go for the opener. Unsurprisingly, it was the more valuable and less competitive of the two heats. Her horse won easily. She then told Beaufort that she'd changed her mind, and intended to run in the second race as well. He took off his hat, bowed to her, and said, "As Your Grace pleases, let it be so." Although her horse won again and his was second, he kept his temper.

Beaufort was an enthusiastic owner, to the point that he set off from Badminton before dawn to see his string work, with a relay of mounts waiting for him at coaching inns on the way to Manton. Mostly, he should have stayed at home. He had numerous slow to useless animals. Among the few exceptions was the filly Rêve d'Or, who carried Beaufort's 'blue, white hoops' to victory in the 1887 1,000 Guineas and Oaks. In Queen Victoria's sixtieth anniversary year, Beaufort also had a tough colt, Carlton, who won the Chester Cup, the Manchester Cup, the Goodwood Stakes and the November handicap. Carlton lit up a season that was to be Taylor's last hurrah. It harked back a third of a century to the golden summer of Teddington and Aphrodite. In the Jubilee year, besides Reve d'Or's two classics and Carlton's handicap wins, Manton won the Lincoln, the Great Metropolitan, the Hunt Cup and the Liverpool Autumn Cup, with four different horses.

Oberon's Lincoln success gave Taylor particular pleasure. His son recalled that at the start of the year, "We had heavy snow for weeks on end. I've never known [weather] like it. There came a foot of snow and it froze hard. The snow that fell afterwards [was] like powder, and after galloping was over each day we chain- and brush-harrowed the surface. We prepared our Lincolnshire handicap horses [for six weeks] on the snow, and tried them on it." Taylor, whom no one could accuse of ostentation, celebrated his season and the Queen's Jubilee by erecting an ornamental lamppost in the middle of his yard. The installers were at work when he saw that from his window, the post obstructed his view of the stable entrance opposite. So he had it moved a few feet off centre. Then, he laid a large circular lawn around it, and warned his staff that it was out of bounds.

Meanwhile, the Duchess of Montrose continued to blow in and out of Manton like a hailstorm, scattering noise and occasional damage. Her stud groom John Griffiths gave a vivid account of her caprice:

"The Duchess was not easy to get on with. She was very hot tempered and changeable. She had a succession of managers of her racing stable, and during the time I was with her, she had ever so many trainers. This is the sort of thing that would happen. When her horses were with a trainer at Newmarket, I was sent to him one afternoon to say that the Duchess would arrive at four o'clock to see her horses. When I delivered the message, the trainer said: 'You can tell the Duchess that stable time is six o'clock, and if she will come then she can see the horses with pleasure.' However, the Duchess duly presented herself at the trainer's house at four o'clock. 'He is playing tennis,' said the servant. 'Then tell him I want to see him.' The trainer refused to leave his tennis court and the Duchess came straight to me in a towering rage. 'Griffiths,' she shouted, 'it's a [damned] fine thing if I cannot see my horses when I want to. I'm not keeping them for him to bet on. Here's a blank cheque. Go and ask him what I owe. When he tells you, put it on the cheque and hand it to him. I'll arrange for my horses to go back to Alec Taylor.' And a few days later I was instructed to send the horses to Manton."

It was about this time that Taylor gave the Duchess a rare piece of poor advice. She asked him to look over her well-bred yearlings at the Sefton stud. There were 10 of them, they were backward, and when the question was put to him, 'keep or sell?' he replied, sell. Captain Machell got wind of the opportunity, and asked the Duchess round for dinner. In due course, he broached the subject of her yearlings. Montrose said that Taylor had valued them at £1,000 each. "Will you give me that?" she asked. After the wine had gone round, Machell offered £9,000 for the youngsters, sight unseen. The Duchess hesitated and countered, "Make it £9,500." "Done," said Machell, and he slapped a sovereign into her hand to close the deal, like a coper at a horse fair: "The yearlings are mine." Machell had several years' close experience of the Duchess. Early the following morning, his trainer appeared at the stud with a note stating that Machell had bought the yearlings and delivered his cheque. All seemed in order, and off went the yearlings. Hardly had they left than a message arrived from Montrose, ordering Griffiths not to release them. She'd changed her mind, as Machell had expected, and she was too late. "The Duchess was annoyed and gave expression to her annoyance in her usual vigorous way."

A few days later, Machell sold on the yearlings at a good profit: "Her Grace was very wroth indeed," noted Griffiths. It was a calamitous sale, and not Taylor's finest hour. The yearlings included Satiety and Seabreeze, who between them won £31,500 in stakes in their first two seasons in training, including Seabreeze's Oaks and St Leger.

Crawfurd's death affected the Duchess deeply. She built a chapel at Sefton Lodge to house his remains, and re-styled herself 'Caroline Stirling-Crawfurd Montrose.' But she was back on form before long. She encouraged a coterie of young men to dance attendance on her at the races. She sent them to place her bets, though one or two errand boys with better blood than brains invariably took the worst odds. She scandalised society by developing an infatuation for Fred Archer, whom she'd so admired as a young jockey.

Together with George Fordham, Archer dominated race riding in the second half of the nineteenth century. He rode an average of 160 winners a season, in an era of far fewer race meetings than nowadays, at a strike rate of 34 per cent. The Duchess pursued Archer ardently, despite being twice his weight and three times his age. He'd be at the races when a telegram arrived: '*Fred Archer Esq. Weighing Room, Racecourse, Leicester. Can you come to a theatre tomorrow, Friday. Montrose.*' For a time, Archer seems to have taken her pursuit seriously. He had a military friend, Arthur de Vere Smith, who advised him on matters of society and etiquette. Over a hastily-convened dinner, Archer revealed his secret: the Duchess had asked him to marry her. "Of course, if I marry her I shall be a Duke," said the jockey. After recovering from the shock, his friend corrected him: "No, you'll still be Mr Archer." It took the entire evening for him to convince Archer, after which marriage to the Duchess lost its appeal.

Sadly, Caroline might later have contributed to Archer's death. She had a good handicapper called St Mirin, trained by Taylor. The horse was fancied for the Cambridgeshire, at a weight below even Archer's starved frame. A fateful telegram was sent from London: '*Fred Archer: my horse runs in Cambridgeshire. I count on you to ride it. Montrose.*' Frantic to make the weight, Archer ate nothing for three days, purged himself and then, weakened, lost on St Mirin by a neck. A few days later, confused and agitated, he shot himself.

Montrose had one more surprise for London's clubs and drawing rooms. Aged 70, she married the 24-year-old Marcus Henry Milner, son of a Leeds banker. Their discreet wedding in Fulham might have passed unnoticed, had not an organ enthusiast wandered in to try out the church's instrument. The financial choreography of the marriage hints that it was something less than a love match. Milner, who was at once dubbed 'Millions' Milner, was in effect a salaried husband, receiving

£3,000 [*£180,000*] a year until Caroline's death, and then notably absent from her will. But having seen the impact of Stirling Crawfurd's death on his bloodstock interests, she did at least transfer ownership of all her horses in training to her new husband.

Soon after, she and Milner arranged with Taylor that they'd be up early on the Heath to see one of their horses have its final workout before a big race. After waiting for an hour, Taylor worked the horse. Only then did the Duchess arrive with Milner. Taylor told her, "You're too late, Your Grace. I've done all there is to be done." Gallop the horse again, she retorted. "Very well, Your Grace, if you insist, but you will lose the race tomorrow." The next morning there was another scene between the two, and Montrose called for her stud groom: "I'll have no more of these flash trainers, Griffiths. Can't you find me someone who's been head lad in a good stable?"

Mat Dawson's head lad Billy Gray was the choice. The final split between Taylor and the Duchess was acrimonious. When the message arrived at Manton to transfer her horses to Newmarket, Taylor refused to release them until her account was settled. Billy Gray lasted a couple of seasons with the Duchess, but she became bored with him, and went through half-a-dozen more trainers in as many years. One was JF Peace, at Lambourn. She called him, 'the Peace that passeth all understanding.'

When Carrie Red died, a rich vein of stories passed with her. Two of the smoking room favourites had a domestic setting. First, she was having her hair combed by a maidservant whom she'd abused once too often. As Montrose daydreamed, the girl plaited her hair in and out of the back of the chair her mistress was sitting on, rendering her a prisoner. The maid slapped the Duchess hard, skipped downstairs to her waiting suitcase and was never seen again. Also in Belgrave Square, Montrose was having a lift installed. She was impatient to try it out. The engineer told her it wasn't ready. She ignored him and stepped into the lift, which dropped to the basement and jammed. One of her manservants had to lower himself down and climb back out, with the red-faced Duchess slung over his shoulder, accompanied by much cursing and shouting.

Caroline had a mostly unremarked good side to her. She built Montrose House on Loch Lomond to provide the children of Glasgow's mean streets with a holiday in the fresh air. Well she might, with her income from Craw's Glasgow property. In Newmarket, she founded the Stableman's Institute, with a reading room and games rooms for stable staff. Her hope was to keep them out of the town's pubs. In her will, the Duchess directed the sale of some of her jewellery, to raise £2,000 [*£114,000*] "for the benefit of the poor of the East End of London." She also left a plea to her executors and to her eldest son:

> "I wish to express my earnest desire that Sefton Lodge Newmarket and all that appertains to it and the gardens and grounds and particularly the plot of land which is the burying place of my late husband William Stuart Stirling Crawfurd [and] is intended to be my own burying place shall never be sold but always retained so as never to leave my family and I sincerely trust that all parties concerned will respect my wishes in this matter."

She was ignored. The new Duke had no interest in racing, and before long, he sold the broodmares and the property.

Caroline Montrose stands alone as a woman in English racing history. Dorothy Paget, the owner of Golden Miller, was a celebrity 50 years later, with her telephone-number bets. Paget was strange, gloomy and nocturnal, but Carrie Red livened up the racecourse and the social whirl in a unique way. She was lampooned in at least two plays of the time: in *The Silver Gauntlet* as Lady Wincastle, a 'fascinating widow'; and *The Sporting Duchess*, later a 1920s movie - a romp around adultery, cards, ruin and redemption. Montrose had the best part of *£17 million* from Craw's estate, and in a decade she whittled it down to *£10 million*. Few pursuits could have offered her autocratic nature as much scope for costly disaster as racing did. At every stage of ownership – breeding, buying, selling, making entries, laying plans, betting – the Duchess interfered, and the results were predictably awful. But she added immeasurably to the colour and verve of everything that she touched. The chapel at Sefton was crammed at her funeral and the mourners spilled far back outside. Every curtain, shutter and blind in the windows of Newmarket was closed in respect as her cortege passed.

Only weeks before, a wreath with a simple message had been laid at the graveside of Alec Taylor: *From Caroline Montrose, to whom he was a kind friend and faithful servant.* Manton's first Master suffered a long, exhausting struggle against cancer. For his last two or three seasons, Taylor mostly trained his own horses, and as his days drew in, his last significant owner, the Duke of Beaufort, sold off all his bloodstock. Taylor was buried in the churchyard at Fyfield, the village where his training career began almost half a century before. The 36 lads still employed at Manton paid their respects, as did the Duke of Beaufort, the new Marquis of Ailesbury, and the neighbouring trainer Sam Darling from Beckhampton. There was a wreath from his satellite yard at Newmarket.

Taylor left a carefully framed legacy, in a will written in longhand by a clerk of his solicitor Merriman. It runs across nine tightly spaced pages, without a comma, as was the way in legal documents back then. Taylor had a dilemma. At that time, aside from exceptional circumstances, the first son inherited: that was Tom, by his first wife Anne. His second surviving son, by his second wife, Ann Maria, was Young Alec. Their father's inheritance was, at first sight, even-handed: "My sons Thomas Alexander Taylor and Alexander Taylor shall carry on my racehorse training and farming businesses so long as [they] shall mutually agree to do so." However, Old Alec outlined a clear preference for Young Alec as his successor at Manton:

> "In consideration of [Alec] having always been at home with me and of his having consequently obtained a thorough knowledge of my racehorse training and farming businesses to the exclusion of any other business to which he might otherwise have turned his hand"

The reference to 'any other business' was pointed. Tom Taylor had set himself up as a corn chandler in Ireland, while Young Alec was at home with the horses. The clearest sign of Taylor's intended succession came in a section that provided for Young Alec buying out Tom's interest in Manton, but not vice versa:

> "If in disregard of [my] earnest desire [my] said two sons shall disagree and in consequence of such disagreement shall be unable to harmoniously carry on the said businesses then I direct that my said son Alexander Taylor shall have full power at any time [to give] Thomas Alexander Taylor three months notice to him in writing and that upon the expiration of such notice eleven thousand pounds [*£630,000*] shall be paid [and] that upon such payment the whole of the said businesses [shall] belong absolutely to my said son Alexander Taylor alone"

For several years, the brothers were the joint Masters of Manton. Tom looked after the office and the administration. Young Alec trained the horses. From the start, the arrangement was doomed. At the end of the 1890s and into a new century, winners from Manton were scarce.

Old Alec Taylor hated what in his era was called 'publicity'. He avoided being photographed, and he didn't give press interviews. His achievements spoke for themselves. He built Manton from the chalk upwards. He spent years painstakingly clearing the downs of stones, to create perfect gallops. He journeyed from a groom's son to the most respected horse master in the country. He trained the winners of 12 classics and numerous other big races, among them the Lincoln and the Cesarewitch twice each, the City and Suburban three times, the Manchester November handicap five times and the Goodwood Stakes six. He would have regarded any analysis of his personality or feelings as intrusive and irrelevant. But Taylor has left an intimate glimpse of himself in the churchyard at Fyfield. His tomb reveals that he and his first wife lost four children in infancy. She herself died aged only 28. Child mortality was commonplace in those days, but the achievements of Taylor's early years are the more remarkable against that backdrop of continuous domestic sadness.

Then consider his jockey Eli Drew, who was killed in a fall at Brighton in 1863, aged 21. Drew was 11 when he arrived at Manton. Taylor and his wife, and the other apprentices and lads were the only family he had. Drew was a promising young jockey. He'd ridden a Cesarewitch winner, and had already won 20 races in the season before the accident that ended his life. *The Sporting Life* called him, "A special favourite with everybody." Drew's headstone reads:

"This stone was erected by his
brother jockeys to mark their sense
of his upright behaviour in his
calling and of his general good conduct
with our earnest hope that God will bless
the humble efforts of an
orphan jockey boy"

George Payne was at the races that day, and supervised the boy's unavailing transfer to Brighton hospital. Alec Taylor mourned Drew by commissioning a lych gate for the Fyfield churchyard. To the left and right of the gate are stones inscribed, 'IN MEMORY' and, 'OF ELI DREW.' To the back of the churchyard is Drew's headstone. Taylor's tomb is immediately behind it: not close, but touching, its base cut around Drew's memorial. It's as if, across time, Taylor has an arm around the shoulder of his orphan apprentice.

Chapter 8

R v Taylor and others

There's no memorial for the boy of 15 who died in the fifth year of Tom and Alec Taylor's partnership. An episode which brought shame to Manton began one Monday morning when a Marlborough GP, Dr JB Maurice, was called to visit James Luddon, a Manchester lad who'd been working at the yard for only three months. Luddon had a high temperature and symptoms resembling influenza. He was taken to Savernake Hospital, where he soon lapsed into a coma. Within a week, he was dead. The cause was given as 'tubercular meningitis.' Ordinarily, that would have been the end of the matter. But there were the bruises to explain. Luddon's legs were a mass of welts. When Dr Maurice examined the boy, he asked how they were caused and noted the reply, "Reeves and Stickler." They were the Manton head lad and second lad.

The next day, Marlborough subscribers to *The Sun* were startled by a story headlined, '*Alleged Brutal Treatment of a Trainer's Apprentice*':

> "A very mysterious affair has just occurred at one of the training stables in Wiltshire. The matter is kept such a profound secret, however, that up to the present it is impossible for us to mention any particular names in connection with it. The facts of the case are as follow:
>
> "On Monday afternoon a message was received at the Savernake Cottage Hospital to the effect that a bed was to be instantly prepared for a patient who was in a most critical condition. Shortly afterwards the patient arrived, and was found to be a small boy. [He] was taken in, and examined by the doctor, who was greatly surprised to find that the boy was covered with bruises from head to foot, and in a very dangerous condition.
>
> "In intervals of consciousness the boy alleges that the head lad at a training stable thrashed him because he did not get up early enough in the morning. The boy also says that his life at the training stable was most terrible.

> "The greatest secrecy is observed in connection with the case, as the doctors believe that it is quite unlikely the boy will recover, and, of course, if he does not, a very serious charge may arise out of it. There is no doubt whatever that the boy has been severely ill-treated, and practically 'thrashed within an inch of his life'."

The following morning, *The Sun* ran another inflammatory headline: '*Dying of Ill-Treatment.*' It reported that the sick boy was called Luddon; that he was employed at 'Messrs Taylor's at Manton'; and that an inspector from the National Society for the Prevention of Cruelty to Children had arrived in Marlborough.

Luddon died five days after being admitted to hospital. By now, *The Sun* had found a source inside the yard, a coachman called Boulton, and he in turn directed the paper to a former Manton apprentice, Thomas Holloway. It quoted a letter that Holloway had written home:

> *"Dear father will you come down at once. I have been badly beating* (sic) *about by Mr T Taylor over nothing at all, he is always knocking me about. [He] never hits big lads only the little lads such as me. I would sooner be in a reformatory than here."*

The Sun sneered at the local papers for not having published a line about the incident. It wasn't until the following weekend that the *Marlborough Times* broke its silence: "During the past week the inhabitants of the district have been passing through a form of sensational excitement which is fortunately rare in the history of the locality." This was after other London papers had followed *The Sun*.

The story gathered pace as lurid tales of mistreatment were reported from an Epsom yard. The *Morning Leader* described the Luddon case as, "Enough to make any man of decent feeling sick with shame and with indignation." The Taylor brothers, it said, were,

> "Sons of the stern old trainer Alec Taylor, who made the place famous in the racing world. The old man also, however, made it notorious. Twenty years ago, it is said, a stable lad was surprised when he found he could lie down without pain."

If that was exaggerated, life for a new lad at Manton at that time was certainly hard. His initiation began with an obligatory fight with all the other lads, and continued with a dunking in a horse trough. At the end of the 1970s, in his hundredth year, a former Old Alec apprentice called Ted Caplan recalled that breakfast consisted of a mug of tea, a slice of bread, and two cuts with a hunting crop: "It was the same for supper and the only second helpings were from the crop."

After Luddon's death, the district Coroner asked three local doctors to carry out a post mortem. They found, 'Excessive inflammation of the membranes of the brain,' and that, 'The lower part of the brain had distinct tubercular spots upon it.' The next day, the Coroner held an inquest at Savernake hospital. A jury of Marlborough tradesmen was sworn in; men with yeoman names like Leather, Glass and Baker. Among them were a cobbler, the town's undertaker Thomas Free, and at least three future Mayors. The jurors insisted on making their own, detailed inspection of the corpse. A nurse and the hospital porter were called to help them. A police superintendent and the NSPCC inspector stood at the back of the inquest. The Coroner told the jury, "It has come to my knowledge that there has been a great deal of talk about this matter. I wish you to come with perfectly clear and unbiased minds and to listen to nothing but what you hear in evidence."

Tom Taylor was the first witness. The Coroner asked him, what had been Luddon's duties? Taylor replied, "The copper hole," explaining that each new boy's first tasks in the yard included lighting and maintaining the furnace that boiled water for the horses, and helping in the dining hall. Taylor added that Luddon, "Was never inclined for work... sometimes he would not have hot water [ready] for the horses." At first, only the Coroner and the jury foreman questioned Taylor, but as his evidence continued, juror after juror joined in.

Taylor was asked, "Did he give any orders for the boy to be chastised?" "Certainly not." "You have no idea how the bruises that he has on his body came about?" "Not the slightest." Had any lad been taken away from Manton in the previous month? "Yes. There was [one] who complained of being ill treated. [As the boy] did not do as he was told I gave him two stripes on the bottom with my cane."

Taylor, under attack from several jurors, confessed to having 'striped' Luddon also. That contradicted his claim not to have any idea how Luddon came by his bruising. He conceded that the lads' housekeeper, Mrs Fanny Boulton, had had 'several hysterical fits' since Luddon's death, and that her husband, a Manton employee for eight years, had been sacked 'for going about making strange statements'. After Taylor came Alfred Stickler, the deputy head lad. In the span of three answers, he denied ever striking

Luddon and then said that he'd given the boy 'a slight tap' for being slow to get up in the morning.

Marian Barrow, the Sister from Savernake Hospital, called Luddon's bruises 'very severe' and said that he complained to her of being whipped out of bed. She was followed by the head lad, Oliver Reeves, aged 70 and an employee of the Taylors for 40 years, going back to Old Alec's yard at Fyfield. He told the inquest that Luddon was lazy and negligent and that, "I had to give him a stripe, and sometimes two," with a riding whip. A juror asked, "Is it usual to whip the lads if they do not do their work?" "Yes. I may just hit them with a stick or a whip." The NSPCC observer challenged Reeves to admit that he struck Luddon shortly before the boy was taken to hospital. Reeves denied it.

Dr Maurice then gave the jury the benefit, as he saw it, of his medical opinion. He testified that he'd visited Manton and that Luddon had accused Reeves and Stickler. He repeated his belief that the cause of death was meningitis. Questions rained down. He was asked, could the beatings have caused, or hastened, the lad's death? Dr Maurice complained of being 'heckled all round.'

He told the jury, "You must remember you are not educated men with regard [to] post mortems." They were outraged. Without quite accusing the doctor of negligence, they opened a new front in their questioning: bruising to the base of Luddon's spine. 'Post mortem marks,' said Dr Maurice. By now, the inquest had run for two hours. The Coroner was aghast when the jury foreman said that he wanted to hear more evidence.

"I don't see any advantage in that," the Coroner said: "You are not here to enquire into the management of Mr Taylor's stables. The post mortem showed that the boy did not die from any bruises on [his] body." The foreman retorted, "I differ," adding that the jury wanted to question the lads who were in Luddon's dormitory when Stickler beat him, and Mrs Boulton, the housekeeper.

"I think, candidly, that the boy's death was due to his having been thrashed," the foreman added. The Coroner made a final attempt at closure. He tried to convince the jurors that 'natural causes' was the proper and only possible outcome. He failed. The jury stayed on at the hospital and insisted on re-examining Luddon's body.

The Coroner resumed the inquest the following afternoon at the Sun Inn in the town. It was an unwise move. Savernake hospital is some way out of Marlborough, up a long, steep hill. In a High Street of many pubs and inns, the Sun is the closest of all to Manton. It drew a large, hostile crowd. Before the hearing began, Dr Maurice handed two anonymous letters to the Coroner, who declined to read them on the grounds that if anyone, "Had anything to say, they know where to come to say it." The letters' contents can be inferred. *The Sun* called Maurice an 'old friend' of the Taylors, with the implication that his evidence couldn't be trusted. The *Morning Leader* dripped sarcasm. It expressed, "The utmost sympathy with poor Dr Maurice, who [has] had to endure the untold agony of a couple of anonymous letters."

The second and third doctors from the post mortem were subjected to lengthy questioning from the jurors about the bruising at the base of Luddon's spine. The exchanges were ill tempered. A juror said he didn't think the doctors had been very thorough, "Seeing that they missed a bruise as large as a man's hand." Eventually, one of the doctors conceded that a blow to the spine sufficient to affect the spinal cord, "Might accelerate death." The housekeeper Mrs Boulton then appeared, to confirm that the boy had been bruised on the back as well as on the legs and buttocks and that he blamed, "Mr Reeves and Master Tom."

The next testimony came from a lad who shared Luddon's dorm. He confirmed Stickler's assault, and added that Luddon had cried that he was 'half dead from being knocked about.' His hands shook so much that he couldn't hold a pen, and another boy wrote a letter for him: *"Dear Mother and Father, just a few lines hoping to find you quite well, but not as it leaves me at present."*

In the letter, Luddon complained that Reeves, Stickler and Taylor had all beaten him. Then James Sprules, a lad of 13, barely three feet tall, stood on a chair to say that Taylor had whipped Luddon as he blew on the fire, and Reeves had assaulted him in the yard with a 'long thong whip.'

The dreadful image taking shape in the inquest room was of a sickly, terrified boy beaten round Manton like a carpet at spring cleaning. After hearing the extra witnesses, the jury withdrew for an hour. When they came back, they delivered a bombshell. They rejected the doctors' report and found that the *'Immediate cause of death was brain disease, caused by the severe thrashings given by Taylor, Reeves and Stickler.'*

"That amounts to a verdict of manslaughter," said the Coroner: "I confess that I don't agree with the jury in this verdict. But these 12 gentlemen have given their time and attention. They have worked out the evidence and heard all that has been said." He bound over the three accused men to appear before a magistrates' court.

A roar went up from the crowd waiting outside. The jurors were cheered as they left. The foreman was lifted shoulder high and carried to his home in triumph. By contrast, Tom Taylor was hissed when he appeared, escorted by six policemen. They had difficulty getting him out of the town. Reeves and Stickler sheltered in the pub until the mob outside had dispersed. The following Saturday, a special sitting of the county magistrates was convened in the Town Hall. The hall was full all day. There was a large, angry crowd outside. Police reinforcements were called in from Hungerford and Devizes.

With prompting from the NSPCC, *The Sun* had decided that if the due process of law didn't serve up Tom Taylor's head on a plate, then it would launch a private prosecution. It invited readers' subscriptions to a legal fighting fund. The foreman of the Coroner's inquest jury pledged a guinea.

A seven-hour hearing began with Taylor, Reeves and Stickler facing a summons for having 'feloniously killed and slain' James Luddon. The prosecutor told the Bench that, "The beating of the deceased was an unlawful act. A parent has a right to chastise his child, and a teacher standing *in loco parentis* might have delegated to him the same right, but a master has no right to chastise a servant."

This was a crucial point for Tom Taylor, and his lawyer stepped in: "The boy was an apprentice and his master had a perfect right to [punish] him." The prosecutor shifted the onus to Reeves and Stickler: "It could not possibly be taken that they had any right [to] chastise the youth who has so unhappily died." His meaning was clear. Tom Taylor might be able to shelter behind the Master and Servant Act: the other two could not.

Sister Barrow from Savernake Hospital confirmed that Luddon had bruises, "From the ankle up to the thigh on both legs. There was much discolouration." Luddon's roommates repeated their evidence from the inquest. None of the three defendants was called. The prosecution simply read out their previous testimony, after which the defence counsel submitted that, "This is a case in which there is absolutely no evidence. All the medical witnesses [say] there was nothing on the body which would account for the [brain] disease or even the acceleration of it."

He went further, asserting that, "The ill-treatment the boy received was infinitesimal." He suggested, to laughter, that there wasn't a magistrate on the Bench who hadn't received 'three or four times' as much punishment in their schooldays. A fag who didn't boil his fag-master's water, he said, 'would be lucky to get off with two stripes.' "Here was a boy with specific duties to do, [one] of them to get the water hot. What [if] he would not do it? The boy must be punished somehow."

The magistrates retired for only 10 minutes before finding that, "The evidence [is] insufficient to justify sending the case for trial on the charge of manslaughter."

Then began the second hearing, into the NSPCC's charge of cruelty against Reeves and Stickler. For the first time in the proceedings, Alec Taylor took the stand. He told the Bench that,

> "When Stickler came into our service [a few weeks ago] I told him he was not to knock the boys about. Reeves has been with me so long that I did not consider it necessary to give him instructions. [When my brother or I] are away, Reeves is in charge of the boys. I should say it would not be outside the limits of Reeves's power to administer a caning to a boy. I should not consider it a violation of my orders if I had heard of it. How is a man to maintain order among a lot of boys if he [does not] have power to punish them?"

After the doctors had reprised their previous evidence, a new witness appeared: Thomas Holloway, the boy interviewed by *The Sun*. His complaints about mistreatment had caused his father to take him from Manton, shortly before Luddon fell ill. Holloway seized his opportunity to settle some scores. He claimed that, "I was in the yard and saw Reeves with a riding whip in his hand. [He] went into the dining hall, to Luddon. I could see in through the window. I saw Reeves flogging Luddon with the thong end of [the] whip."

Luddon was shrieking, he said, "Very loudly, all the time [Reeves] was hitting him… I saw Luddon [in] the kitchen. I saw Reeves go in with the same whip in his hand. He chased Luddon out of the kitchen, flogging him with the thong again. The thong was about four feet long. Luddon stopped outside the dining hall and held his hands up. While he did so, Reeves was hitting him." Holloway claimed to have seen Reeves hit Luddon 10 or 11 times that day: "As hard as he could strike."

Holloway hadn't finished. He said that, from several rooms away, 'with thick walls between them,' he'd heard Luddon crying at night, "Shouting out loudly." He raised doubts about his testimony when he insisted that he heard, through those thick walls, Stickler hit Luddon 'about a dozen blows.' "That's as true as the rest of my evidence. If others say there were only two blows they must be mistaken." The 'others' were the three boys who were in the room when Stickler hit Luddon.

"The boy Holloway manifestly lied," the defence lawyer snapped. He then threw in the towel, saying that he didn't plan to call Reeves and Stickler as witnesses, because their evidence was sure to contradict. The two men were charged with cruelty and committed to appear at Wiltshire's winter Assizes. As Tom Taylor left the Town Hall, the waiting crowd, estimated at between 400 and 500 strong, jeered and jostled him all along the High Street.

The Assizes convened a fortnight later. Mr Justice Grantham arrived from London to tell a grand jury that despite the rejection of the manslaughter charge in the magistrates' court, the Coroner's inquest verdict obliged them to reconsider it. He then waved it aside: "On the doctors' evidence there can be no justification for [pursuing] manslaughter. It would be [a] waste of time."

The defendants then faced their second charges: assault against Taylor and Stickler, 'assault causing grievous bodily harm' against Reeves. Taylor pleaded not guilty, the other two, guilty. Grantham conceded that there was an argument as to, 'What amount of chastisement [Taylor] was justified in administering to his apprentices,' but on balance felt there was insufficient evidence against him. The jury acquitted Taylor. The judge said of Reeves and Stickler, "The suggestion that a boy was somewhat late in the morning, or that the hot water in the afternoon was not as hot as it ought to be, [was] no justification for any man taking a horse whip and a big stick and knocking a boy about."

Stickler escaped lightly because he had only one, relatively minor assault against him, the caning in the dormitory. He was fined £5, and bound over to keep the peace. That left Reeves. Grantham told him that, "You had no right to use a whip in the way in which you did. It is necessary that men in your position should know, if you are guilty of cruelty to lads placed under your care, you will be punished for it." Reeves was sentenced to three months' hard labour. The public gallery burst into cheers.

Grantham hadn't finished with Manton. He described the Luddon case in scathing terms as, "Certainly [indicating] that in these stables there was sometimes a great deal of cruelty going on."

"I can only picture to myself [what] we have all read of as the unfortunate and unhappy way [in] which the negroes lived in America before they were emancipated." The conduct of Reeves, he said, "Seems to have been that of what might vulgarly be called a nigger-driver, the superintendent of slaves who went about with a cruel whip to keep the slaves in order. The life of this boy seems to have been that of a slave, so far as you were concerned."

Charles Gianella was an apprentice, in the years before the first world war, at another prominent Wiltshire training yard of the time, Druid's Lodge. It was a byword for isolation and secrecy. It was also a tribute to Alec Taylor. Most details of its design were closely modelled on Manton, and its owners adopted Old Alec's precautions of opening the lads' mail and locking them up at night. It was put to Gianella that life at Druid's Lodge had been harsh? Yes, he replied, "But never cruel." Then he winced: "Not like Manton."

The horses jointly owned by the Taylors were all sold. An advertisement appeared in the local paper:

THE MANTON TRAINING STABLES.

DISSOLUTION OF PARTNERSHIP.

NOTICE IS HEREBY GIVEN,—That the PARTNERSHIP heretofore subsisting between the undersigned, T. A. and ALEXANDER TAYLOR, of MANTON, in the County of Wilts, under the style of Messrs. T. and A. TAYLOR, has been DISSOLVED by mutual consent since the 30th June last; and ALL ACCOUNTS owing to Tradesmen and others, if sent in at once, will be LIQUIDATED.

Dated this 7th day of July.

T. A. TAYLOR,
ALEXANDER TAYLOR.

No man's reputation can survive an association with 'slave whipping.' The townsfolk of Marlborough paid no heed to Tom Taylor's acquittal. In the court of their opinion, he was a murderer. They were in no mood for mitigating circumstances, and in truth, apart from the sanction provided by the Master and Servant Act, there weren't any.

But, just as poor James Luddon had a fatal illness at the time when he was being beaten for idleness, so it seems that Tom Taylor himself suffered from a brain illness, probably a tumour. He had an ungovernable temper. It mostly expressed itself in a furious war against touts. He used to ride round the downs loosing off his shotgun into any patch of bramble that overlooked a gallop. Years after, venerable 'men of observation' showed their pellet scars in the Marlborough pubs.

Tom Taylor left Manton after the severance of his partnership with his half-brother. He had no choice. He couldn't show his face in Marlborough. He died two years later, aged only 52.

Chapter 9

The good luck fairy

The Luddon scandal would have finished off most trainers, the more so as the Taylors had struggled for winners during their shared mastership of Manton. Together, their best year produced only 18 winners from between 50 and 60 horses, with prize money of £5,308. It was a poor return, and a sharp drop back from their father's time. The only races of significance that the brothers won were the Gold Cup and the Jockey Club Stakes, both with Love Wisely, who'd in any case begun in training with Old Alec.

Young Alec had the pedigree to be a great trainer. His life had been spent at his father's side, beginning as a child at Fyfield. For many years, he was assistant trainer in all but name. Before he could stake his own claim, Young Alec had to be free from the distraction of his brother. Once Tom had left, Alec was in a sense on probation. He was the sole owner of Manton. The yard's success or failure was his alone. At that tipping point, he had the great good fortune to take over the training of one of the best mares in the history of racing: the peerless Sceptre.

The bay Sceptre was by Persimmon out of Ornament, a full sister to the unbeaten 1885 triple crown winner Ormonde. Persimmon won the Derby and St Leger, followed by the Gold Cup and Eclipse as a four-year-old. When his daughter appeared in the Duke of Westminster's dispersal sale, she was sure to command a stellar price. The auction provided two surprises. The first was her purchaser: Robert Sievier, a controversial figure who at one time or another antagonised most of the racing establishment. His biographer John Welcome provides a lively sketch: "At the age of 40 he had two marriages behind him [and lived] with a well-connected woman who was not his wife, whom he had filched from her rightful husband. [If] that were not enough, he had been bankrupt three times, struck off the roll of those permitted to attend Court, been involved in heaven knew how many racing scandals and was still likely to seduce your wife or run away with your daughter."

Sievier's enemies included Tattersalls, who'd implied that he wasn't creditworthy. On the eve of Sceptre's sale, Sievier, who liked to get even, preferably in front of an audience, approached the auctioneer Somerville Tattersall with £20,000 [*£1.13 million*] in £500 notes, 'Just so you know I'm good for the money.' Tattersall, with nowhere secure to put the notes overnight, tried to wave Sievier away, but the cash was pressed on him. Tattersall hid the notes on the top of the wardrobe in his room and spent an anxious night, sleeping fitfully and watching the furniture.

A high price had been expected for Sceptre, but no one had imagined that the hammer would fall on a bid of 10,000 guineas [*£621,000*]. It was the highest price ever paid for a yearling, and it stood as the record for 20 years. Sievier waxed lyrical:

> "There she stood, what I can only describe as a mass of perfection. Such a mare as perhaps for many years would not be offered for sale again. The value of money was lost in admiration; I fell in love with her! Her prospective qualities, either on the Turf or for the stud, appeared flawless."

The first time that Sceptre worked seriously as a two-year-old, her trainer Charles Morton put her in a gallop with a five-year-old handicapper. She was weighted to receive 14lb from the older horse, 34lb worse than weight-for-age, and won in a hack canter by half a dozen lengths. Sceptre ran three times in her first season, winning twice. Then Morton accepted an offer to train privately.

Sievier never suffered from self-doubt: he bought a yard at Shrewton on Salisbury Plain, and trained Sceptre himself. As a warm-up for her classic season, he ran Sceptre in the Lincoln. Sievier's lifestyle required regular infusions of cash, and they came from betting. The Lincoln provided a strong market, and Sceptre was allotted just 7st in the handicap, reduced by 7lb when a young apprentice was booked. Sievier hired an assistant trainer and went away for a few days. In his absence, Sceptre was galloped at racing pace every day. He came back to find her, 'Off her feed, nervous, restless and upset.' It was touch and go as to whether he could build her up again in time for the Lincoln. He wrote a letter to scratch her. Then he tore it up. She took her chance, and started a hot favourite at 11-4, with Sievier's own bets standing to win him over £30,000 [*£1.7 million*]. Despite her arduous training, Sceptre nearly won, going down by only a head.

Sceptre's next race was the 2,000 Guineas, where she beat the colts by two lengths and three, in a record time for the race. Two days later, she set another race record when winning the 1,000 Guineas, despite losing a shoe at the start. In both races, she was ridden by Bert Randall, an inexperienced jockey in his first season as a professional. Sievier never explained why he chose not to use one of the many senior riders who would've jumped at the chance to ride Sceptre. Most likely, as a well-informed punter and layer, he simply didn't trust them. Captain Machell used to say, "The jockeys will always beat you."

Sievier badly needed to win the Derby, and not just for the prize. He hadn't recouped his Lincoln losses in the two Guineas, and he'd backed Sceptre for Epsom for months past, beginning with £1,000 to £30 and supporting her all the way down to 5-2. On Derby day, she was even money, despite having been confined to her box with a stone bruise 10 days before the race. Sievier didn't hedge any of his bets: he stood to win £33,000 [*£1.92 million*]. His filly was drawn on the wide outside, and started slowly. Randall lost his head and drove her up the hill to close on the race leaders. She turned into the straight in a share of the lead, but her earlier exertions and the missed work caught up with her, and she faded into fourth. The first and second were Ard Patrick and Rising Glass, whom she'd beaten comfortably in the 2,000 Guineas.

Sievier turned Sceptre out again two days later for the Oaks, and she won easily by three lengths at 5-2. Sievier had run out of money to back her, but he had the satisfaction of a tremendous reception from the Epsom crowd. The cheering continued for long after the race. Applause pays no bills, and Sievier had to go cap in hand to have his prize money paid out at once, so that he could settle his bookmakers' accounts on the Monday.

Having run in four classics, winning three of them, Sceptre then went to Paris for the Grand Prix, 10 days after the Derby. Sievier won heavily betting on minor races before the Grand Prix, and put the proceeds on Sceptre. To his horror, Randall never put her in the race with a chance. Perhaps mindful of the rough treatment that English riders used to suffer in Paris, Randall had nothing outside him but the Bois de Boulogne. Sceptre was still beaten only two or three lengths. Sievier said, "[Randall] did not display that nerve which one likes to see in a jockey. I am as certain as it is possible for a man to be that Sceptre went at least 200 yards further than the winner."

His filly had now run in three Group One races in 11 days. She was only warming up. Sievier sent her from Paris straight to Ascot's Coronation Stakes, where she unseated Randall at the start. He again gave the outside to no one, coming with a run when it was all too late. The first three fillies home had all finished miles behind Sceptre in the Oaks. That was all Sievier wanted to see or hear of Randall, and a new jockey rode Sceptre the next day, when she won the St James's Palace Stakes.

In the second half of the season, she won the Nassau Stakes by four lengths, giving weight all round, and reasserting her superiority over the fillies who'd beaten her in the Coronation Stakes. She won the St Leger in soft ground and then finished second, again giving plenty of weight, in the Park Hill Stakes. So in her second season Sceptre, trained by a beginner, ran 12 times: in the Lincoln, then in 11 consecutive Group One or Two races, winning six of the Group Ones, over distances from a mile to 14 furlongs. Her four outright English classic wins made her unique in racing history. Only the filly Formosa has claimed the same four races, in 1868, though she dead-heated in the 2,000 Guineas.

Despite all the rich purses Sceptre won him, Sievier was broke. With a heavy heart, he sent her to Tattersalls in December with a reserve of 24,000 guineas. She looked woolly and unkempt, and there was no bid for her. Back she went with Sievier to Shrewton for, as he put it, "A final shot in the Lincolnshire Handicap. Financial matters were in a critical state with me. Win, and I could retain her. Lose, or not run, and she must go. Therefore the Lincoln had to decide a lot for me."

There was no happy ending. As he must've known after her wins over middle distances, the flat mile of the Carholme was now too short a trip for her. She also carried vastly more weight than the previous year. She finished fifth, not beaten far. Soon after, Sievier met the racing manager of Sir William Bass, son of Old Alec's owner, Hamar Bass. He told the man that Sceptre was for sale. Sir William was serving with his regiment in India. A cable was sent, the reply came within a day, and for £25,000, Sceptre had a new owner. Young Alec went to Shrewton to collect her personally from Sievier, who 'bore it very well, all things considered.'

Sceptre's transfer to Manton was a local sensation. When she was walked through the town on her way to the yard, the boys from Marlborough College spilled out onto the road to cheer her as she passed. More out of courtesy than to seek advice, Taylor wrote asking Sievier,

'How should I train her?' Sievier wired back, "Train her like you would a [selling] plater." The Sceptre that Taylor looked at was hardly more than a hat-rack. He decided to back off her and encourage her to put on weight. As a supplement to her feed, she was given two gallons of milk each day. She blossomed, and Taylor waited until Royal Ascot before her first run for Manton, in the Hardwicke Stakes. She won by five lengths, and blew hard in the unsaddling enclosure. She ran next in the Eclipse.

The race brought together Sceptre and Ard Patrick, the two horses who'd won all the previous year's classics, and set them against the best three-year-old, the 2,000 Guineas and Derby winner Rock Sand. The younger horse was swamped by the four-year-olds as they turned for home. Sceptre took a slight lead. The Sandown crowd stood on tiptoes and roared her home. In the last half-furlong, Ard Patrick's rider forced him upsides, then ahead. Sceptre went down by a neck.

There were no excuses. But where a 10-furlong race comes down to a winning margin of two feet, it's permissible to consider the strength of the two jockeys. Ard Patrick had the experienced senior rider Otto Madden, Sceptre the young jockey who'd ridden her as a 7lb claimer in the previous year's Lincoln. George Lambton thought that Madden, 'Rode the best race of his life.' The Eclipse gave Ard Patrick a 2-1 advantage over Sceptre in their three meetings. Sadly, he then broke down and never ran again.

It was evident after the race that Sceptre, again, blew hard. Bob Sievier was in the throng around her, and he thought that Young Alec hadn't given her the work she needed. Sir William Bass's racing manager suffered a loss of nerve. He dithered back and forth between Manton and Shrewton. Eventually he asked Taylor to let Sievier advise on Sceptre's preparation for her next race. Taylor agreed: he had little choice. Sievier was in his element at Manton, directing a gallop here and a gallop there. In one spin over a mile and a half, Sceptre was chased along by a sprinter for the first stage and then joined by another of Bass's horses, the stayer Grey Tick. The exercise was repeated the following day.

Sceptre's next target was Newmarket's valuable Jockey Club Stakes at the beginning of October. In it, she re-opposed Rock Sand, who had underlined his claim to be the top three-year-old by winning the St Leger. Sceptre was never beaten at Newmarket, and she toyed with the triple crown winner, beating him by four lengths before returning to another rapturous reception. Sievier had scraped together every remaining coin that he possessed to lump on Sceptre at 5-4, and he was overcome in the unsaddling enclosure. Once recovered, he said that, "In training her, [I can] claim to have run a dead-heat with the Lord of the Manor of Manton."

The wonderful mare ran three times more that October, winning on each occasion. First in a valuable stakes race at Kempton, where she was repeatedly baulked before getting up in the last inches, giving 40lb to the runner-up. Then she went back to Newmarket and won a small-field Champion Stakes by 10 lengths. The following day, her lead horse Grey Tick won the Cesarewitch. Finally, Sceptre won a match by eight lengths at 1-100. It was a day without compare in English racing history, because the race after Sceptre's was won by the two-year-old Pretty Polly, who the year after won the 1,000 Guineas, Oaks, St Leger and five other Group Ones. In the space of half an hour, racegoers at Newmarket saw two of the best fillies and mares ever to race in this country.

To all intents and purposes, that was the end of Sceptre's career. Young Alec ran her three times as a five-year-old, but she wasn't kept in training beyond June, when it was clear that she was, at last, feeling the effects of all the hard races that had gone before, though she still showed high-class form in the Coronation Cup and in the Gold Cup. She was game, sound and tough. One of her daughters would win the Oaks for Taylor, and in the next generation, she in turn produced a 2,000 Guineas winner.

Sceptre brought redemption to Manton. Young Alec had taken on a training challenge with limited scope for glory, but much risk of a banana skin. He trained Sceptre to win five races and return £12,633 to Sir William Bass for his £25,000 investment. Just as important, Manton was again talked of as a racing stable, after it had made decidedly uncomfortable news. In its review of the season, the *Sporting Times* declared that,

> "The change of front [man at] the Manton stable is one of an entirely satisfactory character, inasmuch as we have no training establishment, with all its surroundings, to equal that built by the late Alec Taylor."

In the year of Tom Taylor's departure, the yard had 12 winners worth £2,305. The following year, thanks to Sceptre and Grey Tick, Alec Taylor recorded 33 winners and £18,731. And in the autumn of the year after, the good luck fairy called.

"What Ho! A Fairy!" was Bob Sievier's ironic salute to Alfred Cox. Sievier, irrepressible, had bounced back from various scrapes to launch a weekly paper called *The Winning Post*. It was priced at 1d: 'a Bob for a penny,' shouted the news sellers, and it offered a potpourri of society gossip, politics, innuendo, and Sievier's own racing news and tips. Among its weekly features was a page called *Celebrities in Glass Houses*. One of its subjects was an owner who took his horses to Manton at the end of 1904: Alfred William Cox, who raced as 'Mr Fairie'.

Even his friends never prised from Cox the reason for his assumed name. It was hardly an attempt to conceal his identity: on and off the racecourse, and on the title page of a breeding book that he published privately, he was known as 'Fairie Cox'. Sometimes the obvious explanation is the right one, and it can be guessed that 'Mr Fairie', registered by Cox in 1887 when he was 30, was his ironic salute to the extraordinary luck by which he acquired his millions.

Cox was the second son of a Liverpool merchant. Like many in his position, his future was in the services, but he failed the Army entrance examination. His father soon tired of supporting him, the more so when his son showed greater interest in racing than in finding a job. Alfred Cox was given £100 and a small allowance, and put on a boat to Australia. After a short time in Melbourne, he was employed as a bookkeeper on a station 200 miles north. It was prosperous country, bloodstock breeding was a popular pastime, and every station and farm had something that could gallop. There were local race meetings. Before long, Cox had a horse, a mare called The Greek. He knew if a horse ran in his name, his father would find out, so The Greek ran in the colours of her trainer, Andy Mitchelson.

New hands on the outback stations were called 'jackeroos,' especially if they hailed from the old country. Cox stood out at the races by wearing a white bowler hat and white kid gloves. The bookmakers dubbed him 'the dandy jackeroo.' News of that kind of curiosity tends to spread quickly, and sure enough, some busybody wrote to Cox senior to let him know that his boy was keeping bad company.

By return, the son had an angry letter telling him that unless he cut all his links with racing, his allowance would stop and he could forget any hopes of an inheritance. Cox seems to have done as instructed. The Greek had borne him a couple of gifts in minor races, but flopped one day when the money was properly down. She was sold without regrets. Cox directed his energy to investments. Those were the early days of mineral discoveries in Australia. Silverton, far to the north of New South Wales, was a boom town with a silver rush in full spate. Cox heard that Mount Gipps station, not far from Silverton, was hiring a jackeroo. He applied to the station manager, a fierce Scot called George McCulloch, and was taken on.

McCulloch's handshake opened the door to an astounding fortune. Prospectors were swarming over the surrounding countryside, driven on by each tale of new-found mineral riches. Among them was one of McCulloch's boundary riders, a German immigrant called Charles Rasp. He'd seen the mine workings round Silverton, he'd listened to all the talk, and he'd been poking around an escarpment that overlooked Mount Gipps. Because of its rugged outline, the locals called it the broken hill. Rasp bought a copy of *The Prospector's Hand Book*. Sitting up on the hill with his book, Rasp was sure the samples he'd collected were rich in tin.

He enlisted two men who were digging a dam nearby. One was a Welsh coalminer, David James. Together, the three pegged out claims for 40 acres. Rasp paid £10 for a year's ownership of the claims. It was one of the best investments that any man has ever made. On his own hunch and after others had looked and moved on, Rasp had found the mammoth silver lode that became The Broken Hill Proprietary company [BHP]. First, though, he had to navigate a tricky meeting with the station manager. He gave notice to George McCulloch and asked for his back pay.

McCulloch was hard-headed, hard-fisted, and capable of volcanic temper: all were needed to manage rootless riders and station hands across an area the size of an English county. He was also intelligent and quick thinking. His opening salvo was, "Ye've been peggin' the hill!" Yes, said Rasp. McCulloch teased out the story, and at once backed the other man's judgement: "Ye'll be wanting money to develop [the claim]."

He proposed that a syndicate be formed from the Mount Gipps staff, to raise capital. Seven men joined in the next day, led by McCulloch, Rasp and James. They pledged to contribute £70 each, and in the next fortnight, they filed claims that took in two miles of the broken hill's ridge. There were delays. A drought meant that the men were occupied with the welfare of their sheep. The assays of their mineral samples produced negative results, because they were being tested for the presence of tin. But there were plenty of people in those feverish times who wanted to buy into any claim near Silverton. The syndicate agreed to divide their holdings in half, so there were 14 shares available for trafficking.

At that moment, Alfred Cox arrived at Mount Gipps. He was caught up in the frenzy. He asked McCulloch, 'Will you sell one of your shares?' "Yes," he told Cox, "£200." That was quite an uplift on a share that McCulloch had put £35 into, and Cox counter-offered £100. McCulloch wouldn't budge. Cox raised his offer to £120. McCulloch still didn't lower his asking price. After much argument, Cox challenged McCulloch to play cards. The fourteenth-share would be sold at the winner's price: £200 [*£10,500*] for the share if McCulloch won, or £120 [*£6,290*] if Cox won. McCulloch agreed.

The game was arranged for the following evening. They were to play euchre, a variant of poker, the best of three. Several of the other syndicate members crowded in to watch. McCulloch dispensed whisky to all, complaining, "It's an awful risk I'm taking." He quickly won the first game. Cox drew level in the second. Then in the decider, fate handed all the cards to Cox. "A good game," he said cheerfully. "It might have been a damn sight better," replied McCulloch. A new 14-man syndicate agreement was drawn up, and among the signatories was 'AW Cox, station hand.'

McCulloch sensed that he'd made a mistake in parting with half his original stake. He was a willing buyer whenever part-shares became available. Not many months after the card game, assays of rock specimens taken from the broken hill showed deposits of up to 1,000 ounces of silver to the ton. Within six years, with BHP floated as a public company, each original fourteenth share, if held in its entirety, had created wealth equivalent to £1,260,000 [*£71 million*] in market value, bonus shares and dividends.

None of the syndicate members had held onto all their holdings. There were regular calls on them to provide more capital after their claim had been filed, and they were besieged with offers. Most mining claims come to nothing. It was natural if some of the syndicate succumbed to the chance of doubling or trebling their investment overnight. The sums were so vast that even a sliver of a fourteenth-part share turned out to be a King's ransom. David James, who drove the first peg in Rasp's claim, sold three-quarters of his original share for £1,900 [*£104,000*]. The remaining quarter set him up for life: he established a stud, and in 1895, he won the Melbourne Cup.

Cox cashed in some of his holdings from an early stage. He was negotiating to sell more, right up to the time of boarding the boat that took him home. The good luck fairy continued to watch over him. The buyer reckoned the asking price was too high, and Cox failed to close the deal.

Just before he sailed, Cox ran into Mitchelson, trainer of his mare The Greek. He bought him lunch and said, "I have big interests here, Andy. I'll be back and I'll bring you a couple of nice horses." But the dandy jackeroo spent his treasure-trove of silver in England. Luckily for Alec Taylor, some of it found its way to Manton.

Chapter 10

Bayardo

When Fairie Cox had gone to a place beyond the help of libel lawyers, the *Sporting Times* seldom mentioned him without prefixing his name, 'the weird and wonderful' Mr Cox. Overnight, the broken hill insulated him for life from financial worries. He didn't give a fig for most of the conventions of the time, and he could afford not to. He wasn't clubbable, and he seldom bothered talking to anyone on the racecourse, apart from Taylor and his jockeys. Society mothers would trail their daughters in front of him at Ascot and Goodwood, and he paid no attention at all. Whatever emotion he felt was hidden behind a huge cigar and an expressionless face.

The first winner in Cox's colours of white, orange sleeves and cap was at Newmarket in 1888. Over the next few seasons, he spent lavishly on yearlings at the sales, without finding a decent horse. He did however buy a mare called Lady Muncaster, who traced back to the Derby-winning northern race mare Blink Bonny. Lady Muncaster had won six races as a two-year-old, among them the Gimcrack and the Seaton Delaval stakes, and three more as a three-year-old. Her first living foal was the filly Isoletta, by Isonomy. Isoletta never raced, but she bred six individual winners, and her importance to Fairie Cox and to English breeding came from the product of her mating with the 1875 Derby winner Galopin: a filly called Galicia. In her first season, she won a valuable Ascot stakes race, and was winning a similar event at Newmarket in a canter, but split a pastern.

As a three-year-old, she was aimed high, as Cox's horses tended to be, and she made no show in the fillies' classics. In the Derby Cup, Galicia looked as if she'd come home alone, but broke down and never ran again. Her first three years at stud were inconclusive.

Founders: the four dominant personalities in the early years of Manton were (clockwise from top left): Old Alec Taylor, George Payne, Stirling Crawfurd – whose financial backing enabled Taylor to build the yard – and Crawfurd's wayward wife, the Duchess of Montrose. Taylor was said to be the only man she feared.

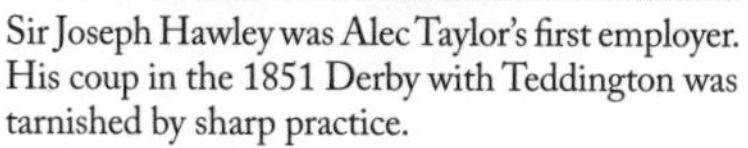

Sir Joseph Hawley was Alec Taylor's first employer. His coup in the 1851 Derby with Teddington was tarnished by sharp practice.

Taylor was famed for frugality, but once established at Manton he treated himself to personalised horse brasses.

Below, Young Alec Taylor, on his hack Alberta, watches over Lord Astor's 1926 Oaks winner Short Story.

Lee C A Wages a/c 1923		£	s	d
Jan 1	By Bonus	2		
Dec 31	Wages	9	14	2
		£11	14	2
Jan 13	To Money		6	
Apl 4			4	6
	Cash		2	
10	Mundy		5	6
Ju 25	N. H.!		10	10
29	Money	1	3	6
Jy 16	Sox		3	
Aug 6	Cash		2	
30	Money		5	3
			19	11
Oct 13	Cash		2	
15	Shirt		9	10
Nov 9	Cash		2	
20	Mon[illegible]		5	
Dec 17			5	6
31	N. H. s		11	3
	Bal[illegible]	5	16	1
		£11	14	2

WARREN COTTAGE,
NEWMARKET.
Oct 19. 1924

Dear Sandy,

I send you a present of £25 with my thanks for your good care of [illegible]. I hope the horse will go on well & that we shall all be still prouder of him next year.

Yours Truly
A. R. Cox.

The wages statement of senior lad Sandy Lee shows that in 1923 he earned the equivalent of £186 today, but he had several times that in a gift from grateful owner Alexander Cox.

Above, Tom and Alec Taylor ran Manton jointly after Old Alec's death in 1894. The partnership stuttered along until the hot-tempered Tom was involved in a damaging court case. Below, Picaroon was rated Young Alec's best horse, despite the rival claims of triple crown winners. Blood poisoning prevented him from ever realising his potential. Taylor is behind the colt's head in the photograph.

Above, champions: Young Alec, Danny Maher and Bayardo, the winner of the 1909 St Leger and 1910 Gold Cup. To Taylor's irritation, Maher employed exaggerated waiting tactics on Fairie Cox's colt. Below, the yard at the end of the nineteenth century. The lawn was laid in 1887 to surround a massive Coalbrookdale lamppost, put up by Old Alec Taylor to celebrate a successful year and Queen Victoria's Jubilee.

The good luck fairy: Alfred Cox owned Bayardo and the consecutive Derby winners Gay Crusader and Lemberg. The cartoon is from *The Winning Post.*

Joseph Watson, leading in his 1921 Oaks winner Love In Idleness. He died soon after buying the yard and taking the title of Lord Manton.

Masters: the quartet who shaped Manton's future at the end of the 1920s:
(left to right) Somerville Tattersall, Young Alec, Lord Astor and Gerald Deane.

The parting of the ways: Young Alec stepped down as Master in 1927, after ill health. In this farewell photograph, his successor Joe Lawson is in the centre of the second row. Taylor is on his left. On Lawson's right is the head lad Tom Ault. Two along from Ault is Jack Brennan, work rider and Lord Astor's jockey.

In the third row, eight from the left, is Ted Caplan, who complained of 'second helpings from the riding crop' at mealtimes. Third from the right in the same row is Sandy Lee, whose wages statement is on page 84. Caplan and several others in the photograph received bequests in Taylor's will.

She was barren; then she produced a winner of two minor races; then she had a colt foal who showed promise at Manton, but went amiss and never saw a racecourse.

At Fairie Cox's initiative, Galicia was then mated with Bay Ronald. It was an unexpected but inspired choice. Bay Ronald was a little below the racing ability of the Derby winners that Cox had been using with his mares. He ran fourth in his 2,000 Guineas, fifth in the Derby and second in the Eclipse. He won five times from 25 starts in four seasons, demonstrating durability and consistency. His best days were when winning the City and Suburban and the Hardwicke. For a fee of only 75 guineas [*£4,700*], his mating with Galicia produced one of the best horses that Young Alec ever trained, one of the champions of the first quarter of the twentieth century: Bayardo.

Fairie Cox had mostly lean years when he was building up his stud. He did win the 1895 1,000 Guineas with Galeottia, but she became ungenuine. It was at the end of a winnerless season in 1904 that he moved his horses to Manton. The next year was hardly better, with just one winner of £140 'owned Mr Fairie, trained A Taylor.' The partnership jelled with four and seven successes in the next two summers, and then came Bayardo's two-year-old season, 1908.

At the beginning of June, following a series of optimistic reports from Taylor, Cox asked his trainer to set up a trial to find out just how good Bayardo was. It was over five furlongs, with three of Cox's other two-year-olds and a reliable three-year-old. Taylor arrived back at Manton from the races the evening before, with a couple of senior jockeys recruited to ride in the trial. Otto Madden was one of them. The trial was held soon after daybreak, to allow the jockeys to get back into Marlborough for an 8am train. Madden partnered Bayardo, who was tried at level weights with the three-year-old, 27lb worse than weight-for-age. Taylor's trials book read, "Won easily by six lengths."

Afterwards, there was a scramble back to the station. Madden didn't have a chance to discuss the morning's work with Taylor. He decided that he must have been on the three-year-old in the gallop, and that as a result Cox's two-year-olds were moderate. It was an expensive mistake. On the opening day of Royal Ascot, he and Taylor met to agree the jockey's rides for Manton during the meeting. Pointing in his list to Bayardo in the *£98,000*-to-the-winner New Stakes, Taylor told Madden, "That's your mount there." No, replied Madden, he'd already been booked for another in the race. Taylor, incredulous, asked him, 'What about the gallop?' Only then did it dawn on Madden that he'd been riding the two-year-old. There was nothing to be done. Bayardo won easily, with Madden looking on miserably from many lengths back.

After the race, Fairie Cox told a friend, "This is undoubtedly the best I've ever owned." Thereafter, the American jockey Danny Maher took the ride, and Bayardo went through the season unbeaten. He won *£235,000* when beating 12 rivals in Sandown's National Breeders' Produce stakes. That frightened off most opposition and all bookmakers. In his remaining five races, including the Richmond and Rous Memorial stakes, the Middle Park and the Dewhurst, he never faced more than five rivals and never started at less than 1-3.

If there was any, tiny hole that could be picked in Bayardo's seven-race first-season spree, it was that he never seemed to win by far. Maher invariably rode Cox's colt from far off the pace, appearing in the closing stages to win, apparently, on the bridle.

Hold-up rides carry self-evident risks, though less in the small fields that Bayardo often faced. They frustrate form students by obscuring a winner's superiority; and over time, they can create the suspicion that perhaps the horse is a 'thinker.' Why else is the rider wearing kid gloves? Quite unfairly, Bayardo came to be spoken of by some observers as a horse with a kink, and all because of Maher. Young Alec used to argue with the jockey that if he went on leaving it so late, it would go wrong one day, and eventually it did.

At the start of the 1909 season, Bayardo was the warm ante-post favourite for the 2,000 Guineas and the Derby. But all wasn't well. It was a cold, dry start to the year on the downs. Bayardo hadn't come in his coat. Rumour had it that he suffered from a physical problem, and he did, described at the time as, 'shelly feet', in fact laminitis, caused or aggravated when he slipped and fell one morning on an icy patch. Taylor couldn't get any worthwhile work into the colt on the prevailing hard ground, and he told Cox that Bayardo wouldn't be ready for the 2,000 Guineas. Mr Fairie wasn't the best recipient of unwelcome advice, and he insisted on running at Newmarket. Such was the public's faith in Bayardo that he went off a solid 8-13 favourite.

It's impossible to believe that the same could happen today, with television pictures, and pre-parade watchers backing their opinions on the betting exchanges. Bayardo was palpably backward. To make matters worse, he sweated heavily. Horses can defy one or the other condition, but seldom both, and certainly not in a classic. He ran well enough to the Bushes, but stopped in a few strides to finish fourth. The winner was King Edward VII's Minoru. He was rated 22lb below Bayardo in the Free Handicap, but all the while that Bayardo was hunched against a cold wind at Manton, Minoru thrived. His trainer Richard Marsh ran him in the Greenham, before which the King's racing manager told Marsh that he was mad to think of the classics: "7st 4lb in the Stewards Cup is more like his class." Minoru won the Greenham and then justified his trainer's confidence by following up in the Guineas.

The third-placed horse, Louviers, beaten three lengths, had twice finished well behind Bayardo the previous season. It was clear that Marsh had conjured a great deal of improvement from Minoru, but the placing of Louviers suggested that Bayardo had run well below his two-year-old form.

Cox's colt still hadn't pleased Taylor as the Derby approached. According to one report, Washington Singer had some big ante-post bets on Bayardo, and induced Cox to insist that his horse ran. The race set up a rematch with Minoru, and there was an intriguing new ingredient, an American colt called Saint Martin, sent across the Atlantic to emulate Iroquois, who won the Derby and St Leger of 1881. Saint Martin won a handicap at Newmarket under a welter weight, and on the strength of that was made 3-1 favourite at Epsom, just ahead of Minoru at 7-2 and Bayardo at 9-2.

It was a race that left the key questions unanswered. Saint Martin fell on the descent to Tattenham Corner. Minoru and Louviers were at the head of the field, away from the trouble. Bayardo, waited with as usual, was badly hampered in the melee behind the faller. Danny Maher reckoned that he lost '16 lengths' in the incident. Bayardo was out of the race, but mercifully unhurt. All the way up the straight, Minoru battled with Louviers, finally prevailing by a head. Half a length back was William The Fourth, with one of that year's big-race regulars, Valens, a further head back in fourth. Bayardo, in his own time, ran on to finish fifth. When Minoru's number went up in the frame, waves of cheering rolled across the enclosures and the downs to celebrate the Royal victory.

The St Leger of that year took on added significance. It offered Minoru a place in the pantheon of triple crown winners, and Bayardo his last chance to win a classic. The two colts tiptoed round each other for the next three months. Both ran at Ascot and both won: Minoru the St James's Palace Stakes and Bayardo the Prince of Wales's Stakes. Later, Bayardo met Louviers in the *£91,500* Sandringham Foal Stakes at Sandown, and the Manton colt took the opportunity offered to show by how much he was prevented from giving his running in the Derby. He won comfortably, with Louviers several lengths back. Bayardo then won the Eclipse, hard held by two lengths, from a small field of older horses.

The race had an embarrassing sequel. Fairie Cox had arranged a celebration dinner at White's that evening. He was supposed to make a speech. He didn't. It wasn't the first time that he'd shown an acute personal failing in public: he was incapably drunk. It was said rather pointedly that Cox was a connoisseur of, 'Racehorses, good Havanas and fine liqueur brandy.' Bob Sievier, less circumspect, wrote in *Celebrities in Glass Houses*, "We [cannot] discover that you are an apostle to teetotalism."

Cox's friend Arthur Portman admitted in a *Horse and Hound* obituary that, "He must have had a marvellous constitution to withstand for so long" a problem that Portman chose not to name. Another said, 'He was an agreeable companion when under self-control,' but much of the time, he wasn't. He was mostly alone on the racecourse, blearily ignoring any attempt to talk to him. "Speechless" was Sievier's cruel summary of the Bayardo dinner.

It says much for both men that Cox's problem never affected his relationship with Alec Taylor. Mr Fairie had plenty of redeeming features. He built a small, choice stud, he became a knowledgeable breeder, and he had the patience to wait 10 years and more for the results to flow. Best of all for Manton and for English bloodstock, he refused almost every offer made to him to sell one of his horses.

Perhaps it was a subconscious tip of his hat to that moment on an Australian quayside when he failed to sell his remaining share in the silver mine. Selling, he may have concluded, was a poor second to standing pat. Fairie would mutter from behind his cigar to a bloodstock agent, "Not for sale." If he was feeling communicative, it might stretch to, "Bayardo is not for sale," his reply to a Frenchman who offered £56,000 [*£2.97 million*] one afternoon.

After winning the Eclipse and *£470,000*, Bayardo won another small-field stakes race, beating Valens by an easy two lengths. That linked to the Derby form: Valens had been only a length or so behind Minoru. As a result, Bayardo was made 10-11 for the St Leger, with Minoru 7-4 and Valens 100-8. The King's colt was fully 'expected'. Like Bayardo, he hadn't been beaten since the Derby. Richard Marsh said that everything had gone according to plan in his preparation: "I know I have a good one to meet in Bayardo, but I can tell you that Bayardo has a good one to meet in mine!"

Alas, Minoru ran no race at all on Town Moor. A furlong from home, Valens and an outsider seemed to have the race between them, but then Danny Maher brought Bayardo to challenge and in three strides, the race was over. Fairie Cox's colt again beat Valens by two lengths. The form of the runner-up confirmed that, on their respective best days, Bayardo was a better horse than the Derby winner. They never met again. Minoru ran and won once more that year, flopped next spring in the City and Suburban and disappeared. Bayardo ran in and won six more races in 1909.

Three of his wins were at Newmarket and in the last of them, he showed that if he didn't have a kink, he had his quirks. He planted himself at the paddock exit onto the course, and resisted all Maher's urgings to go to post. Eventually the stewards gave permission for Bayardo to go round behind the stands, and the colt seemed happy picking his way through the onlookers and the carriages. He came back 15 lengths in front.

It was an open secret that, every now and then, Bayardo reminded his connections that he was the one in charge. In a magazine profile written before the 1909 classics, the racing writer Sidney Galtrey had drooled over Bayardo's looks: "What a deep rich bay he is, and what symmetry of outline! What a healthy gloss is on his coat, and how well and contented he looks in himself!"

There was more in the same vein. Galtrey conformed to the conventions of the time. Readers of the horse-by-horse stable tours in today's racing press might gape at his assertion that, *"To ask questions about the [Manton] horses would have been an impertinence and abusing a privilege."* Still, he was an experienced judge. He might have found words to hint to his readers that the colt he saw was uncooperative,unfit and a most unlikely Guineas horse. Galtrey left it until his 1934 memoirs to reveal:

> "The horses that cold morning in March had just filed into the stable yard on their return from exercise. All except one had dutifully gone to their respective

boxes. The exception was the great horse himself. There he was, standing as stubbornly as a mule. They could not get him into his box. What was to be done? Why, wait until Bayardo thought the moment had arrived [for him] to enter. Until [then] he would pay no heed to any amount of coaxing."

Another of Bayardo's quirks was to bang his chin repeatedly on his manger. He did the same while being travelled to race meetings. The Manton lads called it 'Bayardo's Drum.' These idiosyncrasies didn't detract from a spectacular season. Bayardo had 18 entries in 1909, met 13 of them and won 11 times, netting Fairie Cox £24,797 [*£1.32 million*]. As a four-year-old, he ran five times, winning four. In the Chester Vase he scrambled home by a neck from William The Fourth, giving 2lb – another line that suggested he would have narrowly won Minoru's Derby, without interference.

Bayardo then faced a dozen rivals at Ascot in the Gold Cup. William The Fourth reopposed. The previous year's Derby favourite Saint Martin was in the field, and the French wouldn't hear of defeat for their wretchedly-named Sea Sick II. They believed that their horse would stay, and Bayardo wouldn't. A pacemaker led for the first half of the race, with Maher as usual restraining Bayardo. Sea Sick II pressed on a mile from home, and Maher moved Bayardo into midfield as the field left Swinley Bottom.

Then for the only time in the colt's racing career, Maher allowed his mount to show the full extent of his superiority. Bayardo pulled his way into the lead six furlongs out. The move was so decisive that, provided he stayed, he'd settled the race in half a dozen strides. He did stay. He galloped resolutely home, winning by four lengths from Sea Sick II in a time fractionally outside the course record.

After a couple of pot-hunts at Newmarket, again taken to post via the back of the stands, Bayardo had one more race, the Goodwood Cup. If Maher had shone at Ascot, here he contrived the most abject ride imaginable. Bayardo had two opponents, both of them moderate three-year-olds: he conceded 17lb and 19lb more than weight-for-age. Maher allowed one of them to establish a long, uncontested lead. Giving away weight and 200 yards at the top of the straight, Bayardo couldn't quite get to the younger horse. He went down by a neck at 1-20. One punter had £3,000 on to win £150 [*£170,000 to win £8,500*]: a bad day at the office.

Alec Taylor was furious with Maher at the unsaddling. He moaned to a friend, "I always told Maher the day would come when something awful would happen through overdoing the waiting and waiting. Danny would reply, 'He doesn't like to be in front'." Taylor gave that short shrift: "[Remember] what happened in the race for the Gold Cup. Bayardo just carried him to the front, and the more he got in front, the further he won by. That upset Maher's theory once and for all, but he [forgot] the lesson when he got to Goodwood."

Cox retired Bayardo and sent him to the Redpost stud at Manton. Bayardo was twice leading sire, and his produce included three classic winners, two of whom won the triple crown that he, but for an interrupted preparation and mishap, would surely have won himself. In his three seasons racing, he won 22 from 25 starts, including six Group One equivalents, at distances from five furlongs to two and a half miles.

As a three-year-old, Bayardo completed a near clean sweep for Cox and Taylor in the season's honours. 'Mr Fairie' was leading owner and breeder, Bayardo was the winning-most horse, and Taylor the top trainer. And there was every sign at Manton that Bayardo's dam Galicia had produced another outstanding colt: Lemberg, the result of her mating with Cyllene, a St Leger winner. In the spring of 1909, Lemberg worked with the same older horse that Bayardo had sparkled against a year earlier. The outcome of the trial was identical, and Lemberg nearly emulated his half brother's unbeaten first season, winning six from seven, including the Dewhurst. His only defeat came in the Champagne Stakes, where he was third to Lord Rosebery's Neil Gow.

The two colts were to meet three times in their classic season, much to the consternation of Fairie Cox, who insisted that wherever possible Danny Maher should ride his horses, and paid Maher £3,000 [*£159,000*] as second retainer. Unfortunately for Cox, Rosebery had first call on Maher, thanks to an even larger retainer, so whenever Neil Gow was in opposition, another jockey had to be found for Lemberg. The choice was Bernard Dillon, a gifted young Irishman who began as an apprentice at Druid's Lodge, where he rode gambled-on winners of the Cambridgeshire and Lincoln.

The season had begun with Neil Gow and Maher pitted against Lemberg and Dillon in the 2,000 Guineas, and Neil Gow winning a prolonged struggle by a short head. As a quick consolation, Taylor saddled the first three home in the 1,000 Guineas, Waldorf Astor's Winkipop winning from Sir William Bass's pair, Maid Of Corinth and Rosedrop.

Lemberg renewed rivalry with Neil Gow in the Derby, and was

preferred to him in the betting, Lord Rosebery's trainer having been admirably open about a splint that his horse had thrown a few days before the race. Dillon kept Lemberg up with the pace throughout, and won cleverly by a neck. Neil Gow was several lengths back in fourth. To complete a wonderful Epsom for Manton, Rosedrop improved on her Guineas form and won the Oaks easily, so that Taylor had trained three of the first four classic winners of 1910.

Lemberg went on to run consistently in the top races. On the Thursday of Royal Ascot, half an hour after Bayardo's Gold Cup romp, Lemberg won the St James's Palace Stakes. He was then sent to Longchamp for the Grand Prix de Paris. The race was run in swamp-like conditions, which he didn't handle. Maher rode him sympathetically to finish fifth, just behind the Derby third, so that Lemberg turned out a fresh horse three weeks later against Neil Gow in the Eclipse. It was a nearly inch-perfect replay of the 2,000 Guineas. At level weights, Dillon against Maher, the two classic winners hammered at each other all the way up the Sandown straight: a dead heat and a credit to two brave, high-class colts.

Neil Gow didn't stand further racing. Lemberg, on the other hand, ran five more times. First, he was only third in the St Leger, seeming not to stay. Then he picked up a massive prize, £7,440 [*£420,000*] in the Jockey Club Stakes. Only the Eclipse, in which Lemberg and Neil Gow ran for a first prize of £8,770, was more valuable: the Derby and St Leger were worth £6,450 each. All the English purses were put in the shade by the £14,406 [*£814,000*] of the Grand Prix de Paris that year.

Lemberg ended the season with wins in the Champion Stakes and the [illegible] *£100,000* Sandown Foal Stakes. His total winnings were £28,224 [*£1.61 million*] and he helped Fairie Cox and Taylor to the same quartet of titles as Bayardo had done: leading breeder, leading owner, leading trainer and most successful horse. Taylor's £52,929 [*£3 million*] in purses was more than double the total of his closest pursuer, George Lambton.

Lemberg was campaigned as a four-year-old, and he won a high-class Coronation Cup, but no new talent was emerging at Manton to replace the star colts and fillies of the two previous seasons. For the future, it was significant that Fairie Cox asked Steve Donoghue to ride for him, but the subsequent 10-times champion jockey had little impact on a year when Taylor fell to fifth in the trainers' list.

The yard was becalmed for the next two years and Taylor dropped out of the top five altogether, but in 1914, as the clouds of war gathered over Europe, he bounced back with 39 winners and £51,722 [*£2.53 million*] in prize money. Sir John Thursby's Kennymore won the 2,000 Guineas. Unfortunately, he proved to be a rogue: an unpleasant bout of ill temper before the Derby, for which he was favourite, culminated in his being left at the start.

The summer's main prize contributor was Fairie Cox's stayer Aleppo, who won the Chester Cup and the Gold Cup. One afternoon, a bloodstock agent pestered Cox: would he take £20,000 [*£980,000*] for the colt? Fairie looked blankly at the man and muttered, "I've not quite made up my mind whether to send Aleppo to my stud – or geld him!"

Chapter 11

Racing in wartime

War was declared on 4 August 1914, and for most of that month racing was suspended. When it resumed, all railway traffic was set aside for the use of the armed forces. The Doncaster September yearling sales showed the extent to which war affected confidence. The St Leger meeting was run in front of empty stands. In the sales ring, the average price realised was 249 guineas. A year earlier, it had been 690 guineas. Adjusted for a fall in the value of sterling, vendors' returns fell 68 per cent. Sentiment was described as 'depressing,' but the 1915 flat season began on schedule at Lincoln, and only a handful of meetings were cancelled.

Part of the grandstand at Epsom had been turned into a hospital for soldiers invalided back from France. Somehow, a story spread that the wounded would be ejected to make room for the top hats of the Derby meeting. It was given credence by the Duke of Portland, who wrote in protest to *The Times*. He made a show of scratching all his horses' Epsom entries. He triggered a flood of letters demanding that racing be banned.

The Jockey Club held an open debate, resulting in a motion that, *"Racing should be carried out where local conditions permit and the feeling of the locality is not averse to the meeting being held."* The tide ran strongly against the Club. The 'antis' argued emotively that racehorses were taking feed from the working animals, 'remounts,' on the battlefields. They also claimed that it was an insult to the dead and the wounded for race meetings to be staged to amuse 'shirkers and loafers.'

At times, the juxtaposition of war and sport was agonising. A small crowd gathered at Newmarket in the first October of the war, to see the Middle Park Stakes. During the afternoon, news spread round the course that a U-boat had sunk the battle cruiser HMS *Hawke*. Over 500 of her crew died. It was inevitable that the Board of Trade, spurred on by the uproar over wounded soldiers being 'thrown out of Epsom,' would take a hostile view of racing.

At the end of May 1915, the Jockey Club was told to,

> "Suspend all race meetings in Great Britain after this week for the duration of the war. The only exceptions to this general suspension should be at Newmarket, the peculiar circumstances of which, dependent as [it is] entirely upon racing, combine to make this exception expedient."

The Club, which had lobbied successfully to protect Newmarket, accepted the directive at once. Five fixtures were added there, to stage wartime substitutes for the Derby, Oaks and St Leger. They were the New Derby, New Oaks and September Stakes. The following year, an expanded but still skeleton schedule was approved. It provided 70 meetings, stretching beyond Newmarket to Gatwick, Lingfield, Newbury and Windsor. It was repeated that trainers would have no access to the railways to transport horses, but most of the rolling stock was in any case in northern France.

As a measure of the extent to which racing activity was curtailed, in 1913, 4,055 horses ran on the flat, for purses totalling £518,673 [*£28.52 million*]. In 1916, the equivalents were 2,362 and £147,955. The population of horses seen on a racecourse had fallen 42 per cent; inflation-adjusted prize money fell by 78 per cent.

Alec Taylor had lean years in 1915 and 1916. In the first of them, he trained just nine winners. In 1916, Taylor trained the winners of 16 races and £8,588 [*£309,000*]. In part, the decline from the pre-war years was because he simply didn't have the horsepower, as sometimes happens to trainers who depend on owner-breeders. About the best was Kwang Su, who ran second in the 2,000 Guineas and New Derby of 1916. The colt was another son of Cox's foundation mare Galicia. More generally, Manton was hamstrung by the regime in which almost all racing was at Newmarket, and travelling horses by rail was forbidden.

It wasn't until the last years of the war that Taylor, with horses good enough to make the effort worthwhile, took a string to Newmarket and based them in a satellite yard, as his father had done to humour the Duchess of Montrose. At the end of the 1916 season, he won a race with a two-year-old who'd been plagued with sore shins. It was a Bayardo colt who showed glimpses of exceptional ability over the winter and into spring. Whether he'd have the chance to show it on the racecourse was far from certain. In March 1917, another storm was gathering on the letters pages of the national press. The level of much of the argument was typified by this offering in *The Times* from an anonymous 'Horse Lover':

> "The contention that horse racing is essential for the maintenance of our breed of horses is absurd. We possess the finest breed of carthorses in the world, our Shire horses being only rivalled, perhaps, by the French Percheron. We maintain the breed without racing. Our Shorthorn and Herefordshire cattle are probably the finest breeds of beef-producing cattle in the world; we have accomplished this result without racing the cattle."

To the dismay of the racing community, expressed by the *Bloodstock Breeders' Review*, "The columns of *The Times* were placed at the disposal of cranks, who, utterly ignorant, [regard racing] as a mere idle and vicious form of amusement." The outcome could be predicted. The authorities, having sanctioned a fixture list of 13 meetings for 1917, exclusively at Newmarket, put pressure on the Jockey Club to act:

> "The Stewards of the Jockey Club, having received an intimation that the War Cabinet considers it undesirable that further racing should take place after the conclusion of the First Spring Meeting [May 1–4], have cancelled all 1917 fixtures after that date."

It was a devastating blow to all whose livelihood depended on racing. Most households in Newmarket were affected. A number of provincial trainers like Taylor had rented stables in Newmarket for the year. Some had settled in the town for the summer and autumn. Their expense was for nothing. The bloodstock industry faced extinction: with no racing, there'd be no market for racehorses. A passer-by in Newmarket articulated the shock and frustration: "It looks like bankruptcy, beggary, starvation."

The Jockey Club, energised as never before, joined the Thoroughbred Breeders Association in arguing, urgently, that racing was essential to maintain an important industry. Without competition to establish the best and soundest horses in each generation, the breed would be weakened. A much-decorated admiral accused the Government of breach of faith, by sanctioning a fixture list and then causing it to be cancelled.

From Dublin came an apocalyptic forecast. A meeting of owners, breeders and trainers concluded that without racing, *"Horse breeding would at once cease in Ireland, where 20,000 men and boys would be thrown out of employment and the entire commercial community would suffer vast monetary loss."*

Their voice caught the Government's attention. The campaign for Irish Home Rule had been a friction point in Westminster politics for two decades. Only a year before, 500 troops had been killed or wounded putting down the Easter Rising. German spies were said to be fomenting trouble across the Irish Sea. It would've been political lunacy to antagonise the Irish people further.

Immediately after the meeting in Dublin, an Irish racing deputation went to London to lobby Parliament and the Government. Within days, there was a u-turn. Meetings at Dundalk and Phoenix Park were allowed to go ahead the following week. Fixtures were reinstated later in the month at Limerick Junction and Baldoyle. The move was inevitable. None-too-secret plans were being made for unlicensed meetings across Ireland. They would have been difficult and dangerous to prevent, and a focus for anti-British sentiment.

The Government's *volte-face* over racing in Ireland made its policy in the rest of Britain untenable. The debate rumbled on through June, with more and louder voices heard in and outside Parliament. Finally, at the beginning of July, the Board of Trade sent a letter to the Jockey Club: "In view of the national importance of horse breeding," it read, "A limited amount of racing may be allowed in England from the middle of this month." There were caveats: no special trains for racegoers or racehorses, no use of scarce petrol to run private cars or cabs to race meetings. But racing had won the argument. The 'antis' were reduced to reporting violations, real or imagined, of the regulations barring cars.

The Times ran a story that at one meeting, 'A large number of motor cars were seen on the racecourse, or travelling from it.' That happened to be on a day when the police carried out a spot check. They wrote to the paper with a correction. They'd noted only 15 cars at the races, of which 14, "Were found to be officers on short leave, or invalided members of His Majesty's Forces holding special permits."

The shaming of a solitary motorist was an apt symbol of the ill-thought-out move to ban racing in wartime. It was greatly to the benefit of English bloodstock, and of Alec Taylor, that the attempt failed. Had there been no substitute classics, there would've been no Gay Crusader, no Gainsborough.

Chapter 12

The Manton neglected

For all Young Alec's success in the dozen years between his brother's departure and the war, and all that he went on to achieve in the 1920s, it's hard to find evidence that it brought him happiness. A visitor painted an inadvertently sombre picture of life at Manton House:

> "The front was heavily creeper-clad. Trees and shrubs had clustered closer and closer until they darkened the interior. Inside there was the unmistakable smell of old furniture, carpets and heavy curtains."

Long after electricity arrived in Marlborough, the rooms in Manton House were lit by paraffin lamps, pulled down by chains for refilling and then hoisted back up to the ceiling. In the gloom sat the bachelor Taylor and his spinster sister. The only decorations of note were some equine portraits. Most of them were inherited: they were of horses from his father's time, gifts to Old Alec from Stirling Crawfurd. A painting of Sceptre with her galloping companion Grey Tick must have been a present from Sir William Bass, because nothing in Young Alec's character suggests that he would have parted with his hard-earned for a few dabs of paint on canvas. He took as much pleasure from a small scrimp as from training a winner.

Young Alec hardly bet, which is strange against the background of his father's rise, via Teddington and many another gamble, from stud groom to Manton. The *Pink 'Un* claimed gleefully that 'the world would shake' if the son had so much as a fiver on a cast-iron certainty. He told a friend that he didn't know how the reporter had come by the story, "But he's not far off the mark."

For a while, Taylor helped a fellow trainer who'd fallen on hard times. It was Jack Fallon, who won hundreds of thousands in bets on the big handicap winners of his heyday at Druid's Lodge, and lost it all in little more time than it takes to tell. Taylor used Fallon as an auxiliary travelling lad. One day at Ascot, he asked him to put £2 [*£110*] on one of his runners, Torpoint. Fallon was agog: he knew this was an event rarer than a total eclipse. He stood, wondering where he could borrow some money to top up Taylor's bet, when Young Alec called him back: "On second thoughts, I don't think I'll have a bet. It's too risky." Torpoint duly won. Telling the story, Fallon added, "There's no doubt that the trainer who doesn't bet is better off in the long run," but he learned the lesson years too late.

Taylor used to say, "There are three good things in this world: old clothes, old boots and old friends." His clothes had been restitched to infinity: nothing was replaced until it fell apart. His saddler Fred Chandler came to the yard twice a week, making and repairing tack. Taylor sent him a broken bootlace, to be spliced and repaired. Sidney Galtrey described Taylor's yard clothes:

> "Old-fashioned cloth leggings, cut wide, so that they spread over the boot-tops [from] unfashionably cut breeches. [There was] the famous old Melton blue coat he wore. Once it had a velvet collar. It was [an] old friend that it would break his heart to discard. Some years later he was still getting the last thread or two of wear out of it."

There were several attempts to persuade Taylor to write his memoirs. His stories of the Duchess of Montrose and Fairie Cox would surely have surpassed, for human interest and turf history, the biographies of John Porter, George Lambton and the other trainer diarists. A newspaper approached him with an offer of £1,000 to serialise his story. No, said Taylor, that didn't appeal to him. As the reporter walked away, Taylor called after him, "I might consider it for £2,000," but the moment had passed.

If Taylor was making a train journey, he saved money by travelling up to London second class. To keep up appearances, he switched to first class when he joined the racing community for the onward journey to Newmarket. He had a running contest of wills with his travelling head lad, Joe Lawson.

Taylor would moan to Lawson, "I suppose you want some expenses?" "Yes, sir, I'd better have something," Lawson would reply. "How much do you think?" "Oh, £20 or £30, sir." "Good gracious!" Taylor would exclaim, and shuffle reluctantly to the office cash box, where Lawson knew there was usually a healthy balance. Taylor would peer at the contents: "I've only got £5. Can't you manage on that?" The final step in the ritual was

Lawson agreeing to do his best. So off he went to Marlborough station and beyond, with valuable horses and their lads, using his own savings to make up the difference between his outgoings and Taylor's five pounds. Whenever he ran out of money, Lawson would go to Taylor's secretary and proffer perhaps £100 worth of receipts. A cheque would be drawn up for Taylor to sign. The signature sometimes took a while to materialise.

One of Taylor's first patrons was Washington Singer, the sewing machine heir. Sir William Bass of brewery fame was the son of Old Alec's owner Hamar Bass. Sir Richard Garton was another prominent brewer. Along came Alfred Cox, and Bob Sievier could quip in *The Winning Post* that Manton, 'Must be a merry place, with a Singer and a Fairie, and Bass to refresh them.' New patrons included Lady James Douglas and Waldorf Astor, who was to become for many years Manton's pre-eminent owner.

Washington Singer first had horses with Taylor in 1905. He arrived at the yard with a reputation for serious betting. Most of his pre-Taylor winners were handicappers, and there was talk of a big SP coup when his horse Telescope won the November handicap. He stepped up to classic company within weeks of moving his string to Manton, his Challacombe winning the St Leger, ridden by Otto Madden.

In truth, it was as bad a renewal of the race as has ever been run: a small field, none of the placed horses from the Derby, a favourite who went in season, and only Challacombe stayed, winning by three lengths at 100-6, a result greeted in silence. Singer then had a series of Royal Ascot winners, beginning with successive Ascot Stakes winners, the second of them Torpoint, the horse Taylor decided not to trust with his £2 bet, and continuing with a Hunt Cup winner.

Lady Douglas was a Frenchwoman, the widow of a son of the Marquess of Queensberry, Lord James Douglas. She was a knowledgeable breeder, who arrived at Manton by chance. It was her policy to consign all her yearlings to the sales. She had a stud near Newbury, where one of her first mares was Sir William Bass's Oaks winner Rosedrop. She was sent to Bayardo in 1914 and produced a colt foal the following January. He was sent to the sales and failed to reach his 2,000 guineas reserve. Lady Douglas took him home. When she was offered 1,800 guineas, she responded by raising the bar to 2,500 guineas.

Even then, her yearling was the subject of an offer close to the asking price, but she decided to put him into training. He was earmarked for

Colledge Leader in Newmarket, but Leader had answered the call to arms. Lady Douglas had to find another trainer, and she chose Taylor because he'd trained her colt's sire and dam. By now, the yearling had a name. Lady Douglas hadn't been able to think of anything apt for the son of Rosedrop and Bayardo, but she found her answer in a railway timetable: Gainsborough. She thought it had, "A good masculine ring about it."

She was lucky that when he was led into the sale ring, the gathering at Tattersalls hadn't yet seen the accomplishments of one of Bayardo's first crop, who was also trained at Manton: Fairie Cox's Gay Crusader, out of Gay Laura, by a Jockey Club and Hardwicke Stakes winner, Beppo.

Before the Government's short-lived ban, Newmarket staged the first two classics of 1917, and the 2,000 Guineas produced a one-two for Manton, with Gay Crusader holding off Waldorf Astor's Magpie by a neck. The two colts had both run at the first spring meeting, and both had been beaten in heavy going, Gay Crusader when unfancied at 14-1. He went down by less than half a length, conceding weight to the winner and 18lb to his stable companion, Aleli, a length behind in third.

There was press talk of Taylor working Gay Crusader and Magpie together before the Guineas, but Fairie Cox never allowed his horses to be tried with those of another owner. Taylor did, however, set up a proxy trial, by galloping Magpie with Aleli, giving Aleli the same weight that Gay Crusader had done at Newmarket. The outcome suggested that there was very little between Gay Crusader and Magpie, but a feeling that Cox's colt was the pick was reflected in the Guineas betting: 9-4 Gay Crusader, 6 1 Magpie.

In the race, the two colts were always prominent, and they drew to the front coming into the last furlong. From there to the line, Gay Crusader always held a slight advantage, winning by a head. Afterwards, Steve Donoghue drew attention to his skill in keeping his horse so close to Magpie that Otto Madden on the runner-up hadn't been able to use his whip. It was ungracious of him, particularly as Madden had come out of retirement to take some of the rides vacated by the younger jockeys going off to war. In truth, Gay Crusader won rather cosily, and likely would still have done so had the jockeys been switched.

Soon after the race, Waldorf Astor sold Magpie to Australia. Astor, who worked on the Prime Minister's staff, evidently didn't believe the ban on racing would be overturned. He was wrong, but it was to be 74 days before the next meeting in England, and the New Derby was run on July 31, a Tuesday. In the interim, Taylor and Cox had lost Bayardo, who died at stud that June, aged only 11. In a macabre gesture of remembrance, Taylor used the champion's hide to cover a set of dining room chairs, and the seat of the weighing scales in the tack room.

Gay Crusader stood out in the paddock before the New Derby. Taylor said that no horse in his experience had improved so rapidly in looks and ability as Gay Crusader had done in the build-up to the race. Cox's colt fairly routed 13 rivals, despite an injudicious ride from Donoghue. Only the last three furlongs of the July course were railed at that time. The rest of the course was marked by solid furlong poles. Three times between poles, Donoghue took Gay Crusader off the course to pass the leaders on their inside. Each time the other jockeys crowded him out, and he had to pull back behind them to avoid running the wrong side of a marker. Finally, he gave up, switched Gay Crusader to the outside, and the colt flew home.

The judge gave the winning distance as four lengths: one observer wrote that, "It looked as if [the horse] could have given a stone to each of his rivals and still beaten them." The fifth-placed horse in the New Derby was the 1,000 Guineas winner Diadem. She turned out two days later in the New Oaks, where she was made favourite to confirm Guineas form with Astor's Sunny Jane, whom she'd beaten by a comfortable half-length. Perhaps not surprisingly after her exertions against Gay Crusader 48 hours earlier, Diadem came out second best to Sunny Jane in the Oaks, so that Taylor had again won three of the first four classics.

Gay Crusader's next appearance was in the replacement St Leger, which because of the delayed Derby was run only six weeks later. The impression he'd made scared off all but two rivals: the Derby second Dansellon, and a recent maiden race winner. It was a surprise that Gay Crusader was only 2-11. He came down the Rowley Mile alone, hard held. He ran four more times at increasingly long odds on, beating small fields without coming off the bridle. Sadly, he wasn't seen as a four-year-old. He was in full training at Manton in the spring of 1918, but he sprang the back tendon off a foreleg. There was a suggestion that perhaps Donoghue had pulled him up too quickly at the end of a gallop.

It's difficult to say what Gay Crusader achieved in that interrupted season of 1917, when racing was dominated more by politics than by events on the racecourse. He didn't have to prove himself over the contours of Epsom, and the St Leger substitute was singularly uncompetitive. However, like the best athletes in any sport and generation, he could only beat what faced him. Steve Donoghue was no stranger to good horses: he rode the winners of six Derbys and eight other classics. So it was quite a compliment that in his memoirs, he described Gay Crusader as, 'The best racehorse I ever rode.' "Not only was Gay Crusader the finest stayer I ever sat on, but at the end of a two-mile gallop he could pull out such speed [as] could only be produced by a five-furlong sprinter."

Thanks entirely to Gay Crusader, Cox and Taylor were restored to their former positions when the 1917 data were collated: winning owner, breeder, trainer and the leading horse. For good measure, Bayardo led the sires and Cox's retained jockey Donoghue was champion jockey, albeit with only 42 winners, compared with his 129 in 1914.

The season could hardly have been better for Taylor: four winners and a second in the classics, and Gainsborough to look forward to in 1918. Lady Douglas's colt had made a promising debut, fourth of 21 in a five-furlong maiden. A month later Gainsborough was a close third in a similar event. He was still a little backward, and both Taylor and his owner were delighted. His final outing as a two-year-old was over six furlongs in a valuable stakes race, run immediately after Gay Crusader's St Leger stroll. Not only did Gainsborough win well: he had five previous winners behind him, and reversed the form with the winner of his previous race.

He was hailed in some quarters as the best two-year-old of the season. One paper wrote, "We have seldom seen a better-looking two-year-old." The point was made in the *Bloodstock Breeders Review* that, had Gainsborough gone to the sales a year later, "The bidding might easily have gone to 4,000 or 5,000 guineas," because buyers would've had the performances of his half-brother Gay Crusader to take into account. After a slow start as a sire, Bayardo suddenly made plenty of appeal. When Gainsborough won his maiden race, Lady Douglas was besieged by owners and agents begging her to name a price. She threatened to post a Fairie Cox-like notice: 'Gainsborough is not for sale at any price!'

The colt's three-year-old season followed the same script that Taylor had written for Gay Crusader. First, Gainsborough started in a heavy-ground sprint at Newmarket on a cold, damp afternoon. He looked backward and didn't seem to have grown at all over the winter. He was ignored at 10-1 and finished fifth of 16, ridden by Joe Childs, a brilliant but short-tempered jockey, 'quick to take offence and sensitive to criticism.' Two weeks, sunshine, good going and some brilliant home work produced a different Gainsborough on 2,000 Guineas day. He was third in the betting, the knowing ones thinking that not even Taylor could transform the ugly duckling they'd seen a fortnight before.

The race didn't go entirely to plan: Gainsborough had to make most of his own running after a stable companion, Astor's Blink, was slowly away. From two furlongs out, Gainsborough gradually asserted, winning by a length and a half, with six lengths more to Blink, running on into third. The result was greeted with delight on and beyond the racecourse: Gainsborough was the first classic winner to be bred and raced by a woman.

In the New Derby, the first three from the 2,000 Guineas reopposed. Young Alec was never a man given to effusion before a race, but on this occasion, he radiated serene confidence. The only surprise in the Guineas, as far as Taylor was concerned, was that Blink hadn't finished second. In their last trial together, Blink had run Gainsborough to less than a length. In their Derby re-match, Gainsborough was 8-13 and Blink 100-8, but only 2-1 to place. When the field came into view, the Manton colts were prominent, and they quickly pulled away from the rest of the field. To the horror of many in the stands, Blink harried the favourite down to the last furlong. For a moment, he drew level. Then Childs got after Gainsborough, and he asserted close home to win by a length and a half. The crowd gave Lady Douglas and her colt another warm reception.

Blink's jockey Jack Colling was one of the few not to share the celebrations. He was a talented apprentice, and Taylor had already asked him to be first jockey at Manton the following year. But even at 18, the tall Colling struggled to do 9st. One day after riding at that weight in the first race, he felt faint, and had 'two water biscuits and a glass of port.' By the third race, he was putting up overweight: "Mr Taylor was not amused." He was forced to give up, and later became a trainer, first at Newmarket, then West Ilsley, for a span of over 40 years, many of them with the Astors among his owners.

In retirement, Colling used to grumble that, "I should have [partnered] the Derby winner of that year if I hadn't ridden to orders. [I'd ridden] Gainsborough and Blink at home and knew that Gainsborough was the better of the two, but that Blink would have the edge of speed in a slow-run race. I was engaged to ride Blink for Astor. Major Gerald Deane, who managed for Astor, took me aside and told me that Blink would have to make all the running for Gainsborough. 'The whole stable is on Gainsborough,' he said, and anyhow, Blink was unlikely to stay. 'Not if I ride him like that, he won't,' I answered."

The adult Jack Colling, trainer of the old school, wouldn't have taken kindly to that piece of lip from a teenaged apprentice. His younger self did as instructed, and pressed the pace to set the race up for Gainsborough. Lady Douglas's colt went on to win the Newmarket Gold Cup and then emulate Gay Crusader by taking the last wartime St Leger, easing up, by three lengths and four lengths from two stable mates, Cox's New Oaks winner My Dear and William Cazalet's Prince Chimay.

Gainsborough's career ended in anti-climax, beaten by Prince Chimay in the Jockey Club Stakes, one of those results filed under 'M' for mystery: Gainsborough was 2-11 and Prince Chimay 20-1. Lady Douglas stood her triple crown winner at her stud, where he sired the brilliant Hyperion, winner of the 1933 Derby and St Leger, and himself six times champion sire.

Prince Chimay was an example of what the racing public used to call the 'Manton neglected': an outsider trained by Taylor beating a fancied stable-mate. Trainers down the years have attracted a reputation for such happenings. In the mind's eye is Captain Ryan Price, his trilby raked at a gravity-defying angle, protesting after some unlikely result that, 'They ran on their merits!' No doubt they did, and likewise Alec Taylor's horses, but upsets happened often enough that backing the Manton second or third string in a big race became a popular system.

The first mutterings were heard as early as 1906 at Ascot, when Washington Singer's Torpoint was installed as ante-post favourite for the Ascot Stakes. It was overlooked that Singer had another entry in the race, Pradella. The two horses had different going preferences. The ground had to be soft for Torpoint, fast for Pradella.

Singer was staying near Ascot the weekend before the meeting. He agreed with Taylor that Torpoint would travel to the races, but that if the course was drying, a telegram would be sent asking for Pradella instead. On the Monday evening, Taylor took Torpoint to Marlborough station. Minutes after the train had left, Singer's message arrived: 'Pradella'. The Marlborough touts had seen Torpoint leave for Ascot. They sent messages to their clients and the newspapers, and went home. Only one of them stayed long enough to see Pradella boxed up on a later train. He was a former Manton apprentice, William Maisey, and he profited mightily from his diligence.

There was surprise the next day at Ascot when Pradella's number went up, and Torpoint was an absentee. Some took the hint and backed her at 100-8. She won cosily from 21 rivals. The result was jeered lustily in the Silver Ring and down the course. In the same race four years later, Taylor's two entries did at least both run. One of them was the warm favourite, Elizabetta. The Manton second string, Declare, had been written off as unlikely to start, but he won as Pradella had done, easily, also at 100-8. Eight lengths behind was Elizabetta. This time there wasn't any demonstration over the result, but it was, 'received in chilling silence.'

Sporting Luck led a chorus of press critics of the 'Manton neglected'. Under the headline 'Discreditable Tactics', it claimed that, "[Manton] has become notorious for winning with the outsider of two." It reminded its readers of Sir William Bass's Oaks success with Rosedrop, a race in which she 'simply romped home' while the owner's other runner carried his first colours and was unplaced. "Loud booing and hissing greeted Rosedrop," said the paper.

> "An irate racing crowd is apt to make things very unpleasant. [Some are] ready to [protest] when they think they have been swindled. It is useless to write any other adjective than this, for you can never persuade the public that they have received fair play when Manton [has] run two and won with the outsider."

The most notorious 'neglected' was in an Eclipse renewal where Lord Astor had two runners: the 7-4 favourite Bold And Bad and a 20-1 outsider, Saltash. Bold And Bad was ridden by Astor's newly retained jockey, the Australian Frank Bullock, Saltash by a Manton apprentice, Jack Brennan. Saltash made all the running and won easily, with the favourite only fourth. Astor's wife Nancy took particular exception to the result. She was sharp-tongued and seldom shy to voice an opinion.

As Saltash was led in, she called out sarcastically, in a voice which all could hear in the vicinity of the unsaddling enclosure, "Oh, Mr Taylor, why didn't you tell us this one would win?" The *Pink 'Un* recorded that, "The master of Manton seemed to be having rather a bad quarter of an hour with Lady Astor, who has surely never been more voluble." Heaven knows why. Her husband never bet, and the Eclipse was worth *£263,000*. It should've been a matter for delight whichever of his colts won.

Some of the racing press worked themselves into a froth over Manton 'neglecteds'. Taylor was never lured into replying to the criticism, though he did have some journalist supporters like Sidney Galtrey, who answered for him. First, financial gain wasn't the motive, they said, since Taylor and Astor didn't bet. Second, different owners' horses were seldom tried together. Third, horses aren't machines. To which came the rejoinder: how can a trainer of Taylor's genius not know the respective merits of his runners? The arguments were dusted off every time Manton was doubly represented in an important race.

Chapter 13

The old order changes

"The racing season of 1919 began under normal conditions. A marvellous beginning it was," wrote *The Field*, "For at no previous period in the history of the Turf had racecourses been so crowded, never had money been so freely spent, never had bloodstock been in such demand. Never, perhaps, had there been such an influx of wealthy men aspiring to become owners of a first-class racehorse."

Manton's success of the previous two seasons continued. Buchan, a colt of Astor's, was placed in the 2,000 Guineas, Derby and St Leger, a sequence that included two jockeys incurring the wrath of Astor's racing manager Gerald Deane. Buchan had won his first three races as a two-year-old, and began his second season by winning the Craven Stakes. He went down by a neck in the 2,000 Guineas to The Panther, an imposing colt out of a temperamental mare.

The two colts met again in the Derby, with The Panther a warm favourite. It seemed that the main danger to Buchan disappeared even before the start. The Panther threw his head about repeatedly, broke the tape and then refused to walk forward. When the starter finally got them away, The Panther was badly left. Buchan also dwelt: going up the hill, he had only two behind him.

It was an afternoon of miserable visibility. So far as those in the stands could see, there were only two horses in the race at Tattenham Corner, one of them Lord Glanely's 33-1 outsider, Grand Parade. Then a challenger loomed up behind them. A relieved roar went up for The Panther, but it was Buchan, flying home from his hopeless perch at the top of the hill. Unseen in the murk, his jockey Jack Brennan had given Buchan a patient ride to get him into the race after his poor start. Now, everything that could go wrong, did.

Buchan came wide into the straight, with a clear run up the leaders' outside. The Epsom camber has sucked down many a horse and rider, but Brennan himself pulled Buchan in behind the leaders, into a pocket. A furlong later, he realised his mistake and took Buchan back to the outside. One of his two rivals fell away, leaving Grand Parade the sole target. Brennan decided to aim at his inside, steered Buchan back to the rails, and made an unavailing challenge where there was no room. He got to within half a length but no further. As Grand Parade was led in, the only sound was the rustling of race cards. Buchan plainly should have won. The unfortunate Brennan had made an awful mess of the race that every breeder dreams of winning.

It said a great deal for Astor that Jack Brennan rode for him in every season up to Brennan's retirement in 1942. Brennan was a rare example at Manton of a young apprentice who progressed to senior jockey. He was esteemed as the best work rider at the yard for a span of over 30 years. He was a superb judge of pace, and his opinions on a horse were listened to intently by the owners.

He was a level-headed man, too: whenever Astor's secretary called to ask him about a payment, Brennan would tell her, 'Please ask his Lordship to invest it for me.' The result was that in due course he had a comfortable retirement income, and enough put by to build himself a house by the entrance to Manton.

There's a fine line between a great horseman and a great jockey, and Brennan didn't cross it. The riders in the stands attributed it to nerves: the ice that flows through the veins of a top jockey on a big race day was missing from Brennan's metabolism. He rode one classic winner, but on eight occasions, covering all five classics, he finished second or third, and he rode a palpable shocker on Buchan.

In his defence, he was a natural lightweight. Even aged 40, he weighed only 7st 11lb. It's an axiom that a good big 'un will always beat a good little 'un, and Brennan's weight can't have helped his mounts in the valuable conditions races that Astor's horses were aimed at, where 9st was, and remains, the standard weight carried. In a close finish, 10lb of lead in the saddle doesn't propel a horse forward in the way that 10lb of a jockey's muscle does.

Possibly the most aggrieved person at Epsom was Gerald Deane. He'd backed Buchan to win tens of thousands. It was one of the mysteries of his service to Astor that while his employer never bet, Deane was a punter. There's no record of what passed between him and Brennan, but it must have been painful. Brennan was replaced by the senior jockey Joe Childs in the Prince of Wales's Stakes and the Eclipse, both of which Buchan won easily, and then it was Childs's turn to feel the force of Deane's displeasure.

Buchan was odds-on for the St Leger. When Childs rode him on the morning of the race, he said the colt was, "All right in every way," but then Buchan sweated badly on the way to post. In the race, Childs reckoned he was beaten by halfway. A filly made all and drew clear in the straight: Childs said he, "Just nursed [Buchan] along so as to get a place," finishing third. He told Astor, Deane and Taylor that he could probably have finished second.

This provoked a furious outburst from Deane: "Well, why the hell didn't you? The second place was worth £400 and the third only £200." Deane had to be held to prevent him attacking Childs, who confined himself to saying that Buchan felt like a sick horse and he'd only looked after him.

Childs was later vindicated: Buchan was found to be suffering from diabetes. Restored to full health, he won a second Eclipse as a four-year-old, but then had the misfortune to lose the Gold Cup on a disqualification. Deane's public rage at the unsaddling had a regrettable side effect: it was widely assumed that Childs had 'stopped' Buchan at Doncaster. Deane saw to it that the jockey never wore the Astor colours again – all for £200 [*£4,200*] place money, a trifle for Astor.

To offset the disappointments of Buchan's Derby and St Leger, Lady Douglas won the Oaks with Bayuda, a daughter of Bayardo. The season ended with Taylor the leading trainer for the third year in a row. Yet behind the accustomed victories, it was a year of uncertainty and change.

For the first time, Manton passed out of the Taylors' ownership. Early in May came the news that Fairie Cox had died. It was hardly a shock: Cox had been intermittently unwell. There were times when Cox was driven from his Newmarket home to the racecourse, where his runners were briefly paraded for him, and off he went without seeing them run, or so much as stepping down from his carriage. In his last years, Fairie became close to Steve Donoghue. The jockey would arrive home from a race meeting, be told by the housekeeper that Cox had been waiting to see him, and find his patron asleep in an armchair. Cox had given Donoghue a painting of Gay Crusader and he sat opposite it, saying it was, 'better than my own.'

He left an enduring legacy in the bloodlines of Bayardo, Gay Crusader, Lemberg and a number of other horses of merit. He also left bequests of £5,000 [*£121,500*] to Taylor and £500 to Joe Lawson. The *Pink 'Un* remarked that, "Alec Taylor is a very wealthy man. The £5,000 that Cox left him is but a fleabite."

The main beneficiary of Fairie's will was his brother, Alexander Robb Cox. Included were all his, 'Horses, carriages, harness, saddlery and stable furniture, and also all my thoroughbred racing stud.' As it happened, Alexander Cox, whose inheritance brought him into racing at the end of one world war, would still be an owner at Manton after the second, a quarter of a century later.

Taylor had no crystal ball. All he could know at the time was that he'd lost his best owner: a man as rich as Croesus, a breeder of judgement and patience, and a determined non-vendor. Besides, Sir William Bass had sold all his horses not long before. Lady Douglas's commitment to racing was a poor second to her breeding interests. Even after Bayuda's Oaks win, it was remarked that she showed no interest in leading her filly in. She was, 'calm, matter-of-fact [and] unenthusiastically acknowledged a few congratulations.'

Young Alec looked at the glass, and saw it half empty. He had no financial need to go on. From the beginning, he was a tireless acquirer of land. Not long after parting from his brother, he bought a large tract of the downs from Lady Meux. Before and during the war, when land prices were depressed, he

MANTON HOUSE
AND
CLATFORD PARK ESTATES.

Close to the Town and Borough of MARLBOROUGH, with easy access to the Great Western and Midland and South Western Junction Railway systems, and intersected by the London and Bath Road and the River Kennett.

EXCEPTIONAL FREEHOLD AGRICULTURAL ESTATE
AND
PRINCELY SPORTING DOMAIN,
OF ABOUT
5500 ACRES,
In a Ring Fence and practically Tithe Free.
INCLUDING
THE MANTON HOUSE
TRAINING ESTABLISHMENT
AND STUD FARM
WITH THE
MATCHLESS DOWNS

Surrounding same, the HOME and TRAINING GROUND of many of the
BEST-KNOWN THOROUGHBREDS of all Time, including the WINNERS, many times repeated, of all the CLASSIC RACES, and carried on with constant and ever-increasing Success through the days of
SCEPTRE, BAYARDO, LEMBERG, GAY CRUSADER, and GAINSBOROUGH, to the present time with MANILARDO, BUCHAN, AIR RAID, beside BAYUDA (Winner of the Oaks), the beautiful and worthy daughter of Bayardo, and many famous Mares whose names are found in the Stud Book.

THE PALATIAL AND SUBSTANTIALLY-BUILT
STABLING AND BOXES,
WITH THE
RESIDENCE, YARDS, COTTAGES, etc.,
Are surrounded by the
PADDOCKS AND DOWNS,
MAKING
A UNIQUE PROPERTY
OF
ABOUT 1500 ACRES,

arranged to the Utmost Advantage for Breeding and Racing Success by Mr. ALEC TAYLOR and his late Father, whose keen judgment and continual care has originated and perfected the Property.

Also to be Disposed of in Separate Lots are
10 OF THE BEST MIXED FARMS
IN WILTSHIRE,
Let at Moderate Rents to excellent Tenants,
COMPRISING
FERTILE, ARABLE & HILL PASTURE,
RICH VALE PASTURE AND MEADOWS,
Watered by the River Kennett, with
HOUSES & BUILDINGS
of the best and most complete description
a Magnificent, Well Timbered COVERT
Of 700 ACRES,
Known as the
WEST WOODS,

being a Favourite meet of Hounds, and capable or rearing 8,000 Pheasants, with some of the finest rises that can be found. Numerous well-built
COTTAGES & SMALL HOLDINGS.
ALSO THE
ADVOWSON OF
OVERTON-CUM-FYFIELD,
with an income of about £450 per Annum.

MESSRS. MARK JEANS & SON are favoured with instructions to submit the foregoing to AUCTION at the
TOWN HALL, MARLBOROUGH,
In Numerous Lots,
ON
TUESDAY, 16TH SEPTEMBER, 1919,
unless a suitable offer should be made for the whole, or the Manton House Estate separately, six weeks prior to day of Sale.

bought farms adjacent to Manton whenever they came on the market. After the German surrender in November 1918, land prices soared. So while it surprised the racing world, it was a statement of his plan to retire when at the start of the following July, estate agents printed preliminary sale details of, "An exceptional freehold agricultural estate and princely sporting domain of about 5,500 acres."

It included, "The Manton House training establishment and stud farm [and] 10 of the best mixed farms in Wiltshire." The advertisement listed the equine greats of Manton: "Many of the best known thoroughbreds of all time." There was a flattering reference to the 'keen judgement and continual care' of the Taylors, and notice was given of a public auction at Marlborough Town Hall in mid-September, unless a suitable offer was received beforehand.

The auction never took place. It was pre-empted by the announcement that Manton had been sold to Joseph Watson. At first, a developer called Waterhouse exchanged contracts with Taylor; he planned to sell off the estate in parcels. Instead, he took a profit from Watson, a businessman turned landowner. The sale price was reported at £130,000 [*£3.16 million*]. A trainer drawing up a template for the perfect owner would be hard pressed to improve on Joseph Watson. He was as rich as Fairie Cox, without Cox's baggage. He was interested in farming and the land. Best of all, at 46 he was a relatively young man, holding out the promise of a generation or more of stability and continuity at Manton.

Watson and Taylor had been introduced a few months earlier at Ascot, where Watson asked if Taylor could buy him a good two-year-old. They're hard to find, Taylor told him. "If a man has the luck to come by a good two-year-old he generally likes to stick with it." "Get hold of one if you can," replied Watson: "I'm in no hurry." Now, instead of a decent colt, he bought Manton.

Cox had one-fourteenth of a silver mine: Watson had all of a large Leeds-based business making soap products. His father had built it up, the son continued its growth, and then he had the opportunity to sell the business to Lever Brothers and redirect his energy and acumen elsewhere. He bought, in quick succession, a sporting and farming estate at Sudbourne on the Suffolk coast; the beautiful Compton Verney in Warwickshire; and then Manton, contingent on Taylor remaining as trainer. Watson wasn't a newcomer to racing. In his early twenties, he had a couple of horses in training with Dobson Peacock at Middleham, and at least one minor winner, but he put that aside at 24, when he became managing director of Joseph Watson & Sons.

He did the country an important service during the war. Artillery shells were in short supply: before just one of the set-piece trench battles, a million and a half shells were fired to soften up the enemy. Watson, on his own initiative and at his own expense, set aside one of his factories for filling shells with explosives. It began in a small way, with 20 or 30 of his production staff. By the time the armistice was signed, he was in charge of several thousand workers at the 'No 1 National Shell Filling Factory.'

He set about racehorse ownership and stable management with the same single-mindedness. The lads' dormitory conditions appalled him. "I intend to make Manton a heaven on earth for those who work here," he said, and he was as good as his word. He built a hostel for the lads and apprentices, a minute's walk from the yard entrance. He brought electricity to Manton, sweeping away the candles and Taylor's paraffin lamps. He also freed up space in a corner of the yard by moving the chapel. There's a small farm building in front of the yard gates, formerly a feed store and piggery. Watson suggested it be converted. The newly consecrated chapel was in the loft; the pigs continued below, their grunts accompanying the preachers' sermons.

At the December sales, Taylor was bidding to levels that no one had seen before; far beyond the 1,000 guineas that he once said was as much as any yearling was worth. Standing with him was a tall, younger man, unrecognised except by some of the Yorkshire fraternity. It was Joseph Watson, and Taylor spent 25,750 guineas [*£655,000*] in his name to buy nine well bred yearlings.

Later, when the nine produced the winners of the Oaks and the Grand Prix de Paris, people wrote about Watson's 'beginner's luck.' They should have been hailing Taylor's unerring eye, to pick those two out of 200 yearlings on offer. As two-year-olds, four of the nine won 11 races between them. That included four in five starts each for Blue Lady and Love In Idleness; and a win in the Champagne Stakes and placings in the Gimcrack and Middle Park for Lemonora, by Lemberg. The total return to Watson from his first season at Manton was £9,056. It contributed to Taylor's fourth consecutive season as champion trainer, in a year when he was short of a decent three-year-old and failed to win a classic.

His standard-bearers were the older horses Manilardo and Buchan. Manilardo had won the Wood Ditton Stakes in a canter the previous season, but his classic entries were voided when Cox died just before the 2,000 Guineas. Now, running for Cox's brother, Manilardo won the Coronation Cup and later ran second in the Ebor, giving 30lb to the winner. The perennially unlucky Buchan won the Chester Vase, Eclipse and Doncaster Cup for Lord Astor, but lost the Gold Cup in the Stewards' room. The blame lay with Buchan's jockey, the Australian Frank Bullock. In an otherwise excellent season, in which he rode 123 winners and pushed Donoghue hard for the jockeys' title, it was unfortunate that Bullock saved a woeful effort for the Gold Cup.

Buchan led into the straight with only one possible danger, Tangiers, who'd run second to Manilardo in the Coronation Cup. In the last three furlongs of the Gold Cup, Buchan hung slightly away from the rails, but still went easily. Bullock kept looking back at Tangiers, and each time he did so, Buchan edged further over towards the stands. Tangiers, hard ridden a length behind, his jockey George Hulme seemingly intent on challenging on the stands side, was taken wider and wider. Inside the last furlong, Hulme staged a dramatic diversion. He snatched up his mount, switched behind Buchan, and charged up his inside. Bullock was slow to see the danger, but Buchan had sufficient in hand to win by a neck. Besides Hulme's theatrics, the stewards took into account that Tangiers had made up at least a length in the last half-furlong. Out went Buchan, from first to last, as the rules then dictated. The horse's final piece of ill luck came when he was sent to Newmarket for what appeared a simple task in the Jockey Club Stakes, but coughed, was withdrawn and retired.

A year that includes Coronation Cup and Eclipse winners can hardly be called disappointing, but much more was expected as Taylor looked forward to 1921, and much was duly delivered. The season got off to a stuttering start because of the miners' strike. During the war, the miners' importance to the nation was second only to that of the armed forces. Coal fired the Navy's ships and fuelled the railways. The Government took control of the mining industry, providing subsidies and guarantees that, inevitably, pushed wages to record levels. When the industry was handed back to the mine owners, without financial support, the payrolls inherited from wartime weren't sustainable. The coal owners gave their workers two weeks' notice that their contracts would be cancelled. It was the required first step before wages could be cut. It emerged that in some cases pay packets would be halved.

A national coal strike was called, and racing was quickly drawn into its wider consequences. The miners asked the railwaymen to join the strike, and the Government acted to reduce rail travel to a minimum, to preserve coal stocks. Which meant that, in peace as in war, trains to race meetings and to transport racehorses were withdrawn.

In the middle of April, as it had done four years earlier, the Jockey Club announced that at the Government's request, it was abandoning all racing under rules, 'till further notice.' There was a cynical view at the time that the Government had a secondary motive when it told the Jockey Club to suspend racing. The conspiracy theorists pointed out that many miners followed racing keenly, and liked a bet. Miners now had time on their hands. If there were no horses to follow and winners to back, the misery and boredom of their unemployment would be magnified.

As it had in the war, the Government made a speedy, undignified about turn, in the face of a simple argument: *"Provided that we don't use the railways, why shouldn't we hold race meetings?"* The Guineas meeting went ahead. Cars and coaches set off from London from five o'clock. Every road into Newmarket was clogged long before racing. A huge crowd saw a 2,000 Guineas that lacked any recent form. Jack Joel's Humorist was made favourite on the strength of his running-on second in the previous autumn's Middle Park. Manton had two 10-1 co-fifth favourites, Lord Astor's Craig an Eran and Joseph Watson's Lemonora. When they were galloped at home, they finished in that order, close together. Lemonora seemed held by Humorist after finishing two places behind that colt in the Middle Park. Craig an Eran was still a maiden after just two runs in his first season.

The form counted for nothing, because in one of his greatest training moments, Taylor saddled Craig an Eran to beat Lemonora by three parts of a length, with Humorist the same distance back in third. There were 26 runners and a consequent strong pace. Steve Donoghue on Humorist came to the front passing the Bushes, looking off to his right, but all the danger was on his left: the Manton pair, running home together on the stands rail. Coming out of the Dip, Humorist faltered, while Craig an Eran mastered Lemonora.

Astor's years of investment in his stud paid off handsomely. At Sir William Bass's dispersal sale, Astor paid 4,500 guineas for Sceptre's daughter Maid Of The Mist, with her filly foal Hamoaze, and it was the mating of Hamoaze with the Derby winner Sunstar that produced Buchan, who despite his mixed fortunes won 11 races, three of them now Group Ones. Maid Of The Mist herself bred the wartime Oaks winner Sunny Jane, by Sunstar. Sent again to Sunstar, she produced the Guineas winner Craig an Eran.

The first three from the 2,000 Guineas all lined up in the Derby, after ante-post betting that see-sawed violently in response to each fresh rumour of a sensational gallop or, conversely, a setback. The Newmarket form was handsomely upheld when Humorist narrowly beat Craig an Eran, the pair three lengths in front of Lemonora. There was a certain amount of soul-searching over Craig an Eran, who was ridden by Jack Brennan. Had he allowed Humorist, who quickened to the front two furlongs out, to get first run on him? Hardly: he came into second place as soon as Humorist made his move. Close home, he drew almost alongside Donoghue, but as Steve said afterwards, "I had a little bit in reserve," and that's how the photograph of the finish looks, with Donoghue half upright, peeping at Brennan, who has Craig an Eran under maximum pressure. Brennan said that he sent his mount along, "For all he was worth. He responded gamely, and when I almost got on terms with Humorist, I thought he might go through with it. But all the time I had a suspicion that Donoghue had a bit up his sleeve, and so it proved."

The race had a sad sequel. Humorist was doing some routine work a fortnight later when he bled slightly. He was taken straight to his stable to rest, and all appeared well, but a few mornings later a lad noticed a pool of blood seeping from underneath the door of Humorist's box. The Derby winner, with that notorious 'bleeder' Hermit present three times in his pedigree, had burst a vessel in his lungs.

Craig an Eran confirmed that he was a high-class horse by winning the St James's Palace Stakes and then the Eclipse. He flopped in the St Leger when considered a certainty, starting at 1-4, and although he'd had plenty of time to recover, it was felt that a hard race on firm ground at Sandown had bottomed him. At stud, he sired the winners of a Derby and two French Derbys.

Joseph Watson's Lemonora had his big day in Paris. His jockey Joe

Childs said after Epsom that the horse wasn't good enough. Not very diplomatic, but vintage Childs. He made amends by suggesting to Watson that the French three-year-olds weren't very strong, and there was a big prize looming, the Grand Prix de Paris. No one had a better line than Childs to the French form. Already that season, he'd ridden placed horses in the Prix de Diane and the Prix du Jockey Club, including finishing a close fourth to the presumed good thing for the Grand Prix, the Jockey Club winner Ksar.

At Longchamp, his mount Lemonara was an 11-2 chance behind the 6-5 favourite Ksar. Afterwards, there was much disbelief in the English racing press at Lemonora's starting price. The explanation was that a handful of English professional punters had travelled to Paris with commissions for Lemonora. They were so appalled by the way the local jockeys murdered Steve Donoghue in an earlier race that they decided it was too risky to back any visiting jockey. On another day, Bernard Dillon had won the Grand Prix on Spearmint by making all the running, so avoiding whatever trouble the locals had planned for him. Childs simply kept Lemonora well to the outside, and won comfortably. Joseph Watson was a fine figure in his white silk topper. There were excited stories about him winning tens of thousands in bets. He laughed them off. He didn't bet, because there wasn't much point.

Watson's second season as an owner exceeded even his first. Lemonora had placed in two classics and won the Grand Prix: the little filly Love In Idleness won him the Oaks. She was the winner of four starts from five as a two-year-old, and though the balance of her form didn't appear top-class, she was made 5-1 favourite for the Oaks in a field of 22. It was a rough race in the early stages, and at one point Love In Idleness was knocked back several lengths, but she had the speed and tenacity to work her back into contention on the descent to Tattenham Corner, and when Childs set her alight three furlongs out, she went clear, winning by three lengths. Taylor's friendly rival Richard Marsh said that, "I shall always remember that diminutive [and] remarkable filly Love In Idleness for the beautiful way she was invariably ridden by Joe Childs. Courage is everything in a racehorse, and one saw what it could do for a pony like Love In Idleness, with her big heart and absolute genuineness."

Joseph Watson showed his appreciation of Taylor's instant success for him by investing again at the autumn yearling sales. Manton's future could hardly have seemed brighter. Despite Taylor's fears, Fairie Cox's brother was carrying on as before, even to the extent of repeating, 'Not for sale' when offered £100,000 for Gay Crusader. Lord Astor had won three races which are now Group Ones with Craig an Eran. The following season beckoned. If anything could improve it, it did, with the announcement in the New Year honours that Joseph Watson had been elevated to the peerage, to acknowledge his prodigious work during the war. He became Baron Manton of Compton Verney.

In less than three months, he was dead. He was a keen huntsman. Out with the Warwickshire, his wife and two of his sons riding close behind, he suffered a heart attack and died immediately. The autopsy showed that this tall, athletic man had an abnormally small heart, with fragile muscle walls. The death of Lord Manton was a tragedy for his family and friends, for the employees on his estates and at Manton; and more generally for the country. He managed a large business from the age of 24, with the single-mindedness to put his interest in racing on one side for two decades. He was tough enough to compete successfully with a giant competitor like Lever Brothers, and sufficiently valued to be asked to stay on as chairman when Lord Leverhulme bought Joseph Watson & Sons. He did his country uncommon service in the war. He was a large-scale benefactor: in 1921, he gave £50,000 [*£1.15 million*] to the Leeds General Infirmary, and he set aside 20,000 acres for research into improving animal and plant strains. Had he been given another 10 or 20 years of life, it's as sure as anything can be that he would have made further contributions to public life. Somerville Tattersall said, "The death of Lord Manton involved the English turf in one of the greatest losses it had experienced in many years," but Watson's early death was a loss far beyond racing.

Chapter 14

Waldorf Astor

When Lord Manton died, his oldest son was only 20, and in no position to take on all his inherited business interests and responsibilities. The executors of his father's will decided that Manton and the bloodstock would have to go. The yard was put up for sale, and the horses went to Tattersalls in three consignments. Eight yearlings sold for just under £1,000 each at the July sales. Ten mares brought in a further 15,510 guineas; Love In Idleness and Lemonora were sold for 7,600 and 7,000 guineas respectively. Eighteen other horses in training with Taylor were sold. The total realised was just short of £60,000 [*£1.7 million*]. Only six fillies were retained. Taylor picked them out as likely to enhance their value if they had the chance to race for another season. His case was argued by Somerville Tattersall. It must have impressed the executors that Tattersall was acting against his own short-term interest in proposing that the fillies' sale be postponed. They agreed to lease the six to Tattersall for the 1922 season: he to bear the training costs, prize money to be shared equally between Tattersall and Lord Manton's estate.

The decision was well rewarded. Five of the six won that summer: 16 races between them, from 34 starts. The largest single prize was Lady Juror's Jockey Club Stakes and £6,573 [*£188,000*]. The fillies' campaigns were notable for their travelling further afield, and more often, than was typical of Taylor. Sister In Law won the Yorkshire Oaks and Liverpool's Atlantic handicap [worth *£75,000*]. Two Step was that rarest of creatures, a Taylor-trained sprinter. She won five times, including the Fern Hill Stakes, the Nunthorpe and the Portland handicap. Two four-year-olds, Blue Lady and Tetrabazzia, won three times each. In all, the five fillies won *£474,000* in purses. They were sent to the sales after being covered by a choice selection of stallions, among them Gay Crusader, and thanks to Taylor's skilful handling, they trebled their original purchase prices. Bought by Joseph Watson for 13,350 guineas, they now sold for 41,900 guineas [*£1.19 million*]. Tetrabazzia was the highest priced of the quintet, at 9,000 guineas. As she later bred a St Leger winner, Singapore, by Gainsborough, it was money well spent. By the end of the year after Lord Manton's death, all his bloodstock interests had been sold. At the time, it was calculated that in his short involvement in breeding and racing, and including prize money, Watson roughly doubled his investment.

Selling Manton itself wasn't so easy, and various of its tenants were given the option to buy their farms or homes. From a training perspective, it was business as usual. In 1922, Alec Taylor was again champion trainer. The most successful owner in the yard was Lord Astor, and it was Astor's racing manager Gerald Deane and his business partner Somerville Tattersall who were, in one guise or another, to shape the fortunes of Manton for the next 25 years.

The two men were a study in contrasts. 'Sommy' Tattersall was the last family member to head the bloodstock auction house. It was said of him that, 'His persuasive tongue would get a weak man to bid for a mule.' "He has at his command a musical voice which carries further than any I can recall. This pleasing delivery is backed up by a store of persuasive eloquence that any political orator might envy. His memory too [is] exceptional." A friend spoke of watching trainers' strings on the Heath with Sommy one morning: "Pointing to a bay three-year-old, quite free from distinctive markings, he said, 'That's a colt by so-and-so out of such-and-such a mare. I remember him passing through the ring as a yearling and I haven't seen him since'." The friend, who had a good eye for a horse himself, was astonished.

Tattersall was a man of many parts. He was passionate about the arts, especially music, and he was a keen mountaineer. His climbing clothes were, 'a belted jacket of thick tweed, baggy knickerbocker trousers of the same fabric, woollen ribbed stockings, hobnailed boots and a peaked cap with ear-flaps.' He used to wear this outfit on cold mornings at Manton.

The foil to this quiet, cultured man was his junior partner, Gerald Deane. Sommy coaxed on the rostrum, Deane bullied. "I can't dwell," he barked at under-bidders: "Quick, or you lose him." *The Story of Tattersalls* offers this portrait: "Gerald Deane was at all times exceptionally mercurial, and his temper had a very low boiling point." He suffered from manic depression:

"He had spells in which he became progressively more excitable, over-confident and overbearing, until he suddenly cracked [and] plunged into depths [in] which he showed strong suicidal tendencies." Deane's fuse was so short that one day he threw a Tattersalls client down the office stairs. A window crashed open: out sailed a smart grey Homburg, accompanied by Deane's roar: "And you can take your bloody hat with you, too!"

The *Sporting Times* referred to the, 'ever-impulsive' Mr Deane, and he himself admitted that, "I go into my bridle rather strong at times." His influence at Manton extended as far back as wartime, when Lord Astor asked him to act as his racing manager. It was Deane who told young Jack Colling to ride Blink as a pacemaker in the 1918 Derby. "Major Deane seemed to have a lot of say in the running of all the horses at Manton," recalled Colling. The meddling made such an impression on Colling that he would look back and say:

> "[It] convinced me that if, when I gave up riding, I was ever lucky enough to find owners to train for, I'd insist on one thing – no managers! If my owners couldn't trust me to see to their horses' best interests without an overseer, then they'd have to find another trainer."

That conclusion was harsh where Lord Astor was concerned. His commitments were so extensive that he could hardly be chided for delegating to others. Astor's father William was reputed to be the richest man in America. After a family feud, he came to England, and took British citizenship in 1899. His eldest son, Waldorf Astor, met Gerald Deane at Eton, and was an undergraduate when he paid £100 for his first broodmare, Conjure. She bred him five winners, including the 1910 1,000 Guineas winner Winkipop, trained by Willie Waugh at Kingsclere.

After Astor's death, the respective obituaries of *The Times* and *The Sporting Life* were headlined, 'A Life of Public Service' and, 'Close of Great Era on Turf,' as if there were two different people. His interests ranged over politics, agriculture, *The Observer* newspaper, international affairs and public health. He was a noted sportsman, representing Oxford at fencing, polo and steeplechasing. He became an MP for Plymouth in 1910. It was unreported at the time, but he strained his heart at university, which put an end to sports. He was unfit for active service in wartime. He asked the War Office for a disagreeable job, and was given the task of inspecting Army camps to report wastage. The apparently healthy young MP, with the rank of major and a nice clean uniform, mysteriously exempt from combat, was resented wherever he went. Bob Sievier, who was almost a caricature of a patriot, wrote a misguided portrait of Astor in *The Winning Post*, headed, "Sir, are you a soldier?" It all but accused him of cowardice. Astor, with his weak heart, quietly went about Salisbury Plain, asking for access to every cookhouse and refuse dump, and helped to achieve substantial savings.

Astor joined Lloyd George's staff as parliamentary private secretary in 1917. In the same year, Astor's father accepted a peerage, without discussing the impact of the title with his son. It caused a rift between the two, because whether sooner or later, it put a ceiling on the younger Astor's Parliamentary aspirations. His father died only two years later. Waldorf became the second Viscount Astor, and to his chagrin was obliged to give up his seat in the Commons. He took legal action to renounce his title, and told his constituents, "Don't get too used to 'Viscount,' in case you have to unlearn it," but he failed.

He was living proof of the saying that, 'If you want a task done, give it to a busy man.' He served in the Lords as parliamentary secretary for the Ministry of Food and then the Ministry for Health. He co-authored four books on farming. He chaired a government committee on policy to combat TB. He was a founder, and for 15 years chairman, of the Royal Institute of International Affairs, Chatham House. Most of all, he retained a great fondness for Plymouth. When he stood down reluctantly as its MP, he was succeeded by his formidable wife Nancy, the first woman to sit in the House of Commons. She had a lethal wit. When she arrived in England as a glamorous American divorcee, a group of English society wives confronted her: was she in England to steal one of their husbands? "My dears," replied the future Lady Astor: "If you only knew the trouble I had getting rid of my own." She became such a persistent butter-in during Commons debates that the all-male press gallery agreed among themselves to limit reports of her interruptions.

When Waldorf Astor married Nancy, his father gave the couple his Thames-side estate, Cliveden, and it was there that Astor built up one of the most successful studs of the twentieth century. Breeding was Astor's chosen distraction from all his commitments to public life. It was said of him, 'Breeding is planning, and in all his activities he had a careful planning mind.' Along with Conjure, Astor's foundation mares were Popinjay and Maid Of The Mist. Popinjay was bought from Lord Rosebery. She was out of Rosebery's high-class filly Chelandry, winner of the 1,000 Guineas and second in the Oaks and St Leger, by the 2,000 Guineas and Eclipse winner St Frusquin. Maid Of The Mist and her filly foal cost Astor 4,500 guineas at auction; she won only three minor races, but she was a daughter of Sceptre, by the Gold Cup winner Cyllene. It's a much-quoted precept that one should breed the best to the best, and hope for the best. That's what Astor did, reducing the 'hope' element to the minimum possible. Popinjay and Maid Of The Mist produced numerous high-class colts and future broodmares. Astor never bought a colt, except to lead work for his other horses at Manton, and he never kept a moderate horse. As he said, "The secret of good breeding is fearlessness and ruthlessness in weeding out bad animals." He seldom bothered to cover his costs by sending a cull to the sales. Gerald Deane would simply be asked to find it a good home.

Having had one horse with Taylor in 1911, Astor moved all his horses in training to Manton two years later. The following season he found himself third in the owners' prize money list, Taylor having trained him four winners of 10 races. The most important was the Jockey Club Stakes, where his Trois Temps won £7,440. Maid Of The Mist's daughter Hamoaze, named after a government building in Plymouth, added another £1,700 for finishing second: a combined haul of *£919,000*. Maid Of The Mist's next foal was Sunny Jane, who ran second in the 1,000 Guineas and won the New Oaks. That was the prelude to several years of success for Astor and Taylor: five individual winners of six classics, all of them bred at Cliveden.

Gerald Deane was involved in most of Astor's bloodstock decisions, and as Astor was the principal owner at Manton, Deane had a great deal of influence inside the yard. It was as well that, most of the time, his furies were directed at the enemies without: the Marlborough touts. Young Alec grew indifferent to them. Some of his owners didn't bet at all, others like Lady Douglas and Somerville Tattersall might have a bet on their own horse, but not a life-changing one. If Taylor saw to it that as far as possible the touts were kept away, it was to protect his owners' confidences, not the price. Fairie Cox didn't allow visitors to Manton even to see his horses, unless he'd given permission. Deane brought urgency to the stable's approach to the 'watchers.'

His particular *bête noire* was William Maisey, the canny one who lingered at Marlborough station to see Manton's late entry Pradella leaving for Ascot. For many years, Maisey published a tipping sheet called *The Wiltshire Opinion*. It was well printed and it had excellent information, gleaned from the expanse of training grounds from Beckhampton across Manton to the Ogbournes. He was said to have won £30,000 [*£1.66 million*] in 1906, backing Pradella in the Ascot Stakes and her stablemate Dinneford in the Hunt Cup, in single bets and doubles. Their combined SPs produced a 103-1 double, so the story wasn't entirely implausible. He was able to build a big house and put plenty aside for the losing days. His touts, some of them carrying the scars of earlier skirmishes at Manton, used to buy drinks for every passing stable lad in the Lord's Arms on the outskirts of Fyfield. Any tradesman with business up at the yard was combed for snippets and rumours. At the top of this pyramid of information gathering was William Maisey.

The scene in the Lord's Arms so enraged Deane that he persuaded Taylor to buy the pub and close it down. The touts moved to The Lamb in Marlborough, where Maisey paid their shilling-a-night lodgings. Several of them were former Manton apprentices who still had friends in the stable. Useful tips came from the special trains. Fred Darling's horses from Beckhampton used to be walked over Manton on their way to Marlborough station for Ascot and the big Newmarket meetings. The two sets of lads travelled together with their horses, and it didn't take them long to find out who fancied what. Deane could prowl the downs, peering balefully into coverts, for all the good it did. The days of the man hidden in the hedge were passing; the stable's secrets were exchanged for a half-crown here and a pound there in the Marlborough pubs. Maisey's skill was to make *The Wiltshire Opinion* sound as if he personally had been camouflaged at the top of a tree, binoculars in one hand and notebook in the other.

Lord Manton's executors had the yard for sale for six years, during which time Young Alec was their tenant. It was hardly what he'd planned when, already thinking of an early retirement, he sold Manton to Joseph Watson, staying on as trainer as part of the sale and purchase agreement. Taylor did, though, have all the backing he could have wished. Alexander Cox and Lady Douglas continued to support the yard. Sommy Tattersall reinvested the prize money from his lease on Manton's fillies in more horses in training. Most importantly, Lord Astor provided a stream of good horses from Cliveden, and built his own 24-box yard at Manton to house them. Young Alec continued to rack up successive trainers' championships. Then along came the colt that Taylor reckoned the best horse he ever trained.

When he was asked to named the best mare, that was easy: Sceptre. Best colt? He thought long and hard: he couldn't separate the two sons of Galicia, Bayardo and Gay Crusader. Sighing, he said he wished he'd been able to train Gay Crusader as a four-year-old. All the Cup races would've been a formality, he implied. "He was equally brilliant at five furlongs or two miles. In fact, I really don't know how good he was. It was just a disaster that I [wasn't] able to train him [for another year]." And then when all the questions seemed answered, he would add, sadly, 'Picaroon.'

After seven consecutive champion trainer titles, the inevitable year came when Taylor slipped back to third place; no Manton owner was in the top five. The season ended, though, with Manton two-year-olds at the top of the Free Handicap. A filly, Saucy Sue, was rated 1lb ahead of a colt, Picaroon, who'd won his three starts, the most taking of them in the Middle Park, where he beat Solario and Manna. Over the winter, Alexander Cox was offered £60,000 [*£1.89 million*] for the colt. Like his brother, he said, 'No sale.' It was a compliment to the handicapper that Astor's Saucy Sue won the next season's 1,000 Guineas and Oaks. A similar level of success beckoned for Picaroon after the Craven Stakes, which he won by an easy length and a half from Astor's Crossbow, conceding 15lb, with a backward-looking Solario two lengths behind. Picaroon had been favourite for the Derby from the day of his win in the Middle Park. Now he was as short as 4-1 for Epsom. A week after the Craven there was a rumour that something was amiss. Taylor confirmed at once that Picaroon was suffering from lymphangitis. A minor cut had become septic: an abscess had formed, swollen and burst. There was no chance that Picaroon could be trained for the 2,000 Guineas, and by mid-May, the Derby had been ruled out.

The frustration of Taylor and Cox can be imagined as they saw Picaroon's Middle Park victim Manna win the 2,000 Guineas and Derby. The Middle Park second, Solario, was fourth in both races. Then Crossbow, over a stone Picaroon's inferior at home, ran the winner of the St James's Palace Stakes to a head. Picaroon got back to the racecourse belatedly in mid-August, losing to a horse that had no business beating him, and then ran fourth in the St Leger. A few days earlier, Taylor had set up a proper trial at home. Two lead horses worked with Crossbow and Astor's dual classic winner

Saucy Sue. Picaroon won the trial so convincingly that Saucy Sue, who'd been second favourite for the St Leger, was promptly scratched.

How that must have been regretted when Picaroon only plugged on at one pace into fourth behind Solario at Doncaster. Picaroon then set off on an end-of-season campaign in small-field conditions races, and won four in a row, all at 10 furlongs. One was the Champion Stakes, from which a line to the second-placed horse in the St Leger implied that, if Taylor had only had another two or three weeks to get Picaroon ready, Cox's colt would have beaten Solario, as he'd done twice before. Every hope was held for Picaroon the following season, but as early as March, *The Wiltshire Opinion* told its subscribers, 'He has given Taylor a lot of trouble over the winter.' "It would not surprise us if it was found impossible to [train] him." Picaroon's blood disorder persisted, and he became too sick even to be saved for stud. The tipster Maisey wrote, "[He] was one of the unluckiest animals imaginable not to win the triple crown." Picaroon's regular jockey Frank Bullock believed that, "If only he could have been trained [without interruption] as a three-year-old and four-year-old, he would have proved himself one of the greatest horses of all time."

If Picaroon was fated never to show he was the best that Young Alec trained, Manton mostly purred through the mid-1920s like a finely tuned engine. Astor provided the fuel. It seemed that his stud produced a disproportionate number of classic-winning fillies, but that can be attributed to his unfortunate sequence of near misses in the Derby. In a seven-year span, Taylor saddled five seconds for Astor at Epsom: Blink [1918], Buchan [1919], Craig an Eran [1921], Tamar [1922] and St Germans [1924]. The only colt's classic that Taylor won for Astor was Craig an Eran's 2,000 Guineas. By contrast, the Cliveden fillies could do little wrong: following Sunny Jane in the 1917 Oaks, Taylor sent out Pogrom to win the race in 1922; in 1925, Saucy Sue and Miss Gadabout gave Astor first and second in the 1,000 Guineas and again in the Oaks. Saucy Sue was that year's leading prize money earner. The following year, Short Story won the Oaks, and the year after, Book Law, like Short Story a daughter of Buchan, was second in both the fillies' classics before beating the colts in the St Leger. Astor was teetotal, and his wife Nancy was a vigorous campaigner for temperance. After the St Leger, it was quipped that at Cliveden, 'The water flowed like champagne.'

Chapter 15

Young Alec's retirement

Book Law was Young Alec's last classic winner. A few weeks before the St Leger, it was announced that Manton had, at last, been sold and that Taylor would retire at the end of the season. Continued success on the racecourse muffled unease among the yard's owners and staff. The 'for sale' advertisements meant that every time a stranger was seen at the yard, a fresh rumour circulated. The most damaging for morale in the hostel and the tack room was the talk that another trainer would buy Manton and bring in his own lads and apprentices, displacing the existing staff. The state of Taylor's health was equally worrying for the owners. In the spring of 1926, the *Sporting Times* said, "It is good to see Alec Taylor back on a racecourse. He has been far from well again of late. [It] is rather pathetic to see Manton still advertised for sale, week after week."

Twelve months on, the paper resumed, "There are again rumours of prospective changes at Manton owing to Alec Taylor's ill-health. He has had a bad time of it of late and [we] can take it that this really will be his last season." The *Marlborough Times* wrote that, "Mr Taylor has been in bad health for some time, caused, no doubt, in part by anxiety as to the ultimate fate of Manton." Uncertainty over yard and trainer created unease among the owners. Matters came to a head when Sommy Tattersall warned of, "A risk that [Manton] might be sold as a place for horses to be deposited before being shipped abroad, and that the training gallops would no longer be used." It was whispered that Astor, rather than waiting to see what transpired, intended to move his horses to Beckhampton.

It was clear that if those closest to the stable didn't act at once, the yard's fate would be taken out of their hands. The hero of the hour was Gerald Deane, described in the *Pink 'Un* not long before as, "A little over-zealous at times in the interests of [Astor] and the Manton establishment, [an] outspoken man who does not mind treading on corns." Zeal was the quality the situation demanded. Deane set about forming a syndicate to buy the estate. When that failed, he turned to his senior partner Tattersall, and persuaded him that Manton should be saved as a training yard. To relief and surprise, it was announced that Tattersalls had bought Manton. The reported sale price of £75,000 [*£2.34 million*] was far short of what Joseph Watson had paid eight years earlier, reflecting the extent to which the estate had been whittled down by the executors' sale of farms to their tenants.

With one problem resolved, the more difficult issue was Taylor's future. Tattersall and Deane weren't altruists. They ran a commercial enterprise, which made them ideal owners for Manton. Having spent their working lives in one large racing institution, they weren't daunted by taking on another. Taylor's health had been as much a cause for unrest as the pending sale of the yard, so they addressed it directly. They told him it was time to make way for a new Master of Manton. To sugar the pill, he would have a role as an adviser. Taylor didn't want to go. He told his staff, "You will realise what a wrench it is for me to leave. I have always hoped that I should live, and die, at Manton, but advancing years and increasing infirmity have compelled me to alter my views. [It is] sad to think it is the parting of the ways."

His sadness was eased by the knowledge that his successor was to be a man whom he'd shaped and taught: his travelling head lad, Joe Lawson. Tattersall and Deane had achieved agreement on a new ownership and a new trainer quickly, and as harmoniously as the circumstances allowed. The only hiccup was a report by the racing correspondent of *The Times*:

> "I was informed yesterday on the best authority that the famous Manton training establishment has been sold by the executors of the late Lord Manton and that the purchasers are Messrs Tattersalls. The establishment will still carry on, with Mr A Taylor as adviser and with J Lawson, who has been associated with Mr Taylor [for] the past 30 years, as trainer. The owners whose horses are trained there now will continue as patrons of Manton [including] Lord Astor, Somerville Tattersall, AR Cox [and] Lady Douglas. Lawson [will] no doubt prove himself, with Mr Taylor close at hand to advise him, an able successor to one of the greatest trainers in the history of the Turf."

The story was accurate in every respect, but it caused Deane to blow his famously short fuse. The next day brought a chastened follow-up:

> "I stated that the present patrons of the stables would continue to have their horses trained there. This was inaccurate and unauthorised. The news of the sale was announced [here] before some of the Manton owners knew of it, and, I am sorry to say, caused considerable use of the telegraph and telephone. I regret that my mistake, owing to a misunderstanding, caused Mr Tattersall and Mr Deane a very busy morning."

A newspaper reporter today would give short shrift, if asked to apologise for a well-sourced story. But Deane's intervention helped ensure that Young Alec's owners transferred their patronage to Lawson. Taylor's last months at Manton showed that, whatever his health, his powers of training and placing his horses were undiminished. Book Law went on from the St Leger to win the Jockey Club Stakes, with Tattersall's filly Foliation a close second. It was the ninth win for Taylor in the race: Book Law's £5,429 [*£169,000*], added to her previous wins, put her fourth in the list of prize-winning fillies, behind a trio of greats: Sceptre, Pretty Polly and the 1892 1,000 Guineas, Oaks and St Leger winner La Flèche. At stud, Book Law produced five winners, the best of them Astor's St James's Palace and Eclipse winner Rhodes Scholar, though her greatest contribution to turf history was to breed Archive, by Nearco: he was a hopeless racehorse, but he sired Arkle.

Taylor had 44 horses in training at the start of his last season, and saddled 29 of them to win 47 races. Half his string were sired by horses that he'd trained, highlighting the continuity that his owner-breeders provided. He couldn't quite sign off as champion trainer, finishing a close second, but his prize money total of £55,196 [*£1.72 million*] was within a whisker of his personal best. In all, Taylor trained the winners of 928 races. His record in the classics was: in the 1,000 Guineas, one winner, six seconds and a third. In the 2,000 Guineas, four winners and seven seconds. There were three Derby or New Derby winners, six seconds and two thirds. In the Oaks and New Oaks, he trained eight winners, four seconds and two thirds. In the St Leger, he had five winners, a second and four thirds. He farmed the Jockey Club Stakes and he trained six Eclipse winners. Then there were the Hunt Cups, and other big handicaps galore. The only significant race that eluded him was the Cambridgeshire. There were other brilliant trainers in his generation, but Taylor was regarded as the first among equals, as the previous quote from *The Times* suggests. A prominent breeder, Alfred Potter, paid him this tribute:

> "We owe much to Alec Taylor for bringing the horses placed under his care slowly but surely to full maturity [and] not over-racing them. No trainer has benefited the Turf more. The sires Bayardo, Lemberg, Gay Crusader, Gainsborough, Buchan, Craig an Eran and Magpie [in Australia] have all been under his care. No trainer of the past – not even the great three, John Scott, Mathew Dawson and John Porter – has passed on from the stable to the stud such a series of sires."

Richard Marsh, who trained Bayardo's great rival Minoru, wrote:

> "The deeds of Alec Taylor speak for themselves in far more eloquent language than is at my command. He has that wonderful instinct that tells a man which horses are likely to improve with time and patience. He waits for these horses to 'come' and he will then get the best possible out of them. He is unquestionably a master of the art of training. I have known him all his life and have always had the greatest admiration for him as a trainer, and the most kindly feelings for him as an honourable man. I have at all times been struck with his simplicity, both in his way of living and in his way of accepting his brilliant success."

For all his modesty, Taylor's reputation had spread beyond the racing press. *Punch* magazine published a celebrity portrait each week: *Mr Punch's Personality.* Shortly before his retirement was announced, Taylor was the subject. A full-page drawing showed him towering over the downs, like a colossus. When the season ended, his owners organised a dinner and presented him with a silver salver. It was inscribed, "*Presented by his patrons to Alec Taylor on his retirement from active training at Manton, as a memento of their esteem and appreciation, and his most wonderful and successful services.*"

Taylor himself, conscious of a page turning in many lives at Manton, gathered all his staff for a commemorative photograph. Finally, in the week before Christmas, he laid on a dinner for them all, and the wives of the married men, at the Castle and Ball hotel in Marlborough. Singers, conjurers and comedians came from London to entertain them. It was a proper festive dinner: roast turkey, goose and beef, followed by plum pudding. There were crackers and party hats: Sommy Tattersall's was in the Astor racing colours of light blue and pink.

At the top table sat Taylor, flanked by Deane and Tattersall, with Joe Lawson and Taylor's other head lad, Tommy Ault. Astor sent his apologies. He'd been looking forward to the party, to celebrate Book Law's wins, but he had to be in London to shepherd a Bill through the House of Lords.

His message read that no man could have had a better experience as an owner than he'd enjoyed at Manton. He thanked Tattersalls for ensuring the stable's survival and counted himself, "Most fortunate that Mr Lawson is to take charge. He has proved himself a skilled trainer, with keen judgement and knowledge." Gerald Deane likened Alec Taylor to, "Two great kings: Solomon for his wisdom and the late King Edward, for his tact and charm." Taylor himself asked the gathering to give, 'A hearty vote of thanks for the way in which Tattersalls have saved us from disaster.'

> "I leave Manton with a hopeful heart. I am giving up the reins to a man who is worthy to take them as trainer. Mr Lawson and I have been in close relationship ever since he came to Manton aged 16. In the whole of that period, he has been a good and faithful servant and a good friend to me. I feel confident that he is very capable. I can testify to his sterling character and abilities. It has been my hope that when I gave up he would succeed me. It is very gratifying to me to know that he is going to do so."

Lawson proposed a toast: "Manton first, the rest a good second." The evening ended with the staff presenting Taylor with a cheque: an extreme example of carrying coals to Newcastle. The following season, Taylor did put in a few appearances, but he'd moved out of the area, and the visits tapered off. Once, Lawson asked him to watch a pre-Derby gallop. A searching trial took place, the classic hopeful finished in front and an elated Lawson asked his mentor, what did he think? "I think you've left the Derby at Manton, Mr Lawson," was the reply.

Young Alec made a firm statement with his photograph of the Manton staff and then the farewell dinner. It was the last wiping clean of his half-brother's slate. The photograph showed that Manton was an orderly place where honest service was respected and rewarded: and, definitely, no whipping at the copper hole. The available evidence is that the camera didn't lie. The frequent cases at the Marlborough courts which had been a feature of Old Alec's time vanished when his son took the reins.

Taylor paid his employees annually, at the beginning of January. The 1923 wages statement on page 84 shows that an experienced lad, Sandy Lee, was paid £9.70 for the year, plus a £2 bonus. After deductions for clothes, and including cash advances amounting to eight shillings, he earned £6.20 [*£186*]. But a few months later, after Picaroon's unbeaten first season, the letter to Lee from Alexander Cox accompanies a present of £25 [*£750*]. Whenever he could, Taylor intercepted gifts such as Cox's, and pooled them to be shared round all the paid lads. There wasn't much he could do to stop benefactors like the jockey Joe Childs, who used to visit at Christmas, and hand all the lads £5 as a 'thank you' for his winning rides. Whenever Sommy Tattersall had a winner, he too liked to hand over his rewards personally. One day, Taylor deputed Joe Lawson to accompany Sommy as he inspected his horses. Tattersall lingered with a favourite filly for so long that Lawson, who'd moved on to the next box, became suspicious. He saw Sommy coming out of his filly's stable, looking sheepish. Once Sommy had moved on, Lawson looked in on the filly. Her head turned back from her manger, with a banknote between her teeth.

Cox's present to Sandy Lee provides a clue to Taylor's own riches. Freed from the responsibilities of Manton, Taylor overcame his poor health, and lived for another 15 years, dying in 1942 aged 81. He left £595,791 [*£15.65 million*], mostly to charities. There was £10,000 [*£262,700*] for Joe Lawson and £400 for Jack Brennan. How did he amass such wealth? Certainly not through training fees. In the 1920s, he charged his owners £2.50 per horse per week; the year's bills were sent each December. With at most 50 horses in training, that meant an annual income of *£195,000* in our money, only *£3,900* per horse. He had a substantial income from his farms; he micro-managed to the extent of arranging the shooting lets himself. His prize money percentages ran into tens of thousands over his years at Manton, but the upkeep and the wages bill would have swallowed that. The most likely explanation for his millions is that he received large presents from his rich owners, whether in cash after their big-race wins, or shares in the stallions that he helped establish.

Taylor saved a surprise for his retirement. After all the years of not betting, he decided to have some fun. He asked Joe Lawson to send him news of strong Manton fancies. They were marked with one star for a win selection, two for each-way. It's unlikely that Taylor suddenly started betting in hundreds, but as Lawson carried on Manton's successes as if nothing had changed, Young Alec must have profited.

Chapter 16

A record year

Joe Lawson faced equal measures of challenge and opportunity as he prepared his string for the start of the 1928 season. The challenge was intimidating: to step out of the long shadow cast by the two Taylors. The opportunity was dazzling. All the main owners remained in place, inclined to give the 'new boy' a chance, not least because he'd been at Manton for 30 years. They'd seen him fill Taylor's shoes when Young Alec was ill, and his role as travelling head lad meant the owners were used to him taking their horses to the races and supervising their preparation at the racecourse.

Lawson came from the north-east, near the Tyne estuary. He was apprenticed as a boy to Major Barrasford, who had a small stable at Marsden Hall. The northern racing and hunting personality Jack Fairfax-Blakeborough thought Barrasford a dilettante: "[He] had no one about him who knew anything about racing, and frankly admitted that he knew nothing himself." His assessment was right: Barrasford soon became bored, and went back to his first love, coursing. Luckily, Fairfax-Blakeborough had been asked to advise on the training side. He saw potential in 'Little Joe' as he called him, and he took time to teach him riding, horse care and general stable work. Lawson had his first ride at Newcastle, but in his mid-teens he was already succumbing to weight problems. There was a short-lived hurdles career, a bad fall, and an introduction to Manton, where Alec Taylor would look back on the arrival of, 'a good-looking boy of 16' in 1898. Taylor had demanding standards, and nothing happened quickly in his yard, but in the troubled years of his partnership with his half-brother Tom, a steady, hard-working newcomer like Lawson was a godsend. Even his later, Scrooge-like negotiations over Lawson's travelling allowances were, likely, his own way of preparing the younger man for greater responsibility: watch every penny, watch your staff, make sure they account fully.

Lawson's other good fortune was having Tattersall and Deane as financial and managerial mentors. 'Sommy' was one of the foremost bloodstock experts of his time. Deane, erratic though he could be, was also a bloodstock auctioneer, had trained and raced his own horses, and managed a successful stud. He had far-sighted views on racing reform: standing in for another Manton owner to make the Gimcrack speech, he called for the appointment of professional stipendiary stewards, and he was 20 years early in advocating the photo-finish.

If Lawson had any gaps in his curriculum vitae, the two Tattersalls partners were admirably qualified to fill them. What they couldn't do was serve him up good horses in his debut year. Joe Lawson took over the worst collection of three-year-olds that Manton had seen in a generation. The colts failed to muster a runner between them in the classics. The fillies provided a next-to-last place for Lady James Douglas in the 1,000 Guineas and, a peak of sorts, Tattersall's La Flégère ran third in the Oaks. Among the older horses, there were high hopes for Astor's Book Law, the star of Taylor's final year, but she flopped when odds on in the Coronation Cup. She was treated for kidney trouble, disappointed again in the Eclipse, and retired. Astor, prominent for so long in the annual winning owners' list, didn't appear in the first dozen.

It was by no means a disastrous season. Lawson finished fourth among that year's trainers, winning 46 races, among them the Dewhurst with Somerville Tattersall's Brienz. One afternoon at Newmarket, Lawson sent out four winners. Gerald Deane was so delighted that he asked for a plate worn by each of the quartet, to have them framed as a gift to the trainer – "As you'll never repeat the performance," added Deane. A more sensitive soul than Lawson might have taken that as a dubious compliment.

The *Bloodstock Breeders Review* thought, "[Lawson] has to be congratulated because of the way he has upheld the prestige of [Manton]. His record is the more satisfactory inasmuch as he had [no classic contenders], while Book Law let him down badly." For a first season, that was rather more than a pass mark, and Lawson began 1929 with 67 horses in training, half as many again as in Young Alec's last year. Astor's disappointments of the previous season were quickly forgotten when his Pennycomequick won the Oaks. Her main rival at Epsom, Sister Anne, had finished second in the 1,000 Guineas, where she had short heads to spare over the third- and fourth-placed horses. Pennycomequick then beat those two with the utmost comfort, and as a result was made 11-10 favourite for the Oaks. She bucked off her jockey Henri Jelliss on the way to the start: Lawson called it, 'Perhaps my worst moment on a racecourse'. He caught hold of her before she could run loose. She then won, eased up, by five lengths.

Pennycomequick was a typical Astor filly: named after an area of Plymouth, and homebred. Sired by the wartime St Leger winner Hurry On, she was by Plymstock, a daughter of Astor's earlier Oaks winner, Winkipop, who in turn was out of Conjure, his £100 foundation mare. The day after the Oaks, an interview with Astor appeared in the London *Evening Standard*. His greatest pride, he told the paper, was that since he started racing, he'd bred 89 horses, of which 54 had been winners and three-quarters had been placed.

> "All my animals can be traced to three mares – Conjure, Maid of the Mist and the twenty-four-year old Popinjay. Every mare [now] in my stud I bred myself, except Popinjay. That adds greatly to the interest. I do not believe in buying horses. The pleasure of breeding is that you always have anticipation. Till you are beaten, you hope that you will win. When you do lose, you go into the paddock and there you see prospective winners. When you see one of your horses win, you have the satisfaction of knowing that you bred it yourself. To my mind that is far better and more satisfying than buying a horse, no matter how successful it may be."

When it was put to him that he'd been unlucky in the Derby, he scoffed:

> "What is luck? Surely if a breeder is fortunate enough to produce five colts good enough to be second in the Derby he really cannot complain very much. It all averages out. My racing [has] cost me practically nothing. There is a balance at the bank [in] my racing account. I never have a sovereign on any of my horses. I go to the races to see good horses, and I wouldn't go to see a race, however exciting, if I knew there were only bad horses in it." Astor was generous in deflecting praise to Joe Lawson: "I am very glad that at the beginning of his career [he] has trained a classic winner. It was a great responsibility for him to take over [from] a successful trainer like Alec Taylor. This is a fine start."

The other highlights of Lawson's second season were a win in the Craven Stakes and second in the 2,000 Guineas for Astor's Cragadour. The only setback was that Tattersall's Dewhurst winner Brienz went backwards after finishing third in the Derby. He was plumb last in the

St James's Palace, unsighted in the St Leger, and hastily sold before his value could reduce any further. Lawson finished the year in fifth place in the trainers' table, with 23 winners of 34 races. He was sixth the year after, having sent out 25 winners of 42 races.

In its annual round-up, the *Bloodstock Breeders' Review* praised him again for, "Upholding the reputation of the Manton stable." It singled out his careful handling of Iliad, another shirker owned by Somerville Tattersall. The colt had been consistently unsound as a two-year-old. When Lawson eventually got him onto the racecourse, Iliad was a promising fifth in a big-field maiden at Newbury and then filled the same position in the 2,000 Guineas, running on strongly at the finish. That augured well for the Derby, and Lawson told Tattersall that if the Guineas winner Diolite didn't stay a mile and a half, then Iliad would win. He also warned that his horse was giving trouble at home, and his temperament might get the better of him.

The trainer was right on one count and almost right on the other. Patiently ridden, Iliad crept into contention from the entrance into the Epsom straight and pounced on Diolite with less than a furlong to the finish. The race seemed over. Then with a long run up the centre of the course came the Aga Khan's Blenheim, ridden by 'the head waiter' Harry Wragg. Just before the line, Blenheim caught Iliad, finishing so fast that he won by a length. Iliad's second completed a frustrating hat trick for Tattersall. His first three runners in the Derby, spread over seven years, finished third, third and second. Alas, so far as Iliad was concerned, his near miss was the peak before the trough. He was odds on in the St James's Palace, but downed tools to finish a disappointing third. He repeated the performance in a four-runner race at York and then flopped in the St Leger. Like Brienz a year earlier, he was speedily offloaded.

By that stage of the season, Tattersall must have regarded anything at all that happened to him as a bonus, because he'd almost lost his life at Ascot. A huge thunderstorm broke as the principals in the Hunt Cup passed the winning post. The deluge that followed was Biblical. It lasted for an hour and a half, leaving lakes in the paddock and on parts of the course. *The Sporting Life* reported that, "Patrons of the cheaper rings were in a hopeless plight, and on the far side of the course the scene was pitiable, with absolutely no shelter available." Racing was abandoned, and thousands of bedraggled racegoers made their uncomfortable way home, soaked through. A bookmaker, sheltering under his umbrella, was struck by lightning and killed. Tattersall was standing in a glass-roofed corridor near the weighing room when a lightning bolt crashed next to his feet. The trainer Fred Darling was among those nearby who, horrified, thought 'Sommy' had been struck, but Tattersall walked away unscathed. The unexpected death of Joseph Watson had plunged Manton into several years of uncertainty. If Somerville Tattersall had followed him into the silent majority, it might have proved impossible for Gerald Deane and the junior Tattersalls partners to go on with Manton.

Besides Pennycomequick, Lawson trained a number of big-race winners that year, for several different owners. Washington Singer's Plantago won the Coronation Cup, and his Lucky Tor carried off two prized handicaps, the City and Suburban and the Jubilee. William Cazalet's Paradine was second in the 2,000 Guineas before winning the Jersey Stakes and the Sussex Stakes. So far so good for Lawson. He went into 1931 with a sharply reduced string of 55, down from 74, and small wonder, given the impact on national wealth of the Great Depression. All his inherited owners were still represented, and there was a new name, Sir John Rutherford.

Most of the drop in stable numbers was in the two-year-olds, but the fall in horsepower counted for nothing. Lawson was to produce one of the greatest seasons enjoyed by any trainer for decades either side. Forty-two years earlier, George Dawson had sent out from Heath House, Newmarket the winners of £77,914 [*£4.62 million*]. Despite the steady upward tug of inflation, Dawson's 1889 record still stood at the beginning of 1931. It didn't seem likely to be challenged by a yard which had no horse ranked in the top dozen of the 1930 Free Handicap.

The collapse of Wall Street in 1929 sent economic shockwaves round the globe. In a case study of how not to tackle a recession, the developed nations rushed to put up protectionist barriers. The unsurprising result was that trade came to a standstill. For an export-based economy like Britain's, the outcomes were catastrophic. Two million people were out of work by September 1930, and three million a year later. Income tax and death duty rose. At the highest income levels, the aggregate tax paid went up to 60 per cent. The impact on breeding and racing was immediate. The average value of lots consigned to the first and second Newmarket July sales fell by 52 per cent and 70 per cent respectively, compared to 1929. At some sales, the average realisations were the worst since the ending of the Great War.

The position was a little better in the autumn, at the Newmarket October sale and the yearling sale, but the averages at both were still a third lower than in 1929. The top end of the market was worst affected, but most vendors were making a loss. Against that gloomy background, 1931 was a most unlikely year for a trainer to set a prize money record.

The 2,000 Guineas brought the first intimation that the Manton horses might be better than their two-year-old ratings suggested. Sir John Rutherford's Orpen finished third, albeit two lengths and three behind the easy winner, Cameronian. Orpen had been rated 22lb below the best in the Free Handicap. The Derby ended as a near re-run of the 2,000 Guineas. Lawson had been hopeful of reversing the form with the winner and second, Cameronian and a French colt, Goyescas, the more so as he didn't expect Cameronian to stay. Orpen stepped up markedly on his Newmarket run, and reduced his five-length deficit there to three parts of a length at Epsom, but Cameronian surprised Lawson by staying on stoutly under pressure. Orpen's rider Bobby Jones said, "I had a beautiful run all the way [and] I got to within a head of Cameronian, but just when I thought I had a chance, the leader found a bit, and my mount couldn't answer. I met a better horse, and that's all there is to it."

The Earl of Rosebery's fast-finishing Sandwich was third, Goyescas fourth. It was strong form. No less than nine of the Derby field that year went on to win at Royal Ascot: they included Cameronian in the St James's Palace, Sandwich in the King Edward VII Stakes, Orpen in the Hardwicke: a good race in which to lose his maiden status.

Before Ascot, Fred Darling's Beckhampton yard looked nailed on to end the season as the leading stable. Thanks mainly to Cameronian's two classics, Darling had won £38,529; Lawson lagged with £14,408. Both men won five races at the Royal meeting, but the biggest prize, £4,600 [*£163,000*] went to Lawson via Brigadier-General Charles Lambton's Trimdon in the Gold Cup. The colt's profile was more that of a novice hurdler than a flat racer; he didn't run at all until he was four, and then only three times, finishing with an easy win at Ascot in the Gold Vase. He began 1931 as he'd left off, with a facile success in the Queen's Prize over two miles at Kempton, and then over two furlongs further went down by a length, receiving 6lb, to the legendary Brown Jack in the Chester Cup.

Trimdon's Gold Cup win attracted controversy. He raced neck and neck with Lord Glanely's St Leger winner Singapore for the last two furlongs, the pair clear. His jockey Joe Childs dropped his whip at the furlong pole, whereupon Trimdon swerved onto Singapore and Gordon Richards, pushing them onto the rails. The margin at the line was a short head in Trimdon's favour. An objection and Stewards' enquiry appeared inevitable. That failed to account for the sportsmanship of Glanely, who told Richards, to the jockey's frustration, that he didn't want an objection to be lodged. Without that lead, the Stewards backed away and did nothing; their inaction attracted much criticism. Trimdon renewed rivalry with Brown Jack in the Goodwood Cup. Apparently going much the better, he split a pastern at the top of the straight.

Manton's other winners at Ascot were Orpen; Lord Astor's maiden filly Sunny Devon, cleverly placed by Lawson to take advantage of previous winners' weight concessions in the Coronation Stakes; and a pair of promising two-year-olds. One was barely larger than a pony: Somerville Tattersall's Spenser. His win in the New Stakes was the middle leg of a five-timer that included Goodwood's Richmond Stakes. The other successful Lawson juvenile ran as, 'The Golden Hair colt,' by Gainsborough. He cost Washington Singer 3,000 guineas as a yearling. He began with a defeat on hard ground, but then recorded a series of brilliant successes in the Chesham Stakes, the National Breeders Produce Stakes at Sandown, the Champagne Stakes, the Imperial Produce Stakes at Kempton and finally the Middle Park. After the Chesham, Singer confided to a friend that maybe, at last, he had a Derby horse. At the end of the season, he gave his colt a name: Orwell, inspired by the artist Gainsborough's paintings in the Orwell valley.

After Ascot, the amount by which Lawson trailed Fred Darling's prize purses was halved. The pair swapped wins during the months of high summer, but Darling was consistently £12,000 to £15,000 ahead. He appeared to have a grip on the St Leger with Cameronian, and that five-figure prize would put the destination of the trainers' title beyond doubt. His colt ran unaccountably badly at Doncaster, edgy at the start, fighting for his head and done with a long way from home. He finished last. At the business end of the race, the Derby form was boosted again, with the strong-finishing Epsom third, Sandwich, beating Manton's Orpen with a deal of ease. When checked, Cameronian was found to be running a temperature. Possibly Beckhampton was harbouring a virus. Before the St Leger meeting, Fred Darling had trained the winners of £68,129. In the remaining two months of the season, he added only £1,000 more.

By contrast, Lawson's already good season was about to become a great deal better. He had three winners at Doncaster, including Orwell in the Champagne Stakes. He added another cluster at Newmarket's first October meeting, sending out six winners of nearly £10,000, including the Jockey Club Stakes with Cazalet's Shell Transport. As a result, he moved to within £580 of Darling. The first of three peaks was in sight: the trainers' championship. Then Dawson's monumental record came within reach, and Orwell took Lawson past it when he won the Imperial Produce Stakes and £5,029 early in October. Tattersall, Deane and their trainer were showered with congratulations. *The Sporting Life* praised Lawson's, "Diligence, close attention to detail and far-sightedness." Gerald Deane said that, "No two men can train a racehorse. The training of every horse at Manton is left to Lawson."

The trainer himself deflected the acclaim. He attributed his success to his mentor - "The friendly co-operation with Mr Taylor is something I shall never forget" - to Tattersalls' stewardship of the yard, and, being a practical man, to two factors beyond his control: fine weather the summer long, and a yard full of healthy horses: "Illness in the stable has been practically nil."

An undreamed-of final achievement presented itself: the possibility that Lawson might become the first trainer in history to top £100,000 in prize money. Discussion of that target was mostly dismissive: there were few big prizes left. But at the next Newmarket fixture Lawson had six more winners, among them Orwell in the Middle Park. Then he won the Autumn Oaks at Lingfield. Going into the Houghton meeting, Manton was a little under £9,000 short of its revised target. Lawson sent a team of 13 horses to Newmarket, but the Fates decided that enough was enough, and none of the party won.

Even in their hour of glory, the stable's owners weren't inclined to overlook outside irritants. After the last horse had been roughed off, one of the country's most eminent barristers represented Tattersalls and Lawson in the High Court, in an application for an injunction against a London laundry owner, Fred Johnson. The injunction sought to restrain Johnson from, "Seducing [the Manton] apprentices and stable lads, and thereby obtaining information on racing matters." Johnson protested that while he was friendly with a number of the lads, he hadn't 'induced' them at all.

That claim was undermined when he undertook to desist from further contact with the lads, and paid both sides' legal costs.

The season ended with Lawson's patrons collecting £93,900 [*£3.325 million*] from 34 winners of 69 races, out of a stable strength of 55 horses. Lawson's record was all the more extraordinary because he didn't win any of the five classics, nor the Eclipse. Amid the universal praise and admiration for the achievement, it was speculated that the most likely trainer to surpass his wonder year was Lawson himself. He ended the year with the first, second and sixth in the Free Handicap: Orwell; Lord Astor's Mannamead, unbeaten in three minor races; and Spenser, winner of five of his six starts.

Records are records because they're hard to beat. Having taken 42 years to pass from George Dawson to Joe Lawson, this one waited a further 26 years before it changed hands again.

Chapter 17

A nominal rent

After the party came the hangover. In the wider context, there was no improvement in the economic situation. That was reflected in more sharp falls in bloodstock values, by another quarter across all auctions, but a precipitous 60 per cent at Newmarket's first October sales. In the circumstances, Lawson began 1932 in a position of great strength. He had 72 horses in training, up from 55 the year before, and the largest number stabled at Manton up to that time. There would've been even more, but for the deaths of William Cazalet and Sir John Rutherford. In his younger days, Cazalet had the honour, presumably never to be repeated, of representing his country at the Olympics at real tennis. Sir John was in his 70s when he started training with Lawson, and he liked it well enough to have seven horses at Manton when he died. Only two of them were bought back at his dispersal sale, at which the stand-out attraction was Solario, the 1925 St Leger winner and at 500 guineas for a covering, the country's most costly stallion. Rutherford had paid 3,500 guineas for Solario: the colt was knocked down to a syndicate led by Lord Glanely for 47,000 guineas, the highest price paid at auction for a stallion. It was a rare glimmer of optimism in the prevailing bloodstock gloom. One of Glanely's co-investors was the banker Sir Victor Sassoon. Not long after, Sassoon too became an owner with Lawson.

The year's farewells included the death of one of Manton's equine greats, Gay Crusader. Fairie Cox's colt didn't come close to matching his racecourse brilliance in the covering shed. Despite having the best mares brought to him, he was never higher than sixth in the annual list of winner-producing stallions. Alexander Cox saw to it, though, that Gay Crusader was remembered fittingly. The champion colt lies in a little glade below the wall of the old yard at Manton. Alongside him is his fellow son of

Galicia and wartime Derby winner, Lemberg. Their graves are overgrown now, but nearly a century on from their fields of dreams, the lettering can still be made out on their headstones.

A year that promised to revolve around Singer's Orwell began as the colt's two-year-old season had ended: victoriously. He won a strongly contested Greenham Stakes over a mile at Newbury, so the consensus opinion was, 'Here's the Guineas winner: what odds the Derby?' Orwell did everything expected of him in the 2,000 Guineas. In a field of only 11, he went off the even money favourite. His supporters saw him still under heavy restraint at the Bushes, and when his jockey Bobby Jones asked him to go to work, he quickly went clear, winning by two lengths. After the Guineas, Orwell was made 2-1 favourite for the Derby, though there was a minority opinion that he was an unlikely winner, because of the influence for speed in his pedigree. His dam was by a Stewards' Cup winner who didn't get an inch beyond six furlongs.

That technicality didn't deter the Epsom crowd from a mammoth plunge on Orwell, from 15-8 on the morning of the race to 5-4 at the off. The breeding pundits won the day. Orwell started well enough, and was steadied into midfield. At the top of the straight, he made up a few places, but his effort lasted barely a furlong before he dropped away, finishing ninth of the 21 runners. Public gloom at the favourite's lacklustre run was replaced by enthusiasm when the number 2 was hoisted, identifying the winner as April The Fifth, trained and co-owned by the theatre manager Tom Walls. It was a popular win: Walls trained at Epsom; he was the best known comedy actor of the time; and he was the epitome of an underdog. Because of illness, he'd cut his string to just four horses, and April The Fifth's closest pursuers were owned by the Aga Khan and Lord Rosebery.

After the race, Walls said, "I feared only two things: Orwell, and the start." Walls liked a bet, and the press talked up a vast coup on his 100-6 winner. This triggered an avalanche of post. He received several thousand letters, most of them asking him for money. One man wanted £500 to open a fish-and-chip shop. Walls said resignedly that his actual winnings were close to £5,000 [*£182,000*], with the same to come from his half of the prize money. 'If I'd answered every call for help, I'd have been down about £150,000.'

The Derby might have suggested to most trainers that a return to 10 furlongs or a mile was the best way forward for Orwell. Lawson wouldn't have that. He reaffirmed his belief in his colt's ability to stay, and nominated the St Leger as Orwell's late-season target. Predictably, he ran a non-staying race, prominent three furlongs out, but weakening and finishing only seventh of 19.

The other good horse at Manton that year was, improbably, Trimdon. After his injury in the Goodwood Cup, Trimdon had been reported as retired to stud, but time and rest had repaired his pastern. He appeared in the Queen's Prize, which he'd won a year earlier, this time finishing in mid-field. Two months later, he won the Yorkshire Cup, giving that year's Chester Cup winner 27lb. Trimdon's final race was back at Ascot for a Gold Cup challenge that had seemed impossible when he limped in at Goodwood. He faced top class opposition: a Coronation Cup winner, Salmon Leap; Goyescas, placed in the previous year's 2,000 Guineas and Derby; Cameronian, the winner of both those races; and Shell Transport, winner of a Prince of Wales's Stakes and a Jockey Club Stakes. The race was notable for a slow early pace and for Joe Childs's decision to make the running after the field had covered three furlongs. He kept Trimdon at an even pace until he was a little over half a mile from home. Childs then asked Trimdon to quicken, and the colt maintained a remorseless gallop to the line. Two lengths back was Salmon Leap; then half a length to Goyescas, a short head to Cameronian, and another head to Shell Transport: a race to rank with the best Gold Cups.

The season ended with Lawson having saddled 20 winners of 26 races and £33,537 [*£1.25 million*], claiming third place in the trainers' list. He posted similar statistics the following year: 20 winners of 37 races and £33,730. In a season without a classic victory, the highlights were a fusillade of winners at Royal Ascot, including Canon Law in the St James's Palace Stakes; and of all races, the Cambridgeshire. It was the only race of any consequence that neither of the Taylors won; Lawson was ending a 60-year jinx. His winner was Sir Abe Bailey's Raymond, who'd run sixth in the Derby and fifth in the Hardwicke. He was ridden in the Cambridgeshire by a jockey on a 71-race losing run. The pair's chance was so little regarded that Raymond started at 33-1, though the fact that Alec Taylor was on the racecourse might have hinted that a good outcome was expected. Soon after the start, the field parted like the Red Sea, with separate races on the stands- and far-side rails. All alone in the middle of the course was Raymond. Relishing the isolation, he made most of the running to win by two lengths. The second and third were both saddled by the veteran Yorkshire trainer Dobson Peacock, who routinely trained the highest number of winners each season, though generally of low-value races at minor meetings. Taylor strode over to Peacock, shook his hand and told him, "We'd rather have beaten anyone else."

In the next two seasons, Lawson's prize-money and winners tally remained remarkably consistent, while he was fourth and then third in the trainers' list. The best horse in the yard was Sir Abe Bailey's Tiberius, who ran second in the St Leger and then won the Gold Cup the following year.

The 1936 season reconfirmed that while Lawson could more than hold his own with an average string, he knew exactly how to handle the good horses when they came along. It was a sensational year in the broader context of British history. At its beginning, there was a January night when the BBC broadcast, every quarter of an hour, the announcement that, "The King's life is moving peacefully towards its close." On the stroke of midnight came the news that George V had died a few minutes earlier. He was much mourned on the Turf. He hadn't been as passionately involved as his father 'Teddy', but he maintained the Sandringham Stud, and with his horses in training he won a Middle Park with Friar Marcus, a 2,000 Guineas with Scuttle, a Jersey Stakes and Hardwicke with Limelight, and a Hunt Cup with Weathervane. His son, now Edward VIII, had ridden winners on the flat at Randwick in New South Wales, in a bumper at Sandown, in point-to-points and in steeplechases. Then after a broken collar-bone and a question in Parliament about Royal risk-taking, he stopped riding and sold his hunters, 'on public grounds.'

The new King quickly reassured the public that the Royal link with racing would continue. He leased all his father's horses in training to Lord Derby, to ensure that their engagements would be met. He moved his stud from Sandringham to Hampton Court, signifying his intention to continue as a breeder, albeit nearer London. Last, he made it known that he didn't want any display of mourning at Ascot: it was to be the usual celebration, not a wake. No one could have foreseen that, having reigned for a little over 11 months, Edward VIII would save his country from a constitutional crisis by abdicating.

Lawson and his owners had happier reasons to look back on 1936. Manton struck in the first classic with Astor's Pay Up, despite a last-minute training scare. The only gallop made available at Newmarket to visiting trainers that year was a three-furlong strip with virtually no grass covering, and a sharp turn on which to pull up. As he did so, Pay Up spread a plate and tore off part of the wall of his foot. Re-shod with great care, he fought out a stirring finish to the 2,000 Guineas with the Aga Khan's Mahmoud, drawing level in the last 50 yards and putting his head in front on the line. Astor's second string, Rhodes Scholar, finished fourth.

There'd been some mutterings before the Guineas that Mahmoud wouldn't stay a mile, what with the speed of The Tetrarch and his daughter Mumtaz Mahal prominent in his pedigree, but he took on Pay Up again in the Derby and confounded the breeding theorists by winning easily, in a record time. Pay Up was only fourth, running 10 lengths below his Guineas form. The blame lay with the Epsom course, hard and rough. Three hours after the race, Pay Up was so lame on his off-fore that he could barely move. The vet advised Astor to retire him at once. Rhodes Scholar stood in for Pay Up in the St James's Palace Stakes and, sensationally, beat Mahmoud by five lengths, in receipt of 7lb. He was Astor's fifth winner of the race. At the end of the season, the official rating of the three-year-olds had Mahmoud on 9st 7lb, Pay Up on 9st 6lb and Rhodes Scholar on 9st 4lb. On the evidence of the St James's Palace, it was a mistaken view of the respective merits of Mahmoud and Rhodes Scholar.

Besides his two good colts, Lawson had the highest-rated three-year-old filly, Astor's Traffic Light. She was wall-eyed, and her affected vision made her nervous when she was out on her own, so she had to be ridden to lead close home. She was fifth in the 1,000 Guineas and fourth in the Oaks, but then won the Coronation Stakes at Ascot and the Park Hill at Doncaster. In the Newmarket Oaks, she showed the extent of her improvement by giving the Epsom winner 9lb and going down by only a head.

Other highlights at Manton that year included Lawson's shrewd placing of Sir Abe Bailey's Raeburn to win the Irish Derby: the poor quality of that year's renewal is suggested by Raeburn having previously been sixth in the King Edward VII Stakes at Ascot, and then last in the St Leger. When the Manchester November meeting was over, Lawson was leading trainer for the second time, with exactly half his string, 32 horses, winning 49 races and £61,381 *[£2.19 million]*. Lord Astor was back in his accustomed position as leading owner and breeder, and he had a promising two-year-old to look forward to for the following season:

Early School, the three-length winner of the Coventry Stakes and two other races. The Ascot sprint had produced the winners of good races like the Gimcrack, on which evidence Early School was made winter favourite for the Derby. That particular bubble was burst early the following season: Early School suffered from tendon trouble and was scratched from the 2,000 Guineas, then from the Derby, and by the end of June Lawson had given up all hope of getting him onto a racecourse again.

By then, Lawson had already won another classic for Manton, with Sir Victor Sassoon's Exhibitionnist, by Solario. Her seasonal debut was in the Free Handicap, where she went down by three quarters of a length to another product of Solario, the colt Mid-Day Sun, giving him 6lb. Not much notice was taken of that form, even after Mid-Day Sun ran third in the 2,000 Guineas. The inference that Exhibitionnist would've gone close in the colts' race was ignored in the betting for the 1,000 Guineas, where she was 10-1. Ridden to great effect by Steve Donoghue, she won by half a length.

The Free Handicap form was shown to be even better when Mid-Day Sun comfortably won the Derby. In the circumstances, it was extraordinary that, two days later, Exhibitionnist should start at 3-1 for the Oaks. Seemingly the only question to be answered was, how well would she stay? Steve Donoghue had no doubts: he told all enquirers that Exhibitionnist was, 'Certain to win.' He moved her into second place a mile from home, led at the entrance to the straight and made the rest of the running to win, unextended, by three lengths.

It was the last classic win in Donoghue's long, brilliant career, and much of the cheering after Exhibitionnist's win was for her rider. The cry, 'Come on, Steve!' was familiar on English racecourses for over 20 years, during which he attracted a huge public following. He'd indicated that 1937 would be his last season in the saddle, aged 52. His 12 previous classic wins hadn't included either of the fillies' races, and Exhibitionnist provided him with both. "Once she struck the front she began to prick her ears and run rather lazily, so I showed her the whip to make her realise the race [wasn't] over. There were no real challengers, and she was still cocking her ears as she went past the post."

With two classics in the trophy cabinet, Lawson continued in tremendous form at Ascot, winning six races. Two of them went to Sir Abe Bailey's Valerian, who won the Ascot Stakes and then, two days later, the Queen Alexandra. Astor's Rhodes Scholar won the Ribblesdale on his seasonal debut, after which a second Eclipse seemed a formality, but two days before the race he fell at Manton, cutting one front knee and bruising the other. They were both swollen, but on the morning of the race, he cantered freely at Sandown. Lawson decided to take a chance with Rhodes Scholar, imagining that the colt wouldn't be pressed to beat his five rivals. He was 1-3. The going was firm, and on his way to post Gordon Richards felt that his mount wasn't moving well. Only for a moment in the race, at the turn into the straight, was Rhodes Scholar involved, and then he fell back, finishing fifth of sixth. The colt was sore afterwards, and it was accepted that it'd been a mistake to run him. He was rested, given an entry for the Champion Stakes, but withdrawn when the ground was firm, and retired to Gerald Deane's Littleton Stud in Hampshire.

That was a statement of the continued closeness of Astor and Deane. Earlier in the summer, it had been announced that Deane was standing down as Astor's racing manager. Astor's wife Nancy had a hand in Deane's departure. She was as high-mettled as Deane, and it was an open secret that she didn't approve of his betting. The official version from Deane was that his doctor had been urging him for years to cut back on his commitments, and that he suffered from, "Overwork and laryngitis."

Lawson couldn't quite claim his third leading trainer title, but he was a clear second. He had 31 winners of 44 races and £52,020. He began that year with 84 horses in training, filling the old yard, the lower yard and the Astor yard. It was the largest string that Manton had ever housed, and it remained so for 50 years. In the next couple of seasons, Lawson retained his high ranking among his rival trainers, but he only stabled one top class horse in that time, Robert Sterling Clark's Galatea II. Clark was American and a friend of the long-term Manton patron Washington Singer. Like Singer, his fortune came from sewing machines. Galatea II was bred at Clark's stud in Normandy. As a two-year-old in 1938, she had just one piece of worthwhile form, when third in the Cheveley Park. On her seasonal debut the following spring, she made all to win easily at Lingfield. That was the best public form in the 1,000 Guineas, but there'd been pigeon-catching reports about an unraced filly of Lord Glanely's, Olein, and she was backed to favourite at Newmarket. For five furlongs, she showed great speed and was still clear at the Bushes. Running down into the Dip, Olein's inexperience told, Galatea II joined her, and on the final incline Clark's filly stormed away.

Olein then justified her tall reputation by pulverising a large field in a Newmarket stakes race. Galatea II went straight to the Oaks, where the betting was reversed from the 1,000 Guineas, with Galatea II a shade of odds on, Olein 11-2 and a French invader, White Fox, well fancied at 9-1. On the descent to Tattenham Corner, Olein took up the running, with Galatea II in a closing fourth. It was as well for both of them that they were prominent, because there was a faller just behind and White Fox was all but brought down. She was detached from the field, with only a tailed-off no-hoper behind. At the sharp end, Olein weakened as quickly as she had in the 1,000 Guineas, and Galatea II was left comfortably in command of her nearest pursuers. Some way from home, her rider Bobby Jones took a peep at his rivals, saw no possible danger, and stopped riding his filly.

Had he looked again, he'd have seen an unlikely apparition. White Fox, having been knocked out of the race by the faller, had made up an extraordinary amount of ground, charged through a gap next to the rail, and began to reel in Galatea II. The favourite's supporters shouted warnings to Jones: they could only watch as Galatea II slowed to a walk and White Fox bore down on her. The line came just in time. Galatea II won her second classic by a head.

Racing during the rest of the summer of 1939 was over-shadowed by the slide towards chaos. When Germany invaded Poland at the start of September, Britain and France declared war. The effects on racing would be the same as they'd been 35 years earlier. Prize money would reduce to the point that few could afford to keep horses in training; stable staff would be depleted by call-ups; and a bitter argument would rage in the press and Whitehall as to whether or not racing was justifiable in wartime.

In the short term, the Doncaster sales were cancelled, to the horror of numerous breeders with no market in which to sell their yearlings; and racing was suspended. Tattersalls found itself in a vice. Its auction business faced an open-ended period of greatly reduced income; and it owned one of the largest training establishments. Three weeks after the declaration of war, the firm sent an anguished plea to Marlborough College, from whom it had rented some 300 acres of downs on the Marlborough side of Manton:

> Dear Sir
>
> Barton Down, Manton
>
> We are writing to enquire, if in view of the high rent we have paid in the past, the College will agree to accept a nominal rent for the Barton Down for the duration of the War.
>
> We feel sure you will appreciate the difficult position in which we find ourselves. At the moment our business here is at a complete standstill, and the number of horses now at Manton is so reduced that, even with a resumption of limited racing, it will be necessary for us to exercise the most stringent economies.
>
> We should be very reluctant to give up the Barton Down considering the vast expense we have put into its improvement, and bringing it up to the perfection in which it is today. [If] it were given up, all the money put into it would be wasted, and it would deteriorate rapidly due to rabbits, moles etc, and its further use as a training gallop would be at an end.

Marlborough's bursar asked, what did Tattersalls propose as their nominal rent? By return, the firm replied, £50 [*£1,650*], as opposed to the £280 which they'd paid annually in the pre-war years. Over and above the rent, Tattersalls said, the upkeep of Barton Down cost them an annual average of £151.50, of which £45 was peat and manure, the rest labour. The usual number of horses in training in recent seasons was between 70 and 90, said Tattersalls. In September 1939, it was 35, plus a handful around the yard who weren't in training. The correspondence lasted into the following summer, when the College Council agreed to reduce Manton's rent to £125 during wartime, with a reminder that the previous rent cheque was four months overdue.

It wasn't until mid-October 1939 that one or two race meetings were staged, notably the Cambridgeshire in two divisions. It proved impossible to rearrange the St Leger. In all, seven weeks and most of the big autumn races were lost. Joe Lawson was again the second-placed trainer, but all the leading yards had fewer winners and less prize money, because of their reduced opportunities.

The 1940 flat season began almost as if there wasn't a war. Two meetings on Easter Monday were followed by the Lincoln at the beginning of April, and a total of 20 fixtures during the month. The Craven meeting went ahead: Lord Astor's Golden Penny, highly ranked as a two-year-old, won her prep race for the 1,000 Guineas convincingly. She was odds on for the Guineas, but beaten pointless by Godiva, ridden by an apprentice, Doug Marks, who went on to become a famously eccentric trainer. On this day, he enraged the senior jockeys by giving them some obscene advice as he swept past. Golden Penny finished second, and then only fourth behind Godiva in the Oaks.

On the broader canvas, Germany had invaded the Benelux countries, yet still racing continued as normal. Large crowds saw the Derby and Oaks run at Newmarket. Meanwhile, the German army was on the outskirts of Paris. Finally, on June 19, the Stewards of the Jockey Club announced that there would no more racing until further notice. The *Racing Calendar* suspended publication the day after. *The Sporting Life*, with little to write about, appeared only on Mondays. Before long, there was an exodus of horses from training and from the country. A procession of mares, foals, yearlings, stallions and horses in training were shipped overseas: over 550 between the declaration of war and the end of 1940. Some of them would doubtless have gone in peacetime: then as now, Britain was an exporter of bloodstock. But the departures included high-profile classic-winning stallions like the Aga Khan's Bahram and Mahmoud, sold to the US. From among Manton's alumni, Rhodes Scholar and Galatea II made the same one-way journey.

In July, the Aga Khan advertised the 11 yearlings at his Irish stud as a job lot, at 400 guineas each. Perhaps the only bright spot in Joe Lawson's year was that a London property developer called Alfred Allnatt launched himself into ownership by buying the yearlings and sending them to Manton. In later years, Allnatt was celebrated for buying a monumental work by Rubens, *The Adoration of the Magi*. He paid a then world record, £275,000. He intended to give the picture to the National Gallery, but lost patience when the Gallery people turned up late for meetings. Whenever he was on his way home from Newmarket races, Allnatt liked to call into the chapel of King's College, Cambridge for evensong. Listening to the choir, he decided to make King's the permanent home of his painting. Around that time, he acquired another bauble, a rare yellow diamond weighing in at 102 carats. Named the Allnatt Diamond and set in a Cartier brooch, it later sold for over $3 million. Evidently, he could afford a few horses and their training fees.

After three empty months, racing finally returned in mid-September at Ripon. It was too late to rescue a miserable year at Manton. The yard sent out 12 winners of just 13 races, and there were no Manton owners or breeders in the top 10 of their respective tables.

Chapter 18

Tattersalls call time

In the second full year of war, racing continued, but at a level far below peacetime. There were just 86 days of flat racing. However, the conflict provided Joe Lawson with a windfall. The ship-owner Lord Glanely had his Newmarket stable requisitioned by the Army. He was forced to move his horses, and he sent them to Manton. Among them was a filly called Dancing Time. Lawson took an immediate liking to her: "I had the impression that she would be a good-class mare, and on her breeding almost certain to stay. I therefore decided to [target] the fillies' classics."

His judgement was sound. Dancing Time, home-bred by Glanely by Colombo out of Show Girl, won the 1,000 Guineas. It was Lawson's eighth classic success. Glanely also had a good two-year-old filly Perfect Peace, who won twice, including the Cheveley Park, and went down by a head to the King's Sun Chariot at level weights in the Queen Mary Stakes. Two of Alfred Allnatt's buys from the Aga Khan won races: Shahpoor won once, and ran third in the Dewhurst. Ujiji won three from four starts, his only defeat coming in the Middle Park, when he was beaten three lengths by Sun Chariot, conceding 3lb.

It had been a good season for Lawson: he had 21 winning horses, successful in 36 races worth £12,736 [*£334,700*]. Lord Glanely was leading owner and breeder. But Manton's two-year-olds were the supporting cast to Sun Chariot; she did as much as any horse or man to keep racing going that year. She was bred at the National Stud, by Hyperion out of an unraced mare. She was sent to Fred Darling at Beckhampton, and then leased to King George VI, who also took a colt called Big Game, another product of the National Stud. The outcomes for the Stud, for Darling and the King were near-miraculous. Big Game was unbeaten in five starts, among them the Coventry and the Champagne Stakes.

Sun Chariot won four from four; she headed the Free Handicap on 9st 7lb, with Big Game 1lb behind. It was a boost to racing to have the best colt and filly in Royal ownership: it silenced most criticism of 'frivolity'.

Royal patronage or not, flat racing continued into 1942 in a restricted form. Fixtures were run regionally, to ration fuel; at Salisbury and Windsor in the south, Pontefract and Stockton in the north. Newmarket comprised its own region. With the exception of a small number of 'open' races such as the classics, all of them run on the July course at Newmarket, no horse was allowed to run outside the area in which it was trained. Rail transport of horses to race meetings was prohibited, and the Ministry of Agriculture encouraged the disposal of as many horses as possible, to conserve feed.

After the second race at Newmarket on 1,000 Guineas day, the crowd noticed something unscheduled. From away to their left, a small convoy of vehicles drove up the course towards the stands, led by a police car. The second car stopped as it reached the Silver Ring, and out stepped the King and Queen, he in the uniform of Marshal of the Royal Air Force. A storm of cheering broke out as the pair walked along the rails. It followed the couple's progress all the way to the Members' enclosure.

The cheering redoubled when Sun Chariot and Gordon Richards duly won the 1,000 Guineas, sprinting away to win by four lengths. Glanely's Perfect Peace was second. The day before, Big Game had initiated a notable Royal double by winning the 2,000 Guineas, also by four lengths and ridden by Richards. Big Game next appeared in the New Derby as odds-on favourite, but the presence of The Tetrarch in his dam's pedigree raised serious stamina doubts. He finished only sixth, behind Lord Derby's Watling Street; Manton's Ujiji and Shahpoor were third and fourth. Watling Street made a small piece of Turf history by winning the first Derby to be run on a Saturday.

Sun Chariot made no mistake in the New Oaks. She lost several lengths at the start, but had plenty of time to make up the lost ground, and led a furlong out to win by a length, Richards just riding her out with hands and heels. After the race, he revealed that, "She's brilliant but erratic. It's a relief it's all over. Nobody knows the anxious times I've had with her on the downs. You simply don't know what she'll do, but there's no doubt about her ability." In the New St Leger, Sun Chariot was all brilliance, without a hint of temperament. In the betting, the Derby winner Watling Street was preferred, but although his rider Harry Wragg described the colt as 'going like a train' when he led three furlongs out, "When Sun Chariot came at me I realised that [she] was the real express."

When Wragg made his move, Richards sent Sun Chariot upsides and, "Was past him in a flash. From that point, I [kept] her going with [my] hands to run out a comfortable winner. She's the best I've ever ridden." Having beaten the Derby winner by three lengths, Sun Chariot was retired, a winner of the fillies' triple crown.

One way and another it was a trying year for Lawson. The previous season's good two-year-olds all trained on, and they won minor races, but the closest they got to winning a classic was Perfect Peace's second in the 1,000 Guineas, while Glanely's Feberion was third in the New Oaks. Ujiji and Shahpoor between them recorded a third, three fourths and a sixth in the colt's classics, for a total return of only £232 [*£6,060*] for Ujiji's third place in the New Derby.

Then, Glanely was killed in an air raid. Alfred Allnatt bought 134 mares, foals, stallions and horses in training from Glanely's executors, for £115,000 [*£3 million*]. None of them were intended for Manton: Allnatt was taking a speculative punt. He planned to sell everything except the stallion Colombo, in the hope that the parts would fetch more than the whole.

There were passings at Tattersalls, too. Terence Watt, who was made partner at the beginning of 1939, was killed in a plane crash during the summer. The long-serving senior partner Somerville Tattersall died in the autumn, having played a crucial role in rescuing and maintaining Manton when it was imperilled in the 1920s. His death left the management of both Tattersalls and Manton over-reliant on Gerald Deane.

The backdrop to racing in 1942 had been mostly gloomy. The German army was camped outside Stalingrad; Rommel advanced in north Africa; and having taken Singapore, the Japanese army was streaming across Burma towards India. The following year saw the tide turn, slowly, in favour of the Allies, but in the interests of the war effort, racing remained tightly restricted. There were fixtures on only 67 days: 25 in the south, 21 in the north and the same at Newmarket. In all, 471 races were run, down from 540 the previous year. In the circumstances, Lawson did well enough to turn out 12 winners of 17, among them the winner of the 2,000 Guineas, Kingsway. This was for a new owner, AE 'Ted' Saunders, who bought the colt at auction and sent him to be trained by Bill Smyth at Epsom.

Kingsway, by Fairway out of Yenna, ran unnamed as 'the Yenna colt' when he made his debut in a five-furlong Windsor maiden. There were 25 runners. Only four of them had raced before. An event that might have been complete guesswork in the betting ring proved to be anything but: 'the Yenna colt' opened at 3-1 and was backed down to 10-11. He made all to win by eight lengths. He won and was second at Salisbury, and then, no thanks to Smyth for that debut gamble, the colt was sent to Lawson.

When he made his three-year-old debut, now named Kingsway, he was again heavily backed, but barely scraped home on firm ground. Lawson had two other Guineas horses that spring: Astor's Way In, and Merchant Navy, brought back to Manton for 2,400 guineas after Allnatt's disposal of Glanely's horses.

Kingsway, Way In and Merchant Navy had the same seasonal profiles. They each ran once and won once, but it was Merchant Navy's win that caught the eye, thrashing 24 rivals by six lengths and eight in a maiden race at Newmarket. Before the 2,000 Guineas, Merchant Navy was second favourite, Way In was 100-6 and Kingsway 18-1.

It was a thrilling race, and nearly a Manton one-two. Merchant Navy made the first move, but was at once passed by Way In and Kingsway. Racing alone on their left was the locally trained Pink Flower. On the rise to the finish, he took a definite lead, but veered off a straight line close home, towards the far rail. 'Caught last stride,' reads the form book, with 'Ran on gamely to lead last stride' describing Kingsway's effort. He was judged to have won by a short head. It was only a head back to Way In and half lengths to the fourth and fifth.

The race was a great spectacle, but even a crystal ball gazer might have struggled to take out of it the colt who would found bloodstock dynasties on both sides of the Atlantic. The more so as his *Raceform* note read, "On bit to Dip: no resolution under pressure." Previous and subsequent comments alongside the colt's name included, "Wilful [in] paddock," "Veered right," "Darted left," and "Not keen under pressure."

All these critical remarks were applied during the season to the Guineas favourite, and eventual fourth, the Aga Khan's Nasrullah. Having serially disappointed on the racecourse, Nasrullah went on to become champion sire, once here and four times in America, producing the winners of over 900 races.

Another racing dynasty was established that year. The season's horses were analysed by Phil Bull in the first hardback edition of *Best Horses*. Bull could be forgiven for feeling sour about Nasrullah. He'd struck a bet of £400 at 5-4 [*£13,100* to *£10,500*] that the colt would finish in the first three in the Guineas: good value about a horse whose SP was 13-8. He wrote witheringly in Nasrullah's essay in *Best Horses of 1943* that, "On not a single occasion did [he] visit the racecourse and leave it without his performance having some blemish."

Kingsway's 2,000 Guineas success was followed by wins for Allnatt's consistent duo Ujiji and Shahpoor, in the Gold Cup and the Jockey Club Stakes respectively. The degree to which war had reduced racing's financial viability was highlighted by Shahpoor's prize of £513 [*£13,475*]. A dozen years earlier in the same race, Manton's Shell Transport won £5,333 [*£188,800*]. Adjusted for inflation, the Jockey Club Stakes of 1943 had declined in value by 93 per cent over that period.

The tide that had run so long against Britain and her allies turned decisively in 1944. The small ships that had carried the troops off the Dunkirk beaches in 1940 were replaced by an armada of British, Commonwealth and American forces that crossed back over the Channel to Normandy in June. Reflecting the mood of the country, the bloodstock market surged as if a brake had been released. The average yearling price rose 60 per cent; foals almost doubled in price. Reward, at last, for breeders who'd struggled on with the elderly and the very young to work on their studs, only to find few buyers for their consignments.

At a time when humorous moments were in short supply, Manton's senior work rider provided one. Most things around the estate were diminished. A skeleton staff looked after only 20 horses. Dilapidation was setting in. Prisoners of war, employed to work the land, were billeted around Manton's cottages. Jack Brennan thought the end had come when he was walking alone on the gallops. Out of nowhere, a voice called, "Hello, Jack." Brennan looked disbelievingly round the empty downs. Then up, to see a pre-war stable lad sailing down below a parachute, in training for D-Day.

The year was, on the face of it, a poor one for Lawson. He and his owners fell out of the top 10 trainers and breeders. His seven three-year-olds were useless. They managed one win between them. Luckily, his older horses won races, as did half his 10 two-year-olds. The best of them was Court Martial, an Astor colt who traced back to one of Cliveden's best broodmares, Winkipop. Court Martial ran just twice in 1944, each time at Ascot, the second time seeing off two good previous winners. Glory beckoned, but as a three-year-old Court Martial was to face a formidable challenger for classic honours, from an unexpected quarter: the north.

No one in the southern training centres could say they hadn't been warned. Phil Bull proclaimed that Middleham housed a colt, "Head and shoulders above his contemporaries": Dante. The former maths teacher Bull was outspoken, belligerent and anti-Establishment, which may have blinded the old guard to the fact that he was transforming the analysis of racehorses' performances.

Bull placed his faith in the time test. There was nothing new in the simple timing of races and gallops: it went back at least 50 years. Bull took it to a new level, factoring in the race distance, the going, the speed and direction of any wind, and the horse's age and weight. The result was what he called a 'racefigure'. Every run of each horse reviewed in *Best Horses* had a rating, expressed as 'fast,' 'slow' or 'no figure'. Six or seven per cent of the racefigures given were 'fast,' in a publication which assessed only the season's winning horses, and others that had caught Bull's attention. It followed that a 'fast' racefigure was noteworthy.

Dante won two maiden sprints at Stockton before an afternoon when Bull timed him in a race against a colt called Langton Abbott, another winner of two from two. Dante didn't only beat the future Lincoln winner Langton Abbott by six lengths: "*Made all, never off bit, canter,*" reads the form book: Bull calculated an astonishing speed figure - "The fastest two-year-old feat in my experience."

The Coventry Stakes, run at Newmarket, was one of the 'open' races to which horses could be sent from outside their training region. It was Dante's first appearance away from Stockton, and Phil Bull followed him avidly south. At 11-8, "I had to have a splash," which can be translated as thousands. Dante won by four lengths in another fast time. Then when the colt beat a small field for the Middle Park, Bull plunged again, this time at odds on. It was a muddling race, and he said the only satisfaction he got from it was, "My bookmaker's offer to take 4-7, and the look of disbelief on his face when I told him how much to put me on."

Over the winter, he set out his case for Dante winning the 2,000 Guineas, 'decisively.' He concluded that, "The prospect that exercises my mind at the moment is whether Dante will prove to be one of the best horses of the century. We shall see!"

Dante's racefigure of 1.41 fast on his third outing surpassed the best performances of the season's classic winners: 1.35 fast for Sun Chariot, 1.22 fast for Watling Street and for Big Game. "A two-year-old with a racefigure of 1.20 fast or better may be regarded as a ready-made classic winner the following season. Dante leaps into this category not on one racefigure, but on two!" exulted Bull.

In contrast to all this euphoria, Manton's Court Martial received a short and restrained essay from Jimmy Park of the *Evening Standard*, whom Bull relied on for reports on the southern two-year-olds. On his second run, Court Martial had to overcome serious interference two furlongs out. He was pulled back and switched round his rivals to make his challenge; he showed a great burst of pace. It was enough for Park to say that, "Few of the southern two-year-olds have impressed me as [he has]. It will require a very good one to beat him in the Two Thousand Guineas."

Phil Bull added a postscript to Park's notes, mocking the rating of Court Martial as only 1lb behind Dante in the Free Handicap. He added that Court Martial's two racefigures were, "No better than any decent plater might accomplish."

If that barb caused Lawson and Astor to choke over their breakfasts, Court Martial provided a ready answer on his seasonal debut in 1945. When not fully wound up, he gave 7lb to another of the previous year's good two-year-olds and went down by a neck. His racefigure was 1.14 fast, which put him close to Bull's 'will win a classic' figure of 1.20 fast. In the event, a near identical performance, 1.13 fast, was enough for him to beat Dante in the 2,000 Guineas.

It was a race run before the largest crowd seen on the July course, in an atmosphere of intense relief. Two days before, on May 7, Germany had surrendered. The next day was Victory in Europe Day, and the 1,000 Guineas was run. The 2,000 Guineas followed on the second day of the Victory public holiday.

There were still restrictions on the use of private cars, so most of the crowd made their way to the course by bus, on bicycle or on foot. The houses they passed had flags out on trees, on gateposts and spread over hedges. And on the way home, racegoers saw street and house lights for the first time in five and a half years.

In the enclosures before the Guineas, Dante was backed from 7-4 to evens; Court Martial drifted out to 13-2. The Manton colt benefitted from a brave, positive ride by Cliff Richards, the younger brother of the champion Gordon, and Astor's newly retained jockey. He kept Court Martial in the leading group and then set him alight going down into the Dip, stealing a two-length lead. Dante found his stride on the rise to the winning post and stayed on gamely, getting to within a neck of Court Martial at the line, but the spoils went to Manton.

Bull took a ribbing from the southern press. The *Daily Express*, "Feared his conspicuous red beard would turn white in the night" after Dante's defeat. "On the contrary," riposted Bull: "it turned a deeper and more Bolshevik red, for within half an hour of the Guineas being run, I developed a most extravagant enthusiasm for Dante in the Derby." Bull promptly had £500 each way on Dante at 4-1 [the win portion was *£51,400 to £12,850*], but the glee with which his bookmaker accepted the bet suggested that he'd been too hasty. Sure enough, "Next day you could have had 10-1 anywhere. [I took] full advantage."

The Derby vindicated him. Dante was ridden up with the pace throughout, and, taking a leaf from Cliff Richards's ride in the Guineas, his jockey sent him on in the Dip, ensuring that his stamina came into full play. He won by an easy two lengths and a head. So little was thought of Court Martial's prospects of staying a mile and a half that he started at 100-9, but after being held up by Richards to get the trip, he ran on well into third.

Dante's racefigure, 1.43 fast, surpassed even the blistering 1.41 he'd recorded as a two-year-old. He earned a place in the records as the only northern-trained winner of the Derby since 1869. He was also Phil Bull's biggest winner to that point, netting the founder of *Timeform* our equivalent of *£360,000*.

Court Martial won two small races and then the Champion Stakes; it featured the first French-trained horse to have run in England for five years. His 2,000 Guineas win was the centrepiece of an excellent season for Joe Lawson. From only 22 horses, he trained 17 individual winners of 34 races to finish second among the leading trainers. There were 15 two-year-olds in the yard, and Lawson won races with 10 of them. The pick was Astor's Aldis Lamp, who followed Court Martial's example in having just two outings and winning both. He was spoken of as a Derby horse, and ranked second in the Free Handicap. Another of Astor's, the filly Wheedler, won three from four.

All in all, there was every possible reason for Lawson to look forward to 1946 with optimism. What transpired was months of uncertainty and disappointment. At the start of the season, his roster of horses in training had risen to 30, but that was small beer for a man who before the war had trained over 80. Bloodstock sales all through the year set records, but the tendency of owners to keep their horses with trainers of their own age or younger didn't help the 65-year-old Lawson to attract new patrons. His older owners like Cox and Astor continued to support him, but on a reduced scale.

It might have been different if he'd been able to win a big race or two in 1946, but fate dealt him a wretched hand when he needed her most. From the previous season's three-year-olds, he had the winners of the Ormonde Stakes and the Yorkshire Cup, but all the hopes reposed in the 1945 two-year-olds came to very little. Astor's Fast And Fair won the Lingfield Derby trial and the Gordon Stakes, and was third in the St Leger. Wheedler won the Falmouth Stakes. That was all: a meagre return. Nor was there any promise among the two-year-olds.

At the end of the season, Phil Bull published a bumper *Best Horses of 1946*. It contained notes on over 1,100 horses. As a reviewer pointed out, there couldn't by any stretch of the imagination be 1,100 'best' horses, but even so, only two of Lawson's youngsters merited inclusion. They won three races between them; the rest managed a handful of minor placings.

At the end of the season, Lawson had dropped to ninth place among the trainers, Astor to fifteenth-placed owner. At another time, they'd have waited patiently for normal service to be resumed. Unfortunately for them, Manton's future was decided by an event beyond their control. Tattersalls' junior partner Bob Needham died in June, aged only 53. That left Gerald Deane as the sole surviving partner. He learned of Needham's death during one of his long bouts of depression. On hearing the news, he cradled his head in his hands and burst into tears. 'We can't go on. We can't go on."

Cash was tight at Tattersalls. Its Knightsbridge premises were sold in a sale and lease-back agreement. The partnership was in critical need of rebuilding, to compensate for Gerald Deane's decline. Manton was a commitment that the firm could no longer support. The outcome was an announcement that the yard and estate were for sale. If no buyer met the asking price, Manton would go to auction.

Joe Lawson was appalled. He'd spent almost half a century at Manton. He was Master for 19 years, though as Gerald Deane's wife cruelly reminded him early in his tenure, he was a salaried employee. Lawson was showing some guests of the Deanes round the yard when he mentioned 'Gerald.' "That's *Major* Deane to you, Lawson," he was rebuked.

With no certainty that a new owner of Manton would keep him on as trainer, Lawson cast around for a friendly purchaser. He told Tattersalls that he had a buyer willing to pay £100,000 *[£2.57 million]* for the estate. An Indian prince was said to be hovering. None of the expressions of interest came to anything and the auction went ahead. Lawson spoke of his anxieties to the local paper.

"I have been here 50 years and I don't want to leave. [If] the estate is sold and the new owner [asks] me to continue as trainer, I should be happy and willing to carry on. Otherwise I shall look for a [yard of] my own, as I have no intention of retiring."

He offered his opinions on the problems of finding dedicated staff: "Labour will always be a problem. [Employees] want the cinema, public houses and very little work these days – and there is a lot of work at Manton. What is wanted is a very rich man to buy Manton and spend a lot of money running it for the employees to have a good social life."

These unfortunate musings attracted a swift, anonymous response from a stable lad:

> "Mr Lawson is right when he says that, 'There is plenty of work at Manton' and heavy work at that, as anyone who has carried 1½ cwt [*50 kgs*] to a height of 18 feet several times in an hour will know, but I have not known any shirker among the staff. Also, the workers do not want a rich man to lose thousands to give them, 'A good social life': only someone who will appreciate their efforts."

It was a sorry note for Lawson to end on, though no one in the yard worked as hard as he did. During all his time as Master, he must have felt pressure. When Tattersalls bought the yard and promoted him to licence-holder, Lawson didn't move into Taylor's house. That, it was clear, was for the use of Somerville Tattersall and Gerald Deane and their friends.

Lawson had a handsome consolation: a fine house, The Lodge, that was built for him alongside the yard, but, symbolically, he was outside.

He suffered from ulcers, and confided to a friend that when his holiday came round, his idea of heaven was to take the train up to Paddington, book a room in the Great Western Hotel, and sleep for three days. He was always exhausted, and that was the start of his annual leave.

Lawson was the equal of the Taylors as a horseman and stableman. Like them, he led a modest, quiet life at Manton, but without their reclusiveness. He had a warm send-off from the *Marlborough Times*: "It will be a matter of great personal regret to the large number of people who knew this familiar and genial figure that within a few days he is leaving the soil of Wiltshire."

Besides numerous well-wishers, he left behind his verdict that the best fillies he trained were Pennycomequick, Exhibitionnist and Galatea II; and the best colts were Orwell, "[My] finest two-year-old," Rhodes Scholar and, his personal favourite, Court Martial. He hardly ever bet on these and the other big-race winners that he trained. Occasionally, he'd have £20 on one of his fancied runners, just so that he could pay for the drinks when they won. He believed in having his bet before he left the yard, because once at the racecourse, there were too many distractions.

The announcement that Manton was to be sold caused an exodus. For Lord Astor, who'd been persuaded to stay loyal to Manton 20 years earlier by the intervention of Tattersalls, this was a change too many. He sent his string to Jack Colling at West Ilsley. Alfred Allnatt sold all his horses in training. Weeks before the yard was auctioned, it was empty. Only Ted Saunders, who'd just leased a yearling called Dramatic, decided to wait and see what the future had in store.

Chapter 19

Todd will never manage

Joe Lawson was only a distant onlooker when Manton was auctioned in London in December 1946. He could've been forgiven a sigh when news came that the bidding had stopped £4,000 short of Tattersalls' reserve price of £48,000 [*£1.23 million*]. If he had any hopes of a reprieve for his tenancy, they were dashed. Tattersalls told the estate agents to sell at any price above the reserve, and for a few days, Manton belonged to a builder, GA Freeman. He'd worked as a foreman on the construction of Lord Astor's yard 20 years earlier, and had promised himself that one day it would all be his. Briefly, it was, but negotiations with Tattersalls broke down when it emerged that he only wanted, or could afford, part of the estate. Then at the beginning of January and to general astonishment, the new Master of Manton was revealed to be George Todd.

Joe Lawson's reaction was typical. He was overheard telling a telephone caller, "George Todd will never be able to manage Manton." Few would have argued with him. The Taylors and Lawson had between them trained the winners of 42 classics. By contrast, Todd was a trainer of selling platers and handicappers, horses that the Taylors wouldn't have kept in the yard for a day.

When Todd arrived at Manton, he'd held a training licence for almost 20 years. He was one of the eight children of a Horncastle pork butcher. His first job, for £7 a year - "£8 if I was good, but I had to pay for my clothes," was with the South Wold Hunt. He lost it when a stove set fire to a hut where he was teaching card games to some of the other workers. He began in racing with Percy Whitaker at Royston just before the first world war. The Stockbridge flat-race trainer Atty Persse used to send a horse or two to Whitaker for a winter's hurdling. After the season ended, Todd took some horses back to Stockbridge and stayed there.

Persse was a canny Irishman who liked a bet. He found out that Todd did as well. It's a moot point as to whether Todd jumped or was pushed. He used to tell a good story about the uproar when Persse intercepted a letter he'd written to another trainer, applying for a job. He soon found himself in uniform, and served in France with the Lincolns. He was put in charge of the regiment's horses and mules. The carnage among the animals was even greater than that suffered by the soldiers. The horses carried ammunition, drew carriages of troop reinforcements and pulled field guns, often through deep mud.

By 1916 a million animals – 'remounts' – were in service, most of them Percheron-breds bought in the United States. Todd and another future trainer, Syd Mercer, skinned many a dead animal before it was rendered down or sent to the field kitchen. It was an extended anatomy class in a horse's muscles, bones and sinews. In 1915, Todd suffered a shrapnel wound. He was invalided out, and discharged in August 1916. He never forgot the horrors of the front, or the conditions on the hospital ship in a storm on the Channel. He swore that he'd never go abroad again and he never did.

He found work with the Exning trainer Bert Lines, and stayed for five years, latterly as head lad, after which he moved to the stable of Tom Coulthwaite in Staffordshire. Coulthwaite was a large, blunt Lancastrian who trained humans before he turned his attention to horses. He was a successful coach for the Salford Harriers. He studied, ahead of his time, how to make his runners fit and bring them to a peak for a particular day.

After he was handed a suspension over the in-and-out running of his horses, it was joked that his athletes too were only 'off' once or twice a year, when the money was down. He was banned in 1913, worked energetically for the Remount Commission during the war, and eventually got his licence back in 1918. After a cry of anguish – "Why have they taken my life?" – he confined himself to saying that he'd been given plenty of time to tend his roses. He was a supreme trainer of staying chasers. He won the Grand Nationals of 1907, 1910 and 1931 with Eremon, Jenkinstown and Grakle. He built a miniature National course on his gallops, and encouraged his neighbours to grow gorse so that his trial fences could be accurate replicas of the Aintree obstacles.

Coulthwaite taught Todd two of the foundations of his training career: the importance of feeding, and the value of long, slow work in conditioning stayers. Coulthwaite's horses started in single file, at a steady pace, drawing upsides about two furlongs from the end of the gallop, and in Coulthwaite's words, "finishin' roonin' away." John Cherry, who began as an apprentice with Todd aged 14 and was to become his last head lad, recalls how similar George's routine was: "Most of the work was half speed, then from half way just increase and increase, moving up alongside, never off the bridle. Three-quarters speed was a gallop for us. Afterwards we had to walk to him and he'd listen to each horse to hear how he was blowing."

Coulthwaite's attention to detail extended to his horses' rail journeys to their races. He travelled with them in their box cars, to ensure that he fed them himself. Coulthwaite was obsessive about feeding, with little variants and supplements to suit each individual animal. At one time, he had a hurdler, Rathlea, who was a picky, reluctant feeder. Through studying him carefully, he found that Rathlea would consent to eat up in the small hours, so Coulthwaite set his alarm for the middle of the night and woke to feed the horse himself. The sequel was that Rathlea thrived, and won a Chester Cup. It was evidently a big winner for Coulthwaite: long after, when he retired to a rose-clad cottage, he named it, not after one of his Grand National horses, but Rathlea. George Todd watched Coulthwaite, and learned. With him was a young Irishman, Bob Shanahan, who was to become his own long-serving head lad. Shanahan had been apprenticed to his father Dennis, who trained on the Curragh but died young, after which Bob moved to England. As another bonus for Todd, who was to finance a long training career by betting, he met a group of heavy-hitting northern punters while he was at Coulthwaite's academy. Men like Billy Carter and Tom Degg placed bets for Todd, and later became owners with him.

Carter was a professional punter who got going by clocking greyhounds, an exercise that called for lightning-fast reactions. Then he took his stopwatch to the racecourse, where he linked up with another formidable clocker and gambler, Alec Bird. Tom Degg began life as a bus driver, took over his father's small haulage firm and built it up into a large business. He bet selectively and heavily, usually on his own horses. After one coup in the 1950s, there was a break-in at the haulage office. A thief who was probably looking for petty cash hit the jackpot. The safe contained £20,000.

Todd left Coulthwaite after winning £800 [*£25,000*] on one of the yard's hurdlers at Liverpool. He gave in his notice and announced that he would set up as a trainer. He lost most of his winnings a few days later, but the die was cast. In March 1928, he was given a licence, and he began at Royston, training four horses on a narrow strip round the outside of a farmer's field. Looking back on that time, Todd would say that three of the horses were unsound and the other was useless. Eventually in the autumn, Todd found a race bad enough for a £40 plater called Social Evening to win. He was on his way, slowly.

The following year he moved to Crossways, on the main road in the middle of East Ilsley. He began the season with eight horses and his first outside owners. By the end of the season, four of the horses hadn't made it to the racecourse and three had been lost to other trainers. His only winner was again with Social Evening in a selling handicap. He began his third year back down to four horses, three of which ran without success in selling hurdles. The other won a seller on the flat and was lost at the auction after the race. Three wins in three years was a demoralising start. Todd made ends meet by breaking yearlings for other trainers. He disliked the chore so much that it made him forever a reluctant trainer of two-year-olds. In 1931, things took several turns for the better. Although, small wonder, none of his previous owners were with him, he somehow found new patrons, and his string was into double figures. One of his new owners was a respected bookmaker, Horace Lester, who served as mayor of his home town, Banbury.

Todd had a horse that he wanted to back, a £22 buy called Wenceslas, but he had no money. He asked another Ilsley trainer, Ernest Lowe, did he know anyone who'd put him in for £100 in exchange for the word that Wenceslas was fancied? Lowe introduced him to Horace Lester. The horse lost, but it made amends over hurdles soon after. Lester began by collecting bets in a munitions factory. Like many a 'runner' in the days of illegal street bookmaking, he started keeping the bets for himself. In due course, he built himself a nice house. He wanted to call it Mug's Mansion, because, he said, "Mugs come up to the door and hand me money," but his wife wouldn't allow it.

Todd himself was married that year. He met Audrey King in Exning during his time with Bert Lines. She was a schoolteacher. They made an odd couple: he was tall and spare, she was short and stout. Their talents were complementary: George hated paperwork, so Audrey handled all the stable's administration. He called her 'Boss.' Money was tight. To help make ends meet, Audrey took on the running of the village post office from a front room at Crossways. It might not have been a direct result of his improved personal and financial footing, but 1931 was the year when Todd first showed what he could do when he had slightly better material to train. Eight of his string ran, and they won eight races between them. Six were selling handicaps and the other two were amateur riders' races, but they paid their way: five of the eight winners were favourites. One of them was the first Todd winner to be ridden by Gordon Richards.

The pattern was set for the remainder of Todd's long training career. The yard's solitary two-year-old didn't run. The trio of three-year-olds didn't win a race between them. All the yard's successes came from the older horses. Over the years, there'd be a few exceptions, but a bookmaker rarely took a risk laying a Todd two-year-old. When another trainer asked him, 'Can you get a two-year-old ready at Manton?' he replied, "Oh, yes, we usually get them ready by September." Todd spent the rest of the 1930s in East Ilsley. After his successful 1931 season, his string more than doubled in 1932, and he had a dozen winners.

The following year, though, his numbers were down again, and he struggled through the rest of the decade with his string as few as 11 and never more than 20. They were still from the bargain basement: 40 per cent of his winners were in sellers. In one bleak year, he was back down to just one winner on the flat, Gordon Richards getting a gambled-on favourite home by a desperate short head. They were a precarious few years for the Todds, and for a while, a hurdler called Priddy Hill kept them afloat. "Whenever we were on the rocks, he got us out of trouble," Audrey Todd would recall.

For all that Todd trained from East Ilsley for 10 years, he never found it ideal. His yard's position on the main road made it a nerve-racking exercise getting his horses in and out. Eventually he created a back entrance that led into, of all things, the police station drive, and out that way. The gallops were a couple of miles away, and he shared them with other trainers in the village. At the end of 1939, he moved the few miles to West Ilsley and The Poplars, a small yard at the entrance to Hodcott House, where Jack Colling later trained, and Dick Hern and Mick Channon after him. Todd shared The Poplars with Eric Stedall, an amiable older man who more or less trained for fun. One of Stedall's routines was to go with a friend to dinner parties, disguised as a visiting parson, and scandalise his hosts by telling risqué stories and sinking decanters of port.

The Poplars didn't tick all the boxes. It had no space for accommodation, so the lads were housed in digs all round the village, freer to chatter about their horses than George would've liked. But it was far quieter than Crossways, and during the war years Todd built up his stable strength to 30 in 1945. His consistency in getting an average of a win a season from his older horses also began to attract a broader range of owners. Bookmakers like Horace Lester and Percy Thompson were joined by some astute businessmen: Sidney Banks, a substantial corn merchant; the insurance broker Tommy Frost; and Sir William Cooke, a landowner and breeder who'd once been Master of Todd's first employer, the South Wold hunt.

By now, Todd was hitting the layers hard and often. He had a three-year-old called Coolnargeat who won four handicaps. First when 7-4 favourite at Thirsk for Gordon Richards, then twice at Newmarket, the second time by 15 lengths, having been backed from 8-1 to 5-2. One might think Coolnargeat was by now on every bookmaker's radar, but at Nottingham, it opened at 6-1 and was cut to 7-2. The following season it was sent to Salisbury, supported from 4-1 to 9-4, and won again. Few of Todd's horses at that time had the ability to go on shrugging aside penalties and weight increases: they required a less exposed campaign. Typical were animals like Cecilina and Precipitate. Cecilina had three 'sighters' when she was 25-1 and upwards. Each time the formbook reported, "Made no show." In those days, there were no extended distances or placings given in the papers or in the formbook. Greatly to the benefit of a betting stable, a large proportion of the field in multi-runner races were dismissed under, "Made no show". Cecilina then went to Windsor for a 10-furlong handicap, was a springer from 16-1 to 7-1, and won comfortably. Noted bets at the returned price amounted to £1,470 to £210 [*£38,600 to £5,500*].

Precipitate had run three times unplaced for another yard. Transferred to Todd, it had two quiet runs at Salisbury, 33-1 both times: "Made no show," and, "Lost place halfway." Then it went to Ascot for a maiden race: "Last off, steady progress, led two furlongs out, easily." The betting spoke volumes: "The ring became alive for Precipitate, who, from useful wagers at longer odds, became all the rage at 7-1 to 4-1." Recorded bets at SP alone were *£37,000 to £9,300*. Not surprisingly, people started to pay attention. The retired Epsom trainer Stanley Wootton, no mean punter himself, sent a horse to Todd. And, after an awkward introduction, Todd took on an owner, Desmond Baring, who made a priceless connection for him.

Chapter 20

Say you don't know

'Dez' Baring was a scion of the banking family, a winning point-to-point rider, and a would-be trainer who built some stables at his home near Wantage. The onset of war put his plans on hold, but in the autumn of 1945, he'd gathered a few horses, and he took them to West Ilsley to work. They were led by a groom who appeared from the fog going the wrong way up George Todd's gallops, shouted, "Morning, guv'nor" to the startled Todd, rode straight through his string, and disappeared back into the mist. Todd made some enquiries, which led quickly to Baring. Their conversation began with George bristling: "Why are your horses using my gallops?"

Over a drink or two, all was soon forgiven. Todd ran the rule over Dez's horses and said they were hopeless. But, he told the crestfallen owner, he'd had his eye on a horse of Eric Stedall's at The Poplars. It was called Gremlin. "It's slow and it's never been fit," he said. "Eric hasn't got a clue about it. But I think it could make up into a stayer." As Todd expected, Stedall was happy to sell Gremlin to Baring for next to nothing. It was an inspired buy. Todd started Gremlin off over hurdles, and on its second run it won at the Cheltenham Festival. The horse was switched to the flat and ridden by John Hislop, who became a leading racing journalist and author, but was of more interest to Todd as the best amateur rider of his time. Between 1946 and his last season, 1956, Hislop had 177 rides on the flat. He won on 87 of them (49 per cent) and placed on a further 53 (30 per cent). Hislop steered Gremlin to an easy win at Salisbury; Dez Baring's horse won once more that season, and there was a big payday the following spring.

Todd's breakthrough year was 1946. He trained over 20 winners, for 10 different owners, and as during the wartime years, he usually made them pay. Almost three-quarters of his winners were favourite or second favourite. The post-war racecourse betting market was strong, too. Crowds were enormous, after the shortage of racing during the war. Almost 104,000 packed into the Roodee for Chester's first meeting in seven years, the day that Horace Lester's backwards-spelt Retsel won the Chester Cup. Cars were backed up two miles out of the town. It was Chester's all-time record crowd. The going was hard. Only an hour before the race, Todd thought of taking out Retsel, who had fragile legs after throwing a splint as a two-year-old. But the combination of a valuable prize and a well-handicapped horse were irresistible.

On-course bets on Retsel included £1,600 to £400, £2,000 to £500 and £800 to £200. In our money, the bets totalled *£28,000* to win *£112,000.* The race was uneventful by Chester Cup standards: it had only two leaders from flag-fall to finish. An outsider led to five furlongs out, where Retsel kicked on. He was soon clear, and won by four lengths without anything getting near him.

Geoffrey Hamlyn, the long-serving *Sporting Life* starting price reporter, wrote that the, "Six or seven years [after the end of the war] saw the greatest volume of betting there has ever been." Not, as some innocently thought, because discharged servicemen were spending their back pay and gratuities, but from the black market: "And this found its way to the racecourse, chiefly in ready money. The bookmakers could truly be said to have never had it so good." It was also handy for a gambling trainer like Todd, able to bet though his bookmaker owners into a Ring that was ready to lay serious wagers without a bother. And thanks to Dez Baring, Todd now had privileged access to the wisdom and wiles of one of the most successful punters of the twentieth century: Ben Warner.

Baring was married to Warner's only child, Mollie. She wrote of her father,

> *"[He] worked very hard and he became first a successful bookmaker... then gradually built up a string of racehorses which, with his careful management [and] shrewd and studious work on the form book, proved to be very lucrative and, rather like a fairy story, kept us all in great comfort ever after."*

Did they ever. Two of Warner's palm-sized betting books survive to this day. Their contents would cause even the boldest layer to wake sweating in the dead of the night. The books cover a period from November 1926 to December 1933. They show that over those seven years, Warner won

£79,352, or in today's money *£2.66 million* - an average *£380,000* a year. What's more, there's a gap where one colossal payout should be. Instead, Warner pencilled: "Tenby not included."

In January 1927, Warner engineered a coup that reverberated for years. The tool was a moderate hurdler that he owned called Oyster Maid, running at the long-gone Tenby racecourse. On the first day of the meeting, there was a relentless downpour, driven by a gale. Marquees were blown over, everyone was wet through, the going became bottomless. Warner's betting book reveals that he lost £216 *[£6,735]*.

The second race the next day was the Licensed Victuallers Selling Hurdle. A local trainer, David Harrison, had three of the eight runners, including Oyster Maid and Bubbly. A couple of the tipping sheets put up Oyster Maid as their outright selection, as did the course correspondent of the *Sporting Chronicle*: "If Oyster Maid reproduces her [latest] running she is likely to be returned the winner."

Bubbly was owned by Ted Arnold, a county cricketer turned bookmaker and punter. When Warner and Arnold openly backed Bubbly with the Tenby bookmakers, it was rushed from evens to 2-5. Oyster Maid drifted out to 100-6. Warner had enlisted some of the on-course bookies to operate a knock-out.

The Sporting Life and the *Chronicle* both had SP price men at Tenby. The *Life* reporter, Geoff Hoole, was in on the coup. His *Chronicle* colleague, Teddy Dawson, declined to join in. It was said that he was locked in a lavatory while the market formed. Afterwards, he had no option but to follow Hoole's account of the betting. Next morning, neither of the papers even named Oyster Maid in their SP reports.

All sorts of lurid stories were told about the race. How the jockeys had been paid off beforehand. How one horse was ridden off the track when it seemed to be going dangerously well. How a man waited by the rails before the last hurdle, to shout a bribe to the jockey of any horse who was in front of Oyster Maid.

Large pinches of salt are needed here, but what's certain is that Oyster Maid travelled close up through the race, collared Bubbly at the last hurdle, and sauntered away to win by five lengths. A nationwide SP coup had been meticulously plotted. Fulke and Helen Walwyn (he became a National Hunt legend; she married Gordon Johnson Houghton and after his death trained a 2,000 Guineas winner) went with their parents in a pony and trap to the post office in Abergavenny, where telegrams were sent to bookmakers far and wide. Ben Warner's 14-year-old daughter Mollie and other family, friends and confederates were repeating the exercise at other post offices. When they remembered the script, their bets were preceded by blocking telegrams containing Biblical quotes and the like. Every telegram handed in was time-stamped, and then the telegraph operators keyed them in, in order of their receipt. First went Ecclesiastes 11.1, then the bets on Oyster Maid. So a telegram to back Oyster Maid would be timed, quite legitimately, before the race, but transmitted and received after she'd already won.

Not all the money got on: a taxi touring London's bookies broke down. But at the crucial moment, Mother Nature gave Ben Warner an extra edge. Tenby had no coverage by 'the blower'. The same detail was central to the Gay Future plot at Cartmel almost 50 years later. Nowadays, mobile phones and internet connections ensure that on-course bookmakers can monitor betting off-course and on the exchanges, from moment to moment. But that afternoon in west Wales, the nearest telephone was in a house above the course, a few hundred yards away.

A tic-tac man was stationed on its balcony. In the last minutes before Oyster Maid's race, the phone began to ring. The SP offices were calling to hedge rapidly increasing liabilities. At that moment, it began to snow. The tic-tac man was invisible. He ran frantically to a gate onto the racecourse and was last seen under restraint from a policeman, yelling, "Oyster Maid! Oyster Maid!" into the white-out.

No one would have known from *The Sporting Life* and *Sporting Chronicle* that anything untoward had taken place at Tenby. In the days that followed, there wasn't a peep from either paper, for good reason. The *Chronicle* had 'lost' its SP reporter in humiliating circumstances. The *Life* had to face up to its man returning a bogus starting price. He was fired.

Meanwhile, other papers were quickly onto the story. The Cardiff *Western Mail* report contained a sentence which fuelled the fury that followed: "Bubbly soon became an odds-on favourite, *but some of the shrewd judges preferred his stable companion Oyster Maid and took 10-1.*" The next day, under the headline 'SP coup landed at Tenby', the paper gave an update: "Several bookmakers in a large way of business will remember that Oyster Maid won when settling their accounts this week."

The Racehorse confirmed that:

"Oyster Maid had been performing fairly well and it was only because Bubbly was all the rage that [she went off] at 100-6. It transpires that Mr Warner's filly who, by the way, was selected by our chief writer, was well backed, and loud were the lamentations when the SP came through."

The off-course bookmakers had telegrams arriving all afternoon with bets on Oyster Maid, and liabilities at 100-6 over a horse which should've been a 3-1 or 4-1 chance, and had evidently been supported at 10-1. They held the on-course bookmakers responsible, as indeed they were. One racing paper under-stated the rage when it wrote that, "There was a bit of a squeal from the SP offices."

Behind the scenes, the bad blood lingered for decades. It was prudent of Warner not to boast of the scale of the coup, even in his own betting book. To the end of his life, he kept a Trappist silence on the subject. It'll never be known how much he won, but the *Sporting Times* gave a clue: "Everybody on and off the racecourse, and notably in SP bookmaking circles, is talking about the coup brought off at Tenby by Ben Warner. Office layers all over the place felt a severe draught and the long price hit them badly. I hear that even as far afield as Dublin, one man had to part with four figures. It was the same in London, Epsom and elsewhere."

The smallest four-figure sum, £1,000, represents over *£31,000* today. It doesn't require a feverish imagination to see Warner winning hundreds of thousands, especially in the context of his *£380,000* profit each year, '*Tenby not included*.' And his commission agents would've added their own bets once his money was on. Prominent among them was a nattily-dressed professional punter called Tommy Westhead. Years later, he was George Todd's putter on when George brought off his own biggest coup.

By the time Dez Baring introduced Todd to Warner, the Oyster Maid winnings were invested in hotels in Torquay, and Ben's racing interests were reduced. But Todd used Warner's help and contacts to get his own bets on, and whenever there was racing at Newbury, he stopped off at Warner's home at Donnington. Ben's granddaughter Anne Dalgety recalls their conversation as, "Racing, racing, racing. George was absolutely charming at home and with his owners' children, but you wouldn't dare approach him on the racecourse. He was remote. It was serious business there."

Todd's attitude to owners wasn't unlike that of an old-fashioned prep school headmaster towards the parents. They were a necessary evil, and mostly kept in the dark. In his dreams, Todd wouldn't have had any owners at all. He would've trained for himself. The high cost of buying and replacing stock and running a yard meant that, reluctantly, he had to accept owners' involvement, with conditions. He described his favourite owner as, "One who's pleased to leave it all to me." Wherever possible, he kept a share in a horse, so that the final decisions on their running plans were his, including when they were trying and when they weren't. Dick Broadway, who rode a Cheltenham winner for Todd, remembers his instructions: "If the owner asks you if it's fancied, just say you don't know."

"He didn't want his owners telling all their friends," laughs Broadway. Sidney Banks had numerous horses with Todd over a 20-year period. Banks was at Lingfield Park one afternoon to see one of his horses run. Todd arrived and said nothing. In the saddling box and the paddock, still nothing. Finally, as Banks was in the stand watching his horse arrive at the start, he couldn't contain himself: "George, do you fancy this today?" "Oh, yes. It'll win." Banks was left with moments to scramble down to the rails for a bet.

One year, Banks signed the cheque for a yearling that Todd had bought at Newmarket. Nothing happened during its two-year-old days, which wasn't a great surprise. As its three-year-old season passed, Banks looked in vain for signs of an entry. Come the summer of its fourth year, Banks sent a polite note to Manton asking, 'Is there any news of my horse?' "Dear Sidney," Todd wrote back: "I thought you were a patient man." After buying a yearling for Tom Degg, Todd told him: "He'll be alright as a four-year-old. We'll get some money from him then."

At times Banks became exasperated with Todd, but a winner would put it right. Never more than when George turned down an invitation to Sidney's silver wedding party, saying he'd saddle a winner for him at Lingfield instead. True to his word, he laid out one of Banks's for the big day, and the celebrations went with an extra swing when the news arrived that the horse had gone in at 100-6.

Dez Baring's son Peter says that most of the time, his father only found out that his horses were running when he saw it in the morning paper. Baring's other son, Nigel, who rode out first lot at Manton, was astonished one morning when Todd told the lad riding the Coronation Cup winner Oncidium, "Get off him. Mr Baring rides Oncidium."

Baring remembers, "He only let me have a canter, but he did it just so that I could say, 'I've ridden Oncidium.' It was a sweet thing to do, to put an amateur on a Group One horse." Oncidium's owner Lord Howard de Walden wasn't told. He used to call Oncidium, "My horse behind the Iron Curtain."

The telephone was high on Todd's list of dislikes. He tried never to answer it: that was Audrey's job. Nor did he willingly make calls. His preferred method of contact with his owners was by hand-written letter. Besides his foible: 'What I really hate about training is telephone calls at night,' he told a journalist, there was a practical reason for avoiding the phone. In those days, calls through rural exchanges were connected by local operators. Indiscreet ears might be listening in when an owner telephoned Marlborough 417. Sidney Banks was on a cruise and called his home, ship-to-shore, to check that all was well. An operator at his local exchange told him, "Oh, they're away."

Todd's friend and fellow trainer Jack Colling was at Manton one day when the phone rang. He heard Audrey say, "It's someone who's just bought a horse for £10,000. He wants you to train it." George responded, "I don't know him. I don't know the horse. I'm damned if I'm going to train for him."

However, Todd could be amenable if he was approached in what he felt was the proper way. Kenneth Mackenzie was one of his later owners. Racing was Mackenzie's relaxation from running British Home Stores. "I took a fancy to Todd as a trainer. I noticed that a lot of the horses he was winning with were very moderate." He met Todd at the races and said, 'I hope I might persuade you to buy a horse for me.'

> "He invited me down to Manton the following day for lunch. There were two horses for me to look at. Both were well-bred two-year-olds. One had been owned by the Astors: presumably they didn't think much of it. It was typical that they'd offer a horse like that to George, often for nothing or for very little, because they knew it'd be well looked after. George said that he'd been thinking of keeping them for himself, but that I couldn't start with better possibilities. He said, 'I'll keep half and guide you into ownership that way.' The two half-shares cost me £1,600 [*£22,400*]. As I was leaving, he said that one of them was entered at Ascot the following Saturday: 'Try to be there. It has a very good chance.' It won. The prize we split was about £2,500, so I had a return of £1,250 in six days."

Looked at another way, Todd had given away £1,250. He could easily have waited a week for the horse to win, and then sold the half-share at a higher price. Todd seems never to have run Manton on conventional commercial lines. Mackenzie was surprised to be told by Audrey that, "The monthly charges are so small that I'll send you a quarterly bill instead." Nowadays, many stables benefit from sponsorship. Back then, Todd and his fellow trainers derived almost all their income from training fees and prize money; to a much lesser extent, from their share of apprentices' riding fees and winning percentages; from commissions on buying and selling horses; and, if they were that way inclined, from betting. Training fees and prize money couldn't have maintained Todd at Manton. His friend and neighbour Noel Murless provided a rare glimpse into the economic facts of a trainer's life when he left Beckhampton in 1952.

Murless calculated that he needed his percentage from a minimum of £30,000 in prize money each year to maintain the yard and provide for his family. That year, Murless had £28,182 *[£533,500]* in prize money and the training fees from 59 horses. A few miles away, Todd's 1952 income was only £5,431 *[£102,800]* in prize money. He had 40 horses, but probably only 20 horses' worth of training fees, since he owned several outright and had a share in others. Ten and 20 years later, his owner Betty Cooke remembers, he was charging £12 a week *[£165]* and £22 a week *[£121]* respectively in training fees.

Based on the number of horses he had in those years, and the ones that didn't generate fees because he owned them himself, his income from training was probably between *£4,000* and *£4,500* a week in 1962 and only *£2,000* a week in 1972. Besides the evidence that neither George nor Audrey fully understood, or allowed for, inflation, the figures confirm that Todd's Manton could never have been financially viable without heavy, successful betting. Occasionally when things went badly, he sold off bits of land. Small wonder that he paid more attention to his horses than to his owners. When his money was down, the horses simply had to deliver.

Mackenzie says of Todd that, "If he was interested in you, he was patience itself. Otherwise, he was an impatient man." And even a favoured owner like Mackenzie hesitated before asking George when one of his horses was going to run: "He didn't like it. He wasn't an easy man unless you treated him the way he liked to be treated." If an owner didn't toe George's line, he or she was shown the door.

He was by no means a woman hater, but by chance, two of the owners that he particularly disliked were Stella Carver, who had a wonderful stayer, Trelawny; and Jean Hislop, the wife of his amateur jockey John Hislop.

The Hislops had a number of horses at Manton during the 1950s, with a fair degree of success. None of them was a world-beater, but the likes of Holy Deadlock and Tickled Pink, trained by one master and ridden in amateur races by another, used to win a race or two every year. The Hislops' last horse with Todd was a filly called La Paiva. She ran three times as a two-year-old, showing promise when fifth in a Newbury maiden on her debut. Her next run wasn't so good, the one after was worse.

As a three-year-old her best form, from four runs, was a second in a weak maiden. Twice that season she was backed and beaten. As far as the stable was concerned, she was a liability. Her last racecourse appearance was at Salisbury, by chance in the Manton maiden plate. She was apprentice ridden, and drifted in the betting. The favourite was trained by Sir Gordon Richards, ridden by Scobie Breasley, and backed by Todd and his entourage into favouritism.

Down at the bottom bend, disaster. La Paiva hung badly into Breasley's mount and all but carried it off the track: it finished only fourth. Scobie was furious. Todd was furious. It wasn't La Paiva's fault. Her enthusiasm was never in question, and it emerged that she was losing her sight in one eye, which explained her hanging as she navigated the Salisbury turn.

Jean Hislop never understood, or chose to ignore, George's dislike for owners' questions, especially if they were put to him by telephone. He couldn't abide her, particularly after an incident at Ascot. He saddled two runners in the same race. One of them was hers: it was the lesser-fancied in the betting.

Within earshot of others, Jean Hislop told George that she supposed he'd given her horse a bucket of water to stop it. That was the last straw. Soon after, Todd told her to take her horse and go – even though her husband was riding work at Manton the next day.

The sacking of Jean Hislop and La Paiva had an intriguing sequel. The Hislops realised their filly had no future on the racecourse, and they sent her to be mated with a series of moderate and mostly unheard-of sires. The Hislops offered La Paiva's first foal to Todd as a pipe of peace, but he brushed it aside. Several years and foals later, La Paiva was sent to Queen's Hussar, a former Sussex Stakes winner who showed his best form in blinkers. Their union produced a great champion: Brigadier Gerard. If he hadn't sent Jean Hislop packing, George Todd might have trained Brigadier Gerard at Manton.

In three seasons in training with Dick Hern, the Brigadier won 17 races from 18 starts. His 11 Group One successes included the 2,000 Guineas of 1970 by three lengths from another champion, Mill Reef. The Brigadier's successes had an unfortunate affect on the Hislops. She became even more overbearing. He, perhaps at her behest, spent much time and printer's ink on mapping out the breeding theory that had prompted them to send La Paiva to Queen's Hussar.

Many in the racing and breeding community were irritated by the Hislops' vigorous self-promotion. The doubters had an obvious question: if the mating of La Paiva with Queen's Hussar was so clever, why did the Hislops send her to several other stallions before him? Some of Todd's owners said that Queen's Hussar was simply the nearest half-decent stallion that the Hislops could afford.

The truth had nothing to do with bloodstock brilliance or budgeting. Jean Hislop had won some money playing bridge with Queen's Hussar's owner, Lord Carnarvon. He offered to pay her with a nomination to his stallion. Brigadier Gerard, the best horse trained in England between Tudor Minstrel and Frankel, was the result of a card game.

Chapter 21

Little things make perfection

The 1946 flat season was Todd's most successful by far, with Retsel's Chester Cup win the centrepiece. As it ended, Todd talked to his owners about the impending sale of Manton. It represented a fulfilment he couldn't have dreamed of when he was working four bad platers on the edge of a field. Two of his owners offered to finance him. One was Horace Lester; the other was Jack King, a Gloucestershire farmer who made a fortune selling some land for development. The trio drove up to London on the morning of Manton's auction. They lunched long and late at the Savoy. Afterwards, the traffic was heavy, and by the time they reached the saleroom, the auction was over.

A chastened group drove back to West Ilsley. Then, they heard that the sale had fallen through. Todd was able, at the second attempt, to buy Manton. He offered £50,000. Tattersalls countered by accepting that price for the estate, less the Redpost stud and 40 or so acres of paddocks. The negotiation ended with Todd paying £57,000 [*£1.46 million*] for the whole estate, with a down payment of £10,000 provided by King and Lester.

There were some loose ends. Joe Lawson's severance agreement with Tattersalls included a provision for him to stay at Manton for the rest of the year. At the start of January, he had talks with Todd about training his reduced string from the Astor yard, with Todd occupying the main yard. The idea of having the old and new Masters training together at Manton was impractical, and Lawson turned his energies to finding a new stable in the area. Even in the post-war recession, few suitable yards were available.

Blewbury, where Steve Donoghue had trained, was auctioned in the middle of a freeze-up. The phones were down, and Lawson had to drive a lorry across the snow to an estate agent's office in Marlborough to bid. He was the under-bidder at £9,600 to Gordon Johnson Houghton. It seemed the last straw. At the end of February *The Sporting Life* carried a story headed, "Lawson decides to retire."

It was unequivocal, but it was wrong. Over the next few months, Lawson changed his mind. In the fiftieth year since his arrival at Manton, he bought the Carlburg yard in Newmarket. It was a brave move for a 66-year-old, and it was rewarded when he won the 1954 Derby with Never Say Die, providing Lester Piggott with the first of his nine winners in the race. Lawson retired in 1957. He lived quietly and much respected in Newmarket until his death there seven years later. Timeform's *The Racing Week* celebrated Lawson as, 'A giant of his profession.' "Lawson was lucky to be given charge of a ready-made stable whose fortune was in the ascendant, but then the foresight and ability of a successful man often looks like luck." "He was an extremely good trainer, and a likeable man; patient during illness or adversity, with an unlimited capacity for hard work, reserved, frugal, and always polite."

Meanwhile, Todd made a sensational start at Manton. He prepared two of his handicappers for the big races at Kempton's Easter meeting. Percy Thompson's French import Philadelphe II was aimed at the Rosebery Stakes on the Saturday, and Dez Baring's Gremlin at the Queen's Prize on Easter Monday. The Rosebery had a French favourite, Epi d'Or VII, but on earlier running together at Longchamp, Philadelphe II had an excellent chance, receiving 3lb for a half-length defeat.

The form worked out exactly, Philadelphe II making most of the running to beat Epi d'Or VII by a length and a half. On Monday, it was Gremlin's turn. Baring was an enthusiastic punter, though seldom a successful one. The atmosphere at his home in Ardington was decidedly tense that morning. It would've been more so if he'd known how rough a race it would be, and how Gremlin would be almost put over the rails. *Best Horses of 1947* described the incident:

> *"Pilot, a hooded lunatic of a horse, misbehaved at the start, collided with* [another runner] *as the gate went up, tore off in front fighting for his head, refused to negotiate the first turn, shot across the course almost knocking* [Gremlin] *over in the process, and then stuck his toes in and put his jockey over his head."*

It was as well that Gremlin had plenty in hand. His jockey Cliff Richards took a lead into the straight before going clear two furlongs out and winning by four lengths. Baring returned to Ardington relieved and enriched. He went to the Boar's Head in the village, and stood the drinks all evening. George Todd had a good bet over Philadelphe II, and put all the proceeds on Gremlin, who was returned at 13-2 after being 'exceedingly popular' from 8-1. The starting-price double was almost 33-1. It didn't attract attention the way that later high-profile Todd gambles did, but it was a serious win. And he wasn't to know it, but the biggest earner of all had been waiting for him at Manton. It was a backward two-year-old: Dramatic, leased from Lady Wentworth by Ted Saunders. Dramatic's lad was Bill McCluskey, who found him hard work: Dramatic sweated heavily, and sometimes Todd would intervene to help get the horse ready for evening stables. It was as if, even before Dramatic had set foot on a racecourse, George had seen something in the horse to interest him.

The apprentices and paid lads who worked for George Todd invariably use the same two words to describe him: 'hard' and 'fair'. Todd had failings that would keep a modern-day industrial tribunal, and occasionally the courts, at full throttle, but the unwritten contract with his staff was clear: work hard and work my way, and you'll be well treated.

"I liked him. He was straight down the line," says McCluskey. "He demanded a standard from you, and it was understood that if you didn't meet that standard, your feet wouldn't touch the ground." Todd's mantra was that, "Little things make perfection, and perfection is no little thing." The Manton that he took over from Joe Lawson was some way short of perfect. The downs were overrun by rabbits, and the last thing a trainer wants is gallops pitted with holes. Todd's keepers netted two or three hundred rabbits each week and sent them to market. Around the yard, there were obvious signs of the shortage of investment in the war years.

Albert Tucker, who started aged 15 with Lawson on two shillings a week, would lie in bed in the hostel looking up where ceiling plaster had fallen, seeing the stars between the roof slates. The boiler was out of action and there were no funds to replace it. Winter in the dormitories was bitterly cold. Breakfast was invariably baked beans on toast. The apprentices like Tucker, who had their indentures transferred from Lawson to Todd, saw immediate improvements. The first was in their pay packets. Todd started his boys off on five shillings a week, rising by half a crown a week in each year of the normal five-year span of their apprenticeship.

The lads' food also improved. Todd remembered the primitive catering in his time at Atty Persse's yard. There, the last two lads to arrive at each meal simply weren't fed. It was a robust incentive to be prompt next time; meanwhile, they had to forage for their food. Audrey Todd hired a new cook for the Manton hostel. By chance, she was the daughter-in-law of the jockey who mistook Bayardo for a three-year-old, Otto Madden. The canteen was transformed overnight. The portions were so generous that Manton mealtimes were reckoned almost as much of a danger to the lads' weight as National Service. Malcolm Hall, who was apprenticed at Manton in the 1950s, says, "The food was too good: how could you expect to be a jockey if you were fed the way we were? In the end, the weight beat me."

In a remote yard like Manton, and with very little money, the apprentices' and lads' evenings could weigh heavily. Todd paid for a free bar in the hostel once a week, and he laid on a coach to the Empire Theatre in Swindon when there was a new show. He might've been less generous if he'd known that his lads enjoyed free drinks and the best seats: the Empire's manager was a keen punter who appreciated his hotline into Manton.

Todd also took a paternal view of the apprentices' clothing needs. They were sent once a year to Slopers, the tailor in Marlborough, to be outfitted with a new suit. Whenever clothing wore through, a boy had only to ask George for a replacement. "Yuss, Yuss," he'd say, and send the boy to Audrey to collect a note for Slopers. There were rules: George selected the cloth each year, so that everyone's suit conformed. Todd insisted that his lads looked the part, and they mostly did. Paddock-watchers could always tell the Todd horse by looking for the smartest lad. His concern with apparel was practical. He liked his staff always to wear a cap around the yard, believing it reduced the risk of them being infected with ringworm when grooming their horses.

When the apprentice John Friar contracted TB, George at once equipped all the work riders with full-length waterproof riding coats. He was fair-minded with bonuses. He operated a winnings pool for the paid lads, with the odds to £1 per lad when a stable 'expected' won. In 1949, the pool paid out £118 [*£2,740*] to each lad. As they started on £4 a week, that was a bonus of almost 60 per cent of their annual salary. The only times that Todd dug in his heels over the pool were when something won unintended and unfancied. There was delight in the hostel the day when a debutant filly dead-heated on her debut at 100-6. Todd was distinctly unjoyful: "I shall have to renege on that one," he said. Taking their lives in their hands, the lads nagged him, and eventually he relented. It was an expensive winner for George, but a *£180* or so windfall for every lad.

The set piece to end each day was evening stables. The Taylors would've recognised most of the detail, and approved. Once each lad had finished grooming his horse, its straw bedding was picked up and built into a square in a corner of the box. The tack and tools were laid out for inspection on this table. For ornamentation, there was a twist of straw at the entrance to the box, and the passage would be sprinkled with bran. So there waiting for Todd would be an immaculate horse, clean and shining, with his semi-immaculate lad. Todd saw half the horses at 16.45 and the other half at 17.30, so the lads had up to 45 minutes to do each of their charges. Todd would look at one side of each horse for a few seconds – it seemed an eternity to a nervous lad; and then have the horse turned, for him to inspect its other side. There was an eruption if some aspect of the tableau displeased him.

The scrutiny of evening stables was the distillation of Todd's work ethic. The pressure was remorseless. Paul Cole, the Derby-winning Whatcombe trainer who was Todd's pupil-assistant for 18 months in the 1960s, believes that Todd, "Used to work you to leave, work you to the point of exhaustion. I started at 05.30, rode out, did all the normal assistant's jobs and ended by making sure the apprentices were all in bed. Most nights I wasn't done until 23.00. Nothing was ever going to be good enough. I knew that whatever happened I would have to try harder just to keep my job. I stuck at it because I knew it would stand me in good stead. He was a tremendous stableman as well as a brilliant trainer." Nigel Baring recalls that Cole used to pester Todd: "'Why are you doing this? Why are you doing that?' One day Todd was being particularly foul to Paul. I asked him, 'Who is this chap?' Todd grunted, 'He's my assistant. I wouldn't mind betting that he'll make a trainer, because he's the only man I've had here who pays attention to what I say'." When Cole left, he was followed by Patrick Haslam.

After evening stables came feeding. The feed house was Todd's holy of holies. As he'd learned from Tom Coulthwaite, he fed meticulously and delegated to no one. The feeding routine of those days was, like evening stables, too labour-intensive to be feasible in a modern yard. Twice a week in winter and once in summer, the horses were fed hot mashes. Linseed was soaked overnight to swell it, and then boiled in a copper. Separately, feed buckets were prepared, with bran at the bottom and crushed oats and salt next. Finally, the linseed was poured on top.

Todd's hay and oats were imported. He had an agreement with his farm partner Harry Johnson to buy all the farm's hay, but then decided it had too much clover in it, so he turned to Norway for rye grass hay. Johnson's oats were never to Todd's liking: stained by the English weather, he claimed. Johnson sold them to Quaker Oats, who found them perfectly fit for human consumption, but they still weren't good enough for Todd's horses. He imported their oats from Australia and Canada. The way that he handled the oats was something of a tip-off. A board in the feed house had details of each horse's feed. At any given time, a handful would be on 'specials'.

If a horse appeared on the 'specials' list, it was time for the yard's punters to sit up. The routine feed contained heavily crushed or rolled oats. The specials were based on just-cracked oats: a feeding bowl of these weighed perhaps twice as much as the same volume of fully rolled-out oats, and provided the horse with far more nutrition. Then in went glucose, olive oil or cod liver oil, malt or molasses, sometimes some boiled corn or carrots. When he'd finished, Todd would call the lads and hand out the buckets with their horses' individually tailored feeds.

"After we'd fed the horse its special, we wiped out the bucket with a wisp of hay and dropped it into the manger, to make sure the horse got the last morsel," says Eric Campbell, who rode hurdles winners for Todd. "Then as like as not you'd find George behind you, patting the horse's neck. You knew all right."

Todd began giving his specials to a fancied horse perhaps a fortnight before its race, at the same time stepping up its work on the gallops. His maxim was, "Always feed a horse up to his work, never work him up to his feed." Similar attention was paid to ventilation and watering. One of Cole's and Haslam's tasks was to adjust the ventilation on their evening rounds. It was another notion that Todd picked up from Tom Coulthwaite.

Todd's assistants found it bewildering. "Could it affect a horse in a race if you moved the ventilator three holes?" wondered Paul Cole. He'd be given a list of the different amounts of water to be given to each horse. It was the same for Patrick Haslam:

> "We used to give every horse different amounts of water: some, none at all. Hydration was very important to George. The water buckets were always taken

> out at various points during the day or night. I can't exaggerate how much my life for two years revolved around feeding and watering. The reason he was obsessed with feeding, and spent as much time with his horses as possible, is that it's the only way you can get a horse to 'speak' to you.
>
> "It'd be easy if a horse could talk: 'How are you feeling?' 'Well, actually, I'm not feeling too bad,' or, 'I'm feeling fantastic. I think I'll win today.' That would be handy, but it's not realistic. You can, though, make a horse 'speak' to you if you have the time to observe him and his behaviour. [Drinking water or] not drinking so much water, resting in his box, not resting in his box, his demeanour when he's out, just the expression on his face. You get to know your horse, and he speaks to you in that way. The majority of the horses in Todd's yard ranged in age from four up to their teens, so over time he got to know them very well indeed."

There are circumstances in which water can have a significant bearing on a horse's performance, and George was fully aware of them. He told Dez Baring that when he was a lad at Exning, the yard had a runner that was forecast favourite. Not long before the race, George was told to fetch a bucket and let the horse drink. It finished out of the money. "That taught me how easy it was to stop horses," Todd said. He didn't, though, use dope, although like any betting trainer he attracted rumours. They may have been encouraged by all the ingredients lined up in his feed house. Even one of his owners said it looked like a pharmacy.

Doping was rife in the late 1940s and the 1950s. In England, it seemed to be mostly to stop horses, in France to give them the hurry-up. A series of cross-channel raiders won big races here when white with lather. There was much suspicion, but no action. A charitable explanation would be that with the war still fresh in people's minds, *entente cordiale* was allowed to prevail. One of Todd's owners, Tommy Frost, bought a horse on the recommendation of the Australian jockey Rae Johnstone, who was riding in France. It was only two and half lengths inferior to a stable companion, Galcador, which Johnstone had just ridden to victory in the Derby.

Frost's purchase spent its first few months at Manton sweating profusely, barely trainable. At length Todd won with it at Lingfield and assumed it would make a nice four-year-old, but it fell away to nothing over the winter. Frost eventually sold it for 180 guineas. Another Manton owner, the bookmaker Percy Thompson, bought some dope on a trip to France. He sat down with Todd at Windsor races and asked him to try it on his horses. Todd told him to take the dope away, and take his horses, too.

The old Yorkshire trainer Tom Hall said, "The best dope is 21lb off a horse's back," and that was all the dope that George Todd used.

It didn't take him long to get Manton as he wanted it. John Hislop said, "It was a revelation to see [the yard] maintained to such perfection. The paintwork fresh, the buildings in first class order, the yard swept clear, the paths raked and the gallops immaculate." It was part of the apprentices' duties to keep the yard in apple-pie order. All round the inside of the yard is a strip of flagstones and cobbles. Inside that, and surrounding Young Alec's Jubilee lawn, the yard is laid with pea gravel. The apprentices had to rake the gravel in neat patterns each day. They wore a shoulder harness to pull a wide rake behind them. Few Japanese rock gardens receive the attention paid to Manton's gravel by George's boys. And woe betide if there was any straw or debris to be seen. The flagstones were picked clean of weeds, particularly if an owner was visiting. John Cherry spent his first day at Manton on his knees on a bran sack, digging out anything green with a hoof-pick.

If they weren't raking or weeding, the boys would be in the loft rolling oats or unloading hay, or out on the downs, cleaning out sheep troughs. On Sundays, all the brass work was polished. Todd fully subscribed to the maxim that the devil makes work for idle hands. He translated that into instant physical punishment if an apprentice or lad shirked or disobeyed. Many a backside felt the full force of George's boot. He had a quick temper and sometimes he handed out severe beatings.

Albert Tucker had an argument one evening with one of the head lads. It escalated to, 'I'll see the guv'nor about this in the morning,' which drew the heated reply from Tucker, "Stuff you and stuff the guv'nor, too." Next morning, Tucker was in the passage outside his horse's box when the door burst open and Todd knocked him over. "He picked me up and gave me a right seeing to. My lip was split, my nose was busted." Another lad was told to get his hair cut. George spotted him a few days later, still untidy. "Come here, you dirty little so-and-so," he barked. He picked the boy up, carried him into the forge, plugged in a horse clipper and sheared him to the scalp: "That'll teach you."

What would be judged today as aberrant behaviour was routine in training yards before and during Todd's time, and into the 1950s. The boys were all required to do National Service: they were no strangers to rough treatment there. And though it explains Todd, rather than excuses him, it has to be said that he dished it out to all and sundry, not just his staff. A new milkman walked innocently across the yard lawn and got a cuff for trespass. One day at the races, Todd felt that another trainer's wife was blocking his access to a saddling box. In the ensuing kerfuffle, he punched her husband. Patrick Haslam says,

> "Related to the modern world, [life at Manton] was medieval. The hidings probably didn't do any harm. I suspect in a funny way [many lads] look back on that as the best time of their lives. Everyone had a job to do, you were always busy and it wasn't for the faint-hearted, but if you had something about you, it was interesting."

David Churchley, who started as an apprentice in 1947, says, "He was a fair man. If I got a hiding, it was because I'd done something wrong." Another apprentice from that time, Graham Stephens, was indentured to Todd for five years and stayed another seven as a paid lad.

> "I never had any regrets because I was taught properly. It was quite a stern regime. You didn't do things that you shouldn't do. Perfection was just about acceptable. And if it was perfect he had no need to speak to you. He didn't waste time on good mornings. If you went to other stables at the time, you found the lads lived like pigs. At one Ogbourne yard, the [lads slept] in the saddle room under horses' rugs. What we had was Spartan, but it was clean, we had sheets. If you did any job outside your normal duties, you got paid. That didn't happen much in those days. And it was the most wonderful grub house you could imagine.
>
> "I went on to ride work for Sir Gordon Richards for five years, and then for Dick Hern. Wherever I took my CV, people only noticed two words: *George Todd*. Everyone knew that if you'd spent time with George Todd you knew how to do it properly, because you didn't know any other way. I was always pleased I served my time at Manton."

Terry Stringer, who served out his apprenticeship with Todd, rode successfully in Scandinavia, and was then head lad to Peter Makin, says:

> "We were looked after. We went to [the equivalent of] the Palace. I was deferred from the Army, and I reckon I got a better training at Manton. When we went to work in the morning, we'd go through the hatch in the door to the yard, and the old man would be in the window of his house opposite, shaving. There was a light above the hatch, and as he shaved and dressed, he saw who came in and who was early and who was late. It was strict, but later on, I viewed it as a passport. If you rang up for a job anywhere, you'd be asked, 'Where did you serve your apprenticeship?' 'Manton.' 'Start tomorrow'."

Take away the hidings and Todd comes out of his lads' recollections as a good, if fearsome, employer. His staff had clean accommodation and good and plentiful food. They were properly clothed, and paid as well as, or better than, their peers in other yards. If they served out their time with him, it spoke volumes to any other employer.

His concern for his apprentices extended to their spiritual welfare. His father had been a Methodist lay preacher, and despite gambling and a fondness for champagne, George too was a devout man, determined to keep the Lord onside. Once a month, a notice went up in the saddle room reminding the boys that the Reverend May was coming up from Marlborough to the Manton chapel on Sunday evening: '*All apprentices* will *attend*'. They knew that George would dock them a day off, if they were missing. While they waited for the reverend to arrive, the boys wrote their own entreaty:

"O Lord and Father way up there
Who gives each dog his daily dinner
Please listen to our humble prayer
And send George Todd another winner"

Chapter 22

A million-pound paper bag

A lifetime's prayers were answered by Dramatic, a chestnut colt by the miler Fair Trial out of a Hyperion mare. On the last day of the 1947 flat season, Todd was at Manchester, saddling a runner in the November Handicap. Down at Lingfield, Dramatic made his debut in a six furlong maiden plate, finishing eight lengths sixth of 20. The *Sporting Chronicle* race-reader liked the race: 'highly promising' was noted against the second- and third-placed horses. Dramatic attracted the comment, 'great speed for four furlongs.' When Todd had digested the form and his travelling lad's report, he told the horse's lad Bill McCluskey, "He ran really well, you know." Dramatic had taken time to get fit. He was rather a gross horse, and a keen feeder. Joe Lawson walked up to the gallops one morning to watch Dramatic. Todd asked Lawson, "What should I do with him?"

"Get stuck in. Give him plenty of work," was Lawson's advice. After the Lingfield run, Todd knew that he had the formula right, and any amount of potential for the following season. In one of his early gallops as a three-year-old, Dramatic worked with some of the other maidens and an older lead horse. Todd's instructions to the riders were, "Bunch up behind [the lead horse]: if you can go with him, fine." Dramatic picked up the older horse, a reliable handicapper, and finished 10 lengths in front of him. The other three-year-olds were another 10 lengths in arrears.

Todd stood open-mouthed. "Bill, did you start off upsides?" "No, I was at the back." "That's nice," said Todd. Dramatic's first three runs in 1948 were a masterpiece of horse management. Todd did all his own work on the form book and the stable's entries, and he put together a sequence of races which gave the impression that he didn't know Dramatic's best distance. First, he stepped the colt straight up to 10 furlongs at Hurst Park, where he faded in the last three furlongs. Then he ran over an extended mile at Epsom. At the beginning of June, Bill McCluskey rode Dramatic over six furlongs on Clatford downs in a softly-softly trial.

The other horses in the trial were Legal Proof and Happy Knight. Legal Proof had just run second to that year's Lincoln winner. Sir William Cooke's Happy Knight was a 2,000 Guineas winner, no less. He won the 1946 renewal by four lengths in a fast time. He disappointed after that. He was favourite for the Derby but failed to stay or to handle Epsom, after which Cooke moved Happy Knight from Newmarket to Manton. The yard regarded him as a thief at the races, but still a good horse in his home work. He and Dramatic were at level weights in the gallop, which on the weight-for-age scale meant that in effect the maiden Dramatic was giving 5lb to a classic winner. The head lad Bob Shanahan rode Happy Knight. Bill McCluskey was on Dramatic, with instructions from Todd that he was on no account to let the horse off the bridle.

Happy Knight led the gallop from Legal Proof and Dramatic in Indian file. After half a mile, Dramatic went easily past Legal Proof and a furlong later, he joined Happy Knight and finished upside, hard held, as Todd had demanded. Todd usually watched the gallops impassively. The only signs of animation were when he waved a handkerchief above his head to signal the work riders to speed up, or by his knees to slow down. That morning, he ran after Dramatic as McCluskey pulled him up, confirmed with the lad the evidence of his own eyes, and said, "Bill, I think he'll win the Stewards' Cup."

At the time, Dramatic wasn't an assured runner in the big Goodwood handicap. McCluskey had £10 to his name. He went to the bookmaker Ted Gardner in Marlborough. Gardner was a Manton old boy, a former jockey who won the 1922 Oaks on Lord Astor's Pogrom and set himself up as a bookie after retiring from the saddle. He laid McCluskey £330 to £10 against Dramatic for the Stewards' Cup. A few days later, Dramatic ran again at Epsom, this time in a seven furlong maiden. He finished only sixth of 10, beaten five lengths after getting boxed in two furlongs out. Dramatic was now eligible for handicaps, and Todd wasted no time in sending him to Newmarket, where he won over seven furlongs under Gordon Richards. It was his first outing for a senior jockey, and he made all to win by a length. McCluskey had £10 at 4-1 that day, and took his winnings off to Ted Gardner.

With a few quid here and a few more there, at long odds, McCluskey stood to win £1,750 [*almost £42,000*] by the eve of the Stewards' Cup. Todd sent him to Goodwood with his horse. Before the race, Dramatic looked magnificent. His odds in the ring tumbled from 100-6 to 9-1, at which price McCluskey had a final £10 to win. Dramatic was always prominent, led a furlong out and ran on strongly, winning by a length and a half. Audrey Todd let slip some time afterwards that George won £30,000 over the race: *£717,000* today. As for McCluskey, every jockey that the lad saw the following day gave him a tip, and five of them won. He added another £350 to his £1,840 from Dramatic: *£52,300* winnings in two days. McCluskey remembers it with a smile and the assessment that, "Dramatic had 21lb in hand."

That was no exaggeration. The handicapper had allotted Happy Knight 9st 7lb in the Stewards' Cup, 25lb above Dramatic's 7st 10lb. It was just as well for his peace of mind that he didn't know about the gallop in which Dramatic had worked comfortably with Happy Knight at worse than weight for age. It took Ted Gardner a month to pay McCluskey all his winnings, including having to borrow some of the money from Gordon Richards.

Dramatic had one more run that season. He faced just two opponents, one of which, Explorer, had finished third in the Stewards' Cup, running on strongly at the finish. In the rematch, Explorer was 10lb better off for just over two lengths, which in theory entitled him to reverse the form. In practice, Dramatic won again, cosily. Todd then put the colt away for the season, with a date at Lincoln uppermost in his mind.

Timeform hailed Dramatic as, "[A] smart young handicapper at 6f to 7f: landed a gamble in the Stewards' Cup and is ideally suited to 'hammer and tongs' races of this type; no reason to doubt his staying 1m if asked to do so." *Timeform* rated Dramatic the second-fastest three-year-old sprinter of 1948, behind only that year's Nunthorpe winner. Then over the winter, Dramatic suffered a setback. He injured himself when cast in his box and developed arthritis. He was confined to his box for weeks and then just walked quietly over the downs for several more. As the tempo increased, he was even popped over hurdles to give him some variety. In mid-June he made a belated reappearance in the Wokingham, 25-1 and unsighted. It was the same story in the Stewards' Cup at the end of July. Then over a mile at Ascot in September in a field of eight, he showed signs of a return to form, staying on strongly into fourth, just three lengths behind two previous winners.

The front-page headline of *The Sporting Life* on 20 March 1950 read, *'Dramatic landed major Lincoln gamble'*. It was George Todd's day of days. After his injury, Dramatic was never hard trained in 1949. But Todd and his owner Ted Saunders had a sound horse again, he was still well handicapped, and for months he was prepared for one race: the Lincolnshire Handicap, run on the Carholme course at the start of the flat. "We backed him every week, all winter," says John Cherry: "One day a lad came down from Yorkshire with a horse from Bobby Renton's yard. He told us they were going to win the Grand National with Freebooter, so we stuck the two in doubles."

The longest price reported about Dramatic was 25-1. Todd entrusted the commission to Ben Warner's principal putter-on from the Oyster Maid coup, Tommy Westhead. Tommy got started by backing a couple of Grand National winners at long odds. After Oyster Maid and others had set him up, including his own horse Punch in the 1937 Cesarewitch, he used to arrive at the races in some style. A monstrous dove-grey Packard limousine drove into the car park. The chauffeur was Ben Warner's former jumps jockey George Pellerin. He wasn't an obvious choice for a driver: he had a conviction for a spectacular misdemeanour in Marlborough, when he ran into several parked cars and a shop front in the High Street, slurred, "I'm drunk" and fell over. On better-behaved days at the races, he held open the rear door of Westhead's limo. Out stepped Tommy, clad in 1940s gangster chic. If it was at Newbury, he'd join Todd and his inner circle in the paddock bar, and they drank quality champagne together all afternoon.

Three months ahead of the Lincoln, Todd asked Gordon Richards, did he want to ride the winner? A fortnight before the race, Richards broke off from a skiing holiday to partner Dramatic in a trial. With Dramatic in the gallop were Philadelphe II, Clever Joe and a consistent handicapper, Owenclane. Philadelpe II had won five times since the Rosebery three years earlier, and had been beaten only five lengths in the 1949 Lincoln. Clever Joe was one of Todd's beloved old stagers. He ran seven times as a two-year-old, never out of the money and winning three. He won as a four-year-old, twice at six, and once more at seven, over distances from five to 12 furlongs. He couldn't wait to get out of his box every morning, and he was still fast enough to lead anything in the yard.

The gallop that the four horses worked on that morning was an elongated 'U' on the Barton downs, a mile and six furlongs long, with a sharp bottom bend and a copse running up the centre of the 'U'. The mile start was just before the bend. After the horses had negotiated the turn, the gallop led more gently left, before a straight five furlong incline to where Todd stood. As they went down to the start of the gallop on a beautiful spring morning, Gordon Richards told the other lads to slow right down, for fear that the super-fit Dramatic would take off: "If we go any quicker I won't be able to hold him." The head lad Bob Shanahan was at the start. He asked, "All right, Gordon?" Richards nodded. Shanahan dropped his flag.

To his horror, Dramatic was left a dozen lengths as Albert Tucker on Owenclane led the four horses to the turn and out of Shanahan's sight. Philadelpe II had taken it up as the trial reached the final, straight portion of the gallop. There, bucking and squealing, waited Clever Joe under another apprentice, David Churchley. His orders were, "Jump in ahead of them and go like hell." Two furlongs from Todd, Churchley heard Dramatic coming to him: "Gordon had a double handful as he went past me. Here's me niggling, he was on the bridle. 'Cheerio,' he called, and he was gone. I thought, there's a winner." Dramatic beat Clever Joe by three lengths, hard held, with another three lengths back to Philadelphe II. Going back to the yard, George was quivering. When he saw Shanahan, he exclaimed, "I've never seen a horse finish a gallop faster than that." Shanahan, who saw only the first furlong of the trial, with Dramatic some way in arrears, asked, "Which horse was that?" "Why, Dramatic, of course!"

Shanahan told him about Dramatic's slow start, and called Tucker over to confirm it. It's likely that Todd already knew: that to put the most extreme question to Dramatic, he'd instructed Richards to dally, telling no one else. It's hard to imagine the multiple champion jockey giving apprentices a start by accident. Dramatic's owner Ted Saunders had a question: "I suppose all we're worried about now is the draw, George?" "The draw?" roared Todd: "He can be drawn in China! He'll still win." As it happened, Dramatic had a good draw on the Carholme, but the way he won, he could indeed have prevailed from anywhere on the course. At the finish, Gordon was easing down and looking round, three lengths clear. The second horse, itself clear of the remainder, was Fair Judgement, who'd won the race the previous year as a strong favourite.

What a trial Todd had set up. In the 1949 Lincoln, Philadelphe II finished five lengths behind Fair Judgement, receiving 6lb. The following year, Fair Judgement was 13lb worse off with Philadelphe II and was set to carry 8st 13lb, level weights with Dramatic. Todd would have calculated that against a seasoned handicapper like Fair Judgement, he needed Dramatic to be a stone in front of Philadelphe II at home. In the trial, Dramatic had pulverised Philadelphe II, very likely giving him two stones and more. What the weights were in the gallop, only Todd and Shanahan knew. In his key trials, Todd used saddles of varying weights to gauge the merits of his horses' work. One can only record that in those days Gordon couldn't get below 8st 3lb, and he had 6lb of lead in his saddle in the gallop: Tucker on Clever Joe and Churchley on Philadelphe II were both about 6st wet through. And for good measure, Dramatic had given his galloping companions a long lead.

The veteran racing reporter Quentin Gilbey wrote in the *Sporting Chronicle* that,

> "I have never seen a race of a mile, in which a big field went to post, won such a long way from home. Before they had gone halfway, although he was not actually in front at the time, it was obvious that Dramatic was cantering over his rivals and that the race was over bar the shouting."

Todd had a few palpitations. He couldn't get onto the stand to watch the race, and, tall as he was, all he could see over the crowd was a white cap coming home alone: "I prayed it was *our* white cap." The post-race quotes were short and to the point. Gordon Richards said, "He gave me a grand ride and was never off the bit." Todd proclaimed that, "Dramatic is a racehorse today for the first time in his life." Saunders thanked the Manton vet. The gamble that *The Sporting Life* headlined had been in the making for many weeks. *The Times* noted in early February that, "Dramatic is increasing steadily in favour for the Lincolnshire Handicap. On Saturday, the odds offered against him were only 8-1, after 20-1 had been taken to substantial amounts a fortnight earlier." Four days later *The Sporting Life* exclaimed, "Money talks! [The] support accorded to Dramatic… has been so sustained that layers are disinclined to trade further. There has been no real money for any beyond Dramatic... heavily backed from 25-1."

Dramatic started at 7-1 second favourite on the Carholme. Tommy Westhead had worked the stable commission long before the race. That didn't stop him striking again after Dramatic's sensational final trial. Eight days before the Lincoln, he waded into one of the big rails bookmakers during a humdrum jumps meeting at Hurst Park. The result was that

Dramatic was briefly advanced to clear favourite, and the bookmaker was left, effectively, bankrupt. He stayed in business only because Westhead let him pay in extended instalments.

A few days after the Lincoln, Jack King drove Todd up to London. On the seat between them was a paper bag. It contained £47,000 in cash. It isn't known how Tattersalls' chief cashier Jack Knight reacted to the *£1,060,000* deposit. They didn't have money-laundering laws in those days. Still, it can't have been an everyday transaction. George Todd had paid the balance outstanding on Manton in one hit, thanks to Dramatic. Audrey was appalled that, "George didn't even bother to get out of the car." But any visitor to Manton House could see Dramatic's place in the Todd hall of fame: a half-life-sized portrait photograph of the colt hung in the hallway at the bottom of the stairs. To show George's priorities, an original Munnings oil painting given to him by a grateful owner was housed in the downstairs lavatory.

Not long after the Lincoln, Freebooter won the Grand National, to bring off the Manton lads' spring doubles. A couple of them won close to £800 (*£18,000*) each. John Hislop wrote in an obituary of Todd that he was, 'A cool, fearless bettor'; in the same piece, he recorded that, 'His horses were never tried at home.' The claim was nonsense. There are apprentices and paid lads who remember today the trials that Hislop himself rode in. When the money was down, Todd needed to know the time of day. And though George was a fearless bettor, he wasn't a cool one. For every masterclass like Dramatic's Lincoln, there was a sharp setback, sometimes several. It wasn't long after Dramatic's win that he heaved £5,000 onto a sprinter called Ulster Friar in a handicap at Kempton. It could only finish third. Over his lifetime, Todd came out far ahead of the bookmakers, but there were some hair-raising passages along the way. He liked to go racing even if he didn't have a runner, he liked to drink champagne, and, surrounded as he was by other gambling trainers and their punters, he bet on other people's horses. That doesn't usually work, and it didn't for George.

Kenneth Mackenzie says, "If he'd stuck to his own horses he would've been a very rich man. As it was, he was making a good living for the professionals like Alec Bird and Billy Carter." Todd wasn't a value punter, either. He'd happily lay long odds on a presumed certainty. Noel Murless started training at Beckhampton at about the same time as George at Manton, and they became close friends. If they both had runners in the same race, they talked it over beforehand. One day at Salisbury, Todd had a moderate two-year-old in a maiden event; Murless was running a much-touted debutant for the King. After looking at the rest of a small field in the paddock, Todd decided that His Majesty's horse only had to go down and come back. He piled in at odds as short as 1-8. The second favourite was 16-1. The Manton 'not expected,' Persian Lord, was 33-1. There was an anxious moment when it seemed to be going at least as well as the Murless horse, but a pull from its jockey ensured that Persian Lord stayed anchored in second place.

Todd convinced himself that Persian Lord was a winner waiting to happen. He ran it twice more that season, each time down the field. On its three-year-old debut off a low weight in a Bath handicap, Persian Lord was the subject of a huge gamble, from 100-8 down to 4-1. To Todd's horror, the horse ran wide off the home turn, wouldn't go through with an effort, and finished well beaten.

One day at Chester in the 1960s, Todd laid 1-14 - £14,000 to win £1,000 – in a two-horse race. It looked a formality. The favourite had run third in the Queen Anne at Royal Ascot. Its opponent had been thrashed in a maiden race at Lanark. The good thing duly won as it pleased, netting George the equivalent today of *£12,000* for his *£168,000* staked. Time was, a number of high rollers used to bet all Gordon Richards' short-priced rides to win a specified sum, say £1,000. If Gordon was riding a 2-1 chance, the bet was £500. One of Todd's later owners, Radha Sigtia, used to stake to win £5,000. Enthusiasm for the system evaporated the day that Gordon rode a 1-25 shot, which whipped round at the start and lost any chance of winning. It left the 'to win £1,000' investors £25,000 out of pocket, and underlined the truth of the old saying that a racing certainty isn't the same as a certainty.

Betting *£168,000* to win *£12,000* isn't for the faint-hearted. George Todd punted as opportunity presented, and certainly not always at short odds. One of his coups with Horace Lester was in a 25-runner three-year-old maiden at Salisbury with a horse called Gala Performance. Its only previous run was seventh of nine, beaten 10 lengths and more, but it was working promisingly at home. Lester worked a commission of £500 each way off course for himself and Todd. Gala Performance was returned at 25-1 and won easing down by four lengths. Todd and Lester divided close to *£300,000.* They were so carried away that they next ran Gala

Performance in Pinza's Derby, where not surprisingly it was unsighted. It then went back to Epsom and won the Diomed Stakes: not a bad tool for a punt in a midweek maiden. On the evening after Gala Performance's first win, another of Todd's owners was staying at Manton. He'd been kept in blissful ignorance. Stacking plates in the kitchen, George told Audrey, "I had it off today – but don't you bloody well look pleased when you go back into the dining room!"

"In the early days it was just a matter of knowing when they were 'off'," says John Cherry. Kenneth MacKenzie confirms, "For the first 10 years that I trained with George, if he said to me, 'Go and back this, it'll win,' it won all right." Once the penny dropped, inside the racing community and outwards to the betting public, everyone wanted a friend at Manton. John Claydon, who was Todd's farm bailiff in the early 1950s, would fall into conversation with strangers in Marlborough: "You went for a drink and there was sure to be someone who'd heard who you were and came up and wanted to talk about the stables. You said what a wonderful place it was and of course that wasn't what they wanted to know at all!"

There were curious eyes in the weighing room, too. George Duffield, who was then an apprentice at Jack Waugh's yard in Newmarket, was offered a ride on Kenneth Mackenzie's Picture Boy. He was approached by Bruce Raymond, a senior jockey. Raymond told him that he'd watched Picture Boy having a quiet run. "The horse could've won a minute [last time]. If you're 'off' today, you'll win." Duffield replied, "If I find out it's trying I'll make a thing of pulling my boots up in the paddock."

"Todd gave me his instructions. They began, 'Just track the leaders' and they ended, 'You'll win.' So I pulled up my boots and Bruce backed it." Sure enough, it won. Eric Campbell was another apprentice to be watched closely. He'd been riding a hurdler called Valley Sun in its 'prep' races, first in one of those big-field Newbury novice hurdles where starters in the pre-camera days are supposed to have called, 'Triers at the front, the rest of you behind.' Valley Sun was in the group behind. A week later, he was dropped into a seller at Kempton and remained at the back. "I had the usual instructions in the paddock, 'Drop him out.' He wasn't really fit, we were just schooling him," says Campbell. Back at Newbury for another seller, Todd decided to find out a little more about Valley Sun. He told Campbell to wait until after the last flight of hurdles in the back straight and then wake his horse up. To Campbell's horror – "I'm in queer street here," he thought - Valley Sun picked up his bit and took off, to such effect that he turned for home in third place and stayed there.

"Why didn't you drop it out?" demanded Todd. "The whole world would've seen, Sir." One who did see was the top hurdles rider Johnny Gilbert. Not long after, Valley Sun ran in a handicap for the first time. "Hey, you" called Gilbert across the weighing room: "You'll win, won't you?" "You know the guv'nor as well as I do. I'll be the last to know," Campbell mumbled. "You should've been hung at Newbury," Gilbert told him: "Anyone could see what was happening." The payday came two runs later at Warwick when another claimer, Ron Cartwright, took the ride. It was one of Todd's favoured tactics when the money was down. If the stewards showed interest in a sudden improvement in form, then the horse had responded to the change of jockey. Valley Sun was backed from 12-1 to 11-2, led two out and won easily. Todd saw Eric Campbell in the yard and asked him over to help in the feed house. Todd held out a clenched fist and said, "There's yours." It was £25 [*£400*] to reward Campbell for the part he'd played in setting up Valley Sun for the coup.

Valley Sun unfolded with happy predictability. Occasionally, though, there was a derailment: persons known or unknown got the price before Todd did. When that happened, vengeance was swift. Even his own punters skated on thin ice, never more so than on the day at Brighton when a filly of Radha Sigtia's called Akash Wani had been set aside for a gamble. All the Manton lads were on. Several of George's familiars turned up at the seaside – Alec Bird, Tom Degg, the sharply dressed Joe Allmark. The apprentice John Friar was getting his final words in the paddock when an anxious commission agent joined them. "The price has gone, George," he told Todd. What had briefly been 10-1 was now 4-1, even shorter to a decent bet.

Todd seethed. The plan changed abruptly. "You don't win anything today," he spat at Friar: "Bloody Alec Bird. He's had the price." The putter-on pointed out, reasonably enough, that, "They've had their money on." "Bugger them. They can lose it." Which they did. Todd had an enlarged lobe on his right ear that went red when he was angry. That day it was scarlet as he tugged at it. Word of the paddock scene spread quickly to the betting ring, where Akash Wani did an about turn and drifted to 8-1. John Friar followed his revised instructions. His filly dwelt and then ran on late without getting near the leaders. The next morning, Todd lined up the apprentices and paid lads to remind them of the pecking order: "Do you little bastards think you're smarter than me? Well, you found out yesterday that you're not!"

On other days, the lads got their money on without denting the price, as Bill McLuskey managed with Dramatic, and without alerting all the punters who followed the yard. Paul Cole remembers, "It was all gambling. Todd gambled. The lads gambled. Everyone was punting in Marlborough. All the [Jeremy] Tree lads [at Beckhampton]. Me, to a tiny extent." Terry Stringer walked in on John Cherry and Graham Stephens one day when they were 'having a roll call.' "I'd never seen so much money in my life. There were bundles of notes all over the bed, big white fivers. I was sworn to secrecy." Cherry had been having a bad run. He borrowed £10, put it on a short-priced favourite that won, and in not much more than a month he ran it up to £1,000. "When I got married, every stick of furniture in the house had a horse's name on it," he says.

Apart from the 'specials' board in the feed house, the gallops provided their own clues to alert lads. Stringer had his first bet long before his first ride in public. It was late autumn. Captain Nelson sent some horses over from Lambourn to work at Manton. Among them was a fancied November Handicap outsider. Todd provided a lead horse, Pelota. He'd been culled from a Newmarket yard after a moderate first season. Todd proceeded to win a race or two a season with the horse, including a Birmingham seller when he was backed from 10-1 to 100-30. Stringer says,

> "Before the gallop with Nelson's horses, Todd came to Pelota's box and told me, 'Lead them a good sensible pace. Then halfway up the straight when they come to you, let them go. Do you understand? I don't want any mistakes. Let them go.' So I led these horses, [one of them] fancied to win the November Handicap. They came to me as he said they would, I took a pull and I finished three lengths behind them: I haven't come off the bridle."

Stringer found out that Pelota was going to run in a seller at Manchester. He didn't have any money, so he told a friend about the gallop. The friend had £5 on for each of them. "This is the first bet of my life. All morning I'm thinking to myself, if this gets beat, I'm broke for months. I couldn't eat my lunch. I ran to the phone box and called the bookie: 'What's won the first at Manchester?'" The answer was, Pelota by six lengths at 9-2. Stringer was on five shillings a week at the time, so he'd won over 18 months' wages.

"I'm away! I ran back to the dining room and had two portions of spotted dick to make up for what I couldn't eat before. Of course I never said a word." But there were all the times that he and others backed one of their rides before leaving for the races, got into the paddock, and found from Todd that their mount wasn't 'off' that day. However, Stringer got it right more often than not: he'd put by £2,800, not far off *£40,000* today, when he came out of his Manton apprenticeship, aged 22.

Occasionally, a horse won on the wrong day. The Marlborough bookie Ted Gardner's son Vic was an apprentice at Manton. He had the leg up at Bath on an unraced and unfancied two-year-old of Sidney Banks's called Piranha. At the post, Piranha was keen to be on his way, the starter didn't let them go, and the horse backed into the tapes. When they eventually started, Piranha showed good early speed. He was travelling smoothly behind the leaders as the field reached the kink in the Bath straight. The leaders veered off the rails, providing Piranha with irresistible daylight. Vic Gardner describes the outcome: "He shot through like a rocket. We got up on the line to win." At the finish, Gardner was standing up like a cavalry officer, desperately trying to subdue Piranha, but failing.

The apprentice was the object of intense suspicion. The marks on the horse's quarters from the starting tape made it look as if Vic had been busy with his whip. Worse, one of Vic's relatives joked to Todd that the various bookmakers in the Gardner family had enjoyed a good touch at Piranha's returned SP of 20-1. Gardner winces: "To have said I was out of favour would've been the understatement of the year." He put as much distance as possible between himself and a tricky situation. He answered an advertisement for a retainer in Pakistan, where he rode for an expatriate trainer who downed rivers of gin, assuring Gardner that, "You have to drink plenty of alcohol to kill the bugs". When Vic came back to England, all had long been forgiven. Todd welcomed him back, and he rode some of the top horses that came to Manton in the early 1960s. Later, Gardner took over his father's betting shop in Marlborough High Street, but he was too kind-hearted for his own good. One afternoon Bob Turnell's lads were in his shop with some good things to bet on. They lost everything they had. Vic felt sorry for them and gave them their money back: "Not the sort of thing a bookmaker does."

Todd himself might not have wanted to be described as 'kind-hearted', but, quite apart from the presents that he gave to any lad who helped with an important winner, he was remarkably tolerant of anyone who showed a glimmer of redemption. Not only did he take Vic Gardner back after his spell lying low in Pakistan. When the day came that Gardner decided to leave Manton for good, he had several hundred pounds owed to him in riding fees and winning percentages. As the employer of an apprentice, Todd was entitled to keep half. Instead, remembers Gardner, "He just said, 'You might as well have it all.' He didn't deduct anything."

Another apprentice, Dickie Bates, began with Todd at West Ilsley and moved with him to Manton. The day came when he'd had enough. He stole away home to Derby and found work in the mines An apprentice breaking his indentures laid himself open to be blacklisted from any job in racing. Months passed, and he decided that the open spaces of the downs were a nicer workplace, after all. He wrote to Todd asking if he could come back to Manton? Todd replied, 'Yes, of course.'

Sixty years later, Dickie Bates said that if he could have his time all over again, it would still be with Todd. On his first ride back, his instructions were as if he'd never been away: "Jump off, keep her in the middle, make a bit of a show at the end." At the unsaddling, he told Todd excitedly, "I could just about have won, Sir!" "Shhh. You'll get me shot."

Chapter 23

Boys and old boys

Despite Dramatic's life-changing wins in the Stewards' Cup and Lincoln, George Todd was happiest training stayers. "I do prefer long-distance horses. I've always thought [staying races] are so much easier to win. So few people concentrate on them." The archetype of a Todd winner was an older horse, running in a handicap, at or beyond a mile and a half, carrying plenty of market support, ridden by an apprentice. He had sound reasons for putting boys up on his runners. He hated horses to be whipped, including when he backed them. He preferred them to lose without whipping than win after taking a thrashing. Terry Stringer won one of Todd's favourite races, the Steve Donoghue Apprentices' handicap at Epsom, beating John Friar into second.

> "There was a picture in *The Sporting Life* of me winning. The next day Todd called us both over to the feed house. He showed the photo to John. You could see his stick up and his horse's ears flat. 'Look at this. Bloody disgrace! He's hating every moment.' I'm thinking, it isn't me he wants, I've got away with this. Then he pulled out another photo and he said to me, 'What the fucking hell do you think you were doing?' Where he got the new picture from, God only knows. It was taken from further down the course. I've gone for my stick, my arse is screwed completely off the horse's back. So he gave us both a real dressing-down. I'd ridden about seven winners in the fortnight before and I was thinking I was King Dick. After that I felt pretty small."

Todd also believed that his apprentices were more likely to obey orders than an outside rider. He didn't trust most senior jockeys. A well-fancied stable hope bit the dust one day, with conspicuous lack of urging from the saddle. As he was leaving the racecourse, Todd remembered that he'd left his raincoat in the weighing room. When he retraced his steps, he came across the jockey deep in conversation with a bookmaker. He once praised Gordon Richards, apparently without irony, as being, "Straight as a die;

he'll stop one if you ask him." George thought that senior jockeys would stop one when they hadn't been asked, and that most of them had their own punters to look after.

His homegrown boys did as they were instructed. Most of the time, it was, "Drop it out." Terry Stringer was told,

> "Where to be, what to do, even what to say if anything went wrong. If we were hauled in by the stewards, I'd been primed. I stopped horses for [as long as] two years. I stopped [Tommy Frost's] Tarquinian so many times I wondered, 'What day is this horse ever going to try?' Eventually George took him to Windsor for a seller and he says, 'Kick on at the furlong pole. It doesn't really matter how far you win, but try not to win too far.' If you could be anywhere near where he told you in a race, you won, and you knew a long way from home that's how it would unfold."

Tarquinian was a tiny horse, bought by Tommy Frost as a yearling for £470. Most unusually for Todd, Tarquinian ran eight times as a two-year-old, all unplaced. He had three more unplaced outings early the following season, then vanished for four months before reappearing in a selling handicap at Windsor. It was a perfect day for a coup: the Friday of Aintree's November meeting, with the eyes of the racing press and public on the Grand Sefton chase. There were seven runners in Tarquinian's race. Only one of them was below him in the weights. The trap was set. There was a huge gamble on Tommy Frost's horse, from 8-1 co-fifth favourite to 11-4 clear favourite, with the blower joining in. *The Sporting Life* betting report read, "A little 8-1, 6-1 and 5-1 was snapped up over Tarquinian, confidently backed at all rates to 11-4 tip-top." The paper's reporter noted that while Todd told him that Tarquinian had been difficult to train, he nonetheless went to *£9,800* to retain the horse at the auction. Terry Stringer surpassed his instructions. He led over a furlong out and kept the winning margin to a comfortable length.

Tarquinian landed another touch in a Salisbury seller the following season and won again back at Windsor, bought in each time. A year later, to underline what a weapon he'd been in those poor contests, he went on to win three staying handicaps under Stringer, including when bolting up in the Newbury Autumn Cup. After the race Todd called him, "[The] most genuine horse I've ever trained; game, genuine and kind and [he] doesn't mind what the going's like." Perhaps for the benefit of any listening stewards, he added, "As there weren't enough suitable sellers I put him in a gallop one day and found he stayed better than I thought". Clearly, it wasn't just his apprentices who had post-race quotes prepared in advance. After the Autumn Cup, Tarquinian became a screen star. Wills cigarettes got hold of a film of the horse winning easily, ears pricked, for all the world like a champion, and used it in a TV advertisement.

The subsequent plan for Tarquinian was the following season's Cesarewitch. Frost went for one of his biggest wins, from 33-1 downwards. The Australian jockey Ron Hutchinson was engaged, he of the distinctive bobbing in the saddle. He got boxed in. Tarquinian was flying at the finish, beaten only two lengths in fourth. Afterwards Hutchinson apologised and told Frost, "I totally goofed it."

George's plots didn't always have a happy ending like Tarquinian's win at Windsor. The apprentice Glyn Foster used to be told, 'Stay on the rails and don't pass anything.' "One season I rode over 30 horses on the trot that weren't trying." He was the rider when one of George's plots backfired horribly. Paul Cole introduced a new owner, Bob Heaton. Foster rode his horse Major Rose four times, and each time it was an 'easy.' In April in a 27-runner maiden at Newbury, Major Rose started at 33-1 and made late headway into sixth: 'never nearer.' At Bath, the horse was third and attracted the form book comment: "Seventh straight, ran on, too much to do." At Salisbury in June, Major Rose made, "Some late headway, no danger." Finally at Windsor it was never nearer than sixth.

Heaton cornered Foster and said, "You've ridden my horse and given him easy races. You could've won every time." Without breathing space to collect his thoughts, Foster blurted out the truth: "Look, Mr Heaton, as long as it doesn't get back to Mr Todd I'll tell you. [He'll] keep that horse for two seasons if he wants to, until he thinks the time's right to have his money on it. Then, in the horse will go." Heaton wasn't putting up with that, and he took Major Rose away forthwith.

The horse went first to Keith Piggott, winning immediately, and ended up with Captain Ryan Price, where to rub salt in Todd's wounds the horse won the Chester Cup and Cesarewitch. Later, it finished second in a Champion Hurdle. There was a prolonged, tense silence at Manton over Major Rose. Like the war, he was best not mentioned. Glyn Foster is probably right to conclude that if his part in Major Rose's removal had got back to Todd, "I'd never have had another ride."

A benefit of Todd's regular use of apprentices was that a horse ridden by an unknown claimer attracted less attention than one piloted by a top jockey. Before one fancied ride, Vic Gardner was told that if anyone asked what chance his mount had, he should reply: "If it had any, Scobie [Breasley] would be riding it." Sometimes the boys made mistakes, or in a close finish, they might lose out to a stronger, senior rider. Todd was philosophical: the benefits of using his apprentices far outweighed the occasional slip-up. He looked after them, but he never developed them into jockeys.

He said, "Trainers don't have time to train lads," and called for an apprentice academy paid for by the Levy Board. His apprentices were at Manton to work. If they rode well they had opportunities on the racecourse and if they obeyed instructions, they were given more rides. But his interest in them was confined to their claims, and he saw each claim as his personal possession. He had no intention of frittering it away on other trainers' winners.

Terry Stringer signed on for five years. At the end, he still had five or six winners to go before he lost his allowance, so he stayed for two more years. "If I'd done what kids at other yards were allowed to do, I'd have lost my claim in two years, but Todd wouldn't allow me to take outside rides. Many times at the races, I stood in the stands and trainers came up and said, 'I rang you to ride one for me in this race and your guv'nor said you weren't available.' I had to accept that was the way it was. He wasn't the sort of man you could go to and say, 'Hey, you're messing up my career'."

Glyn Foster remembers, 'The biggest winner I should've ridden.' Major Lionel Holliday, the leading owner of the time, asked Foster to ride his horse Avon's Pride in the Cesarewitch. "I said, 'Yes, but you'll have to verify it with Mr Todd, because he doesn't let us book our own rides.' I saw the Major again and he said, 'It's all right, I've had a word with Mr Todd.' "About a week before the race, Mr Todd called me into the office and he said, 'You know the ride you had in the Cesarewitch?' 'Yes, guv'nor.' 'Well, you haven't. I've told Major Holliday that you can't ride for him because I need you at home to ride work.'" Avon's Pride won.

The following season, Todd's and Holliday's paths crossed again, when one of George's old geldings, Badmash, was sold for a surprising *£15,500* after winning at Kempton. The incident is described in Peter Willett's biography of Dick Hern. Hern had been looking for a horse to lead work for Holliday's Derby favourite, Hethersett:

"[Hern was] at Kempton when Holliday announced, 'I've got you a lead horse'. It was the seven-year-old Badmash, whom he had bought for 1,050 guineas after he had won the selling handicap. Dick was horrified. Badmash was trained by George Todd, who loved his old platers and kept them going for years, and it was tacitly accepted that nobody bid for them. Dick hastened to see George, explained what had happened and said that he had not even known that [Holliday] was bidding. George was unforgiving. 'Well', he said, 'when Major Holliday dies there will be no need for them to put, 'No flowers by request', because he won't get any fucking flowers'."

Although Todd had the consolation of a good bet on Badmash, including £100 for John Cherry, Holliday's intervention rankled for some time. "The bastard's got 70 horses of his own," he growled: "Why does he need one of mine?"

Kenneth Mackenzie knew a few things about man management from his retail business. He says of Todd's pupil-assistants, "Only Cole and Haslam of those who came in wanting to be trainers stuck it out. George didn't take the trouble to teach [the assistants]. It was a great pity, because his methods were so much better than the average trainer of his time." His remark applies with equal force to the boys. Few senior jockeys emerged from Todd apprenticeships. Among them were Tommy Carter and Terry Stringer. Carter cottoned on quicker than most to Todd's lack of plans for his youngsters. He told Stringer, "You make what you can, because as soon as your claim's gone you'll be finished." Sure enough, by the end of Stringer's time, he was in demand to ride work for several other local trainers. Todd called him in and said, "Young man, you seem to be spending a lot of time riding work for other people. Perhaps you'd better find yourself another job."

Todd preferred animals to people. He treated his boys and his paid lads well enough, but that had an element of self-interest. Well-fed and well-clothed staff would do a better job around his horses than hungry wretches in rags. His affection for animals was all-embracing. With the possible exception of rabbits and moles, George Todd loved all God's creatures. He took after his father Richard, who despite butchering pigs was devoted to them. Long into retirement, he kept a few sows on his allotment. During the Horncastle floods of 1953, he was found sitting in a sty in 18 inches of water, chatting to his pigs to comfort them.

Todd's love of his old horses showed in the doting retirements that he gave to them. "They lived the life of absolute Reilly," says Patrick Haslam:

"There were about six of them that had been retired for years, turned out in fields. We used to get them in every night and they had a lovely hot mash." Another sign of George's love of his horses was that he wouldn't train steeplechasers. He certainly bet on them: he liked to watch the field cross the first few fences of a 'chase, decide which had settled into the best jumping rhythm, and then bet in running. But he only ever had one runner over fences, and that was because Jack King had a horse on his farm that he was sure would make a great 'lepper', if only Todd would train it. King pestered, the token run took place, the horse flopped and Todd said, 'Never again.' He hated to see horses injured, and that prejudiced him against 'chasing. It followed that he didn't like hunting, yet he had owners who were keen huntsmen and women.

Todd used to walk the gallops diligently before his horses worked. If he found a lark's nest, he marked it so that the riders passed it safely by. His gallops man noticed a wren's nest in a hurdle. When Todd found out, nothing was allowed to jump the obstacle until the last fledgling had flown. He had the same zero enthusiasm for shooting as he did for hunting. Jack King was given the rights over Manton, but George insisted that only the best shots were invited: he didn't want to find wounded birds the next day.

In the yard, before evening stables, there was the ritual of feeding the cats. When George banged the tin, hardened mousers rushed to him from every corner. At his back door, it was the pheasants' turn, chuck-chucking over their corn.

One day when the keeper caught a badger, Todd was appalled: had it suffered? What would happen to its young? When a suspected rabid dog ran loose in Marlborough, all anyone in the town could think of was to rush up to Manton and ask Todd to come quickly, 'Because you're so good with animals.' Driving to the races, usually late, Todd added more delay if he saw a starved-looking horse in a field; he invariably noted the details to report to the RSPCA.

To complete the Manton menagerie, the Todds always had two dogs around the yard, an Airedale for George and a Cairn for Audrey. When one of them died, Todd buried it with full honours next to Gay Crusader and Lemberg. George told a lad to fetch a rug to wrap the departed. The lad came back with the oldest rug he could find. George sent him back: only a brand new rug would do.

At the heart of Todd's animal kingdom were what Dick Hern had called, 'George's old platers.' Todd could see unrealised, distant potential in the most unlikely of horses and he had the patience of Job. In the twilight of Todd's career, a reporter asked him to name the best horses he'd trained. He insisted on adding his *favourite* horses.

They're nowhere to be found in jockeys' memoirs or annual 'best of' lists. They were all geldings; they often raced to the veteran stage; he owned or had a share in most of them; and they were mostly stayers. When some veteran had been forgotten for so long that anyone giving it a thought would assume it was dead, it would pop up at Bath or Salisbury with a boy on board, and win. The favourites that he named included Blazing Scent, Bradfield, Caught Out and Penharbour.

Blazing Scent's haphazard conception is described in a hilarious chapter of Michael Pope's memoirs, *All Such Fun*. The sire was a moderate sprinter, Blason. The dam, 'Had nothing to recommend her as a broodmare.' The mating was forgotten when, a couple of years later, a friend asked Pope if he'd be interested in a Blason yearling, 'Looking for a good home and a hundred quid.' Pope found him in a field with some cattle: "A pathetic-looking article. Very small, narrow, no bone, light in condition." Nothing that happened at home improved the outlook.

Pope concluded that the horse was either useless or bone idle. The jockey Greville Starkey suggested blinkers. Blazing Scent made his debut in a Nottingham seller. Pope recalled it: "Blazing Scent was soon in arrears, with Greville booting and scrubbing but going nowhere. As a last resort, he gave him one slap. Whoosh! The horse took off and flew past the field."

By chance, some of the sharpest eyes on the racecourse were at Nottingham that day. Alec Bird clocked a much faster time than he expected for a seller. He advised two fellow professionals, the Todd owners Billy Ball and Billy Carter, to buy the horse. Off went Blazing Scent to Manton. He was buried in midfield in a couple of non-sellers. Dropped back to selling company, he won by six lengths. Then Ball and Carter fell out and the horse went to another of the yard's owners, the farmer Bob Capon. There were two more quiet runs in nursery handicaps and then Capon and Todd put on their betting boots. On the last day of the season at Manchester, Blazing Scent was rushed in from 5-1 to 7-4 favourite and drew steadily clear in the last furlong.

As a four-year-old, Blazing Scent won handicaps at Kempton and Ascot, a heavily-backed favourite each time. Aged five, he began with a disappointing run in a big field at Newbury. That led to his being ignored at 25-1 in the Victoria Cup, where he flew home in the last furlong and nosed ahead on the line. Todd called it, "The biggest shock I've ever had. Of all the horses I've trained, this little chap is the most surprising. I didn't think he was capable of running such a race." In the next two seasons, Blazing Scent won at Goodwood and Epsom. At nine, he inspired John Lawrence [later Lord Oaksey] to describe an ordinary Newmarket handicap in his *Horse and Hound* column:

> "Having, as usual, been last for more than half a mile, the old so and so came scampering up the wide outside to [win by] half a length. If ever I saw a horse who knew what he was doing, this was the one. As he passed the leaders, his wise old head was cocked sideways watching them and if a horse's face could show emotion his, I'm prepared to bet, would have worn a smug smile of unconcealed delight. By far the most important quality in a racehorse is invisible. After 48 races, 7 seasons and 11 victories, Blazing Scent still has that priceless quality intact. You can give it any name you please: guts, honesty, ambition or just the will to win."

'Old so and so' was right. He was sometimes savage. He chased one of Todd's assistants up into his manger and trapped him there. Blazing Scent epitomised Todd's ability to keep horses interested for season after season, and every now and then, usually when wanted, they would win. Todd trained a contemporary of Blazing Scent for Bob Capon, with the same longevity: he was called I Claudius. He was offered to Todd by Noel Murless. He had very small feet, and needed firm ground. He ran 45 times over 10 seasons, winning just the once, every year. Sir Peter O'Sullevan said of Todd, "I admired enormously his gift for having horses right at the right time. George had a target every year. They didn't always win, but they were right on the day. He could bring a horse into bloom like a hardy annual."

In Todd's handling of I Claudius, 'the day' was usually the Trundle Stakes handicap at Glorious Goodwood. It was Todd's favourite meeting. He used to stay the week in some style with Tommy Frost and his family at a rented house, or at the Metropole in Brighton. To pay the expenses, he always laid out one or two of his horses for the meeting. Kenneth Mackenzie believes that the outcomes would decide, as often as not, whether George had a winning or losing year. One less than glorious year, "He'd expected three or four winners, and didn't have one. He'd said before the meeting that he wasn't going to Epsom on the Saturday, but on the way home he asked me if I'd drive him there: 'I have to find out how much I owe that bookmaker'."

One of Sir William Cooke's horses provided another Sussex day that didn't go entirely to plan. He had a handicapper called Wheatley, a one-time strong fancy for the Triumph Hurdle. Todd had set Wheatley aside for one of the handicaps. Sir William was deaf and not very mobile. He couldn't cope with all the stages of attending the saddling, going to the paddock, visiting the Ring and then getting up into the stands. He hobbled to the edge of the paddock and came up short. He called out, "George! George!" Todd beckoned him into the paddock. Cooke continued to call to him. A crowd of amused and curious racegoers watched. Todd relented and joined his owner: "All I want to know, George, is will he win?" Todd was torn between speaking loudly enough for Cooke to hear, and sufficiently quietly to keep his message private.

Red-faced, he muttered, "He has a good chance, Sir William," which cued a stampede to the bookmakers, with Cooke tottering on behind as fast as he could manage. Alas, Wheatley fly-jumped on his way to the start, unshipped his jockey, galloped all the way up the straight and back, ran up Trundle Hill, unfenced in those days, and then shot up the straight again. He delayed the start by half an hour before being caught and withdrawn, the bets and the paddock-side whispers to no avail.

I Claudius first ran in, and won, the Trundle Stakes as a four-year-old under Ron Hutchinson. The following year he was second. Four years went by and I Claudius made no show at Epsom in April, went missing until Goodwood in August, and, again ridden by Hutchinson, he dotted up in the Trundle. He wasn't a reliable horse for punting. His first win was a banner day, when Todd and Capon backed him from 100-7 to 9-1 at Kempton. But in the same season, two big gambles went astray on him. Another time he was heavily supported, only to be run over by a horse belonging to Todd's sometime owner Tom Degg and trained by Todd's good friend Towser Gosden. Things were quiet between the trio afterwards. I Claudius had one last go at the Trundle, unplaced as a 10-year-old, after which he went back to Bob Capon's farm with Blazing Scent for a happy retirement.

I Claudius's costly collision with a fancied horse of Gosden's was unusual. During the long years of his climb through the training ranks, Todd got to know which of his fellow trainers liked a bet. Once a friendship was formed, it was only natural that if he and the other trainer had horses running in the same race, they found out each other's plans before risking their money. Terry Stringer rode Todd's regular selling-plate winner Badmash in a race where his instructions were, 'Not today,' and watched on from midfield as a Gosden runner landed a punt. "I could have won that," he told Todd at the unsaddling: "I know," said George.

Towser Gosden was one of Todd's closest trainer friends. If the gallops at Lewes became rock hard in high summer, he sent his horses to work at Manton. Among them was Aggressor, who won the 1960 King George VI and Queen Elizabeth Stakes. Gosden trained many a winner for those titanic punters Alec Bird and Tom Degg, and it was said of him that one flat season he put his own money down on 15 occasions, and picked it up again every time. If true, that made him a far more disciplined punter than Todd, who liked his action fast and furious.

Tom Masson was another Lewes trainer who sent his horses to Manton for two or three weeks each summer. Fulke Walwyn took 'the big horse,' Mill House, to Manton to work him before the first of his epic clashes with Arkle. Noel Murless sent a number of horses to Todd; sometimes for George to train, sometimes just for a change and a break. In the second category was his 1960 Derby winner St Paddy, who had a holiday at Manton to freshen him up for the St Leger. The horse loved it. Murless' then head lad Clive Brittain remembers that St Paddy would plant himself on the downs, quietly take in everything, and then consent to move on. Jeremy Tree brought horses over from Beckhampton, as did Sir Gordon Richards from Ogbourne and later from Whitsbury.

Sometimes they worked with Todd's own string, which Todd's lads enjoyed but Scobie Breasley didn't. Sir Gordon's horses were never as fit as George's, and Scobie told the Manton lads, 'You boys, when I sing out to you, slow down.' They weren't having that. They just called to each other to 'nanny along,' and upped the tempo. As for Todd, he'd be peeling an apple at the top of his gallops, the dogs at his feet, watching intently as his neighbours' horses worked.

Chapter 24

Heaven's pastures

The inclusion of Penharbour in the 'favourites' list highlights Todd's versatility. Despite his refusal to train 'chasers, he was a dual-purpose trainer. He liked to have a hurdler or two to warm up the winter. The best down the years were Iron Blue and three of his Cheltenham Festival winners: Gremlin, Blue Mountain and Nosey. Eric Stedall didn't bear any grudge against Todd for pinching Gremlin from under his nose: he and his wife later sent horses to George at Manton. But it still must have come as a surprise to him when, within three months of his selling it, his backward ugly duckling won a division of the Gloucestershire Hurdle. Dez Baring claimed some of the credit for Gremlin's Festival win. In the weeks before, the Manton gallops were frozen. Baring decided that a trip to the seaside was the answer. Todd wasn't keen, so Baring took charge. He loaded the horse up, drove it to the beach at Selsey and galloped it. He was pleased with himself when Gremlin won, particularly as it was heavily backed.

The win came in the second race of the day. The first was the optimistically named High Class Selling Hurdle, and Todd won it with Flying Mascot. Both of the winners were ridden by a young Irish jockey, Phil Canty, who made all the running in the seller, and did well to get Gremlin home by a hard-fought length after several mistakes. Canty had his own punters, and not long after he enraged Todd by winning on a horse that wasn't supposed to be 'off.' It started at 20-1, which was nice for Canty's pals but ruined Todd's plans for the horse. Canty was shown the door, left a rude farewell message on the hostel ceiling, and went home to Ireland, where he rode two classic winners and later trained with some success.

Iron Blue was an example of Todd's ability to find and nurture talent in strange guises. The horse was transferred to Manton by his owner Sir Foster Robinson, from John Oxley's yard at Newmarket. His *Timeform* profile was damning: "Has the ability to win good races, but is not a battler and failed to score in 12 starts in 1961… Should've won [a Newmarket handicap] but threw the race away by refusing to exert himself under pressure."

The owner's decision was soon vindicated. Iron Blue was sent over hurdles to sweeten him, and won a 24-runner novice hurdle at Newbury by half a length under John Worrall. The jockey's instructions from Todd were on no account to touch the horse with his whip, and the visored Iron Blue came up the straight with his ears flat back: "I had to sit and suffer and kid him so that he would stay on the bridle, and it just worked." The following season, ridden by Dick Broadway, he was a close third in the inaugural running of the Schweppes Gold Trophy, when the apprentice had the misfortune to be sandwiched between two hardened senior jockeys on the run-in: not the ideal place for a horse of doubtful courage.

It was the most valuable hurdle race of the season. There were 41 runners, and the winner was Rosyth, one of Captain Ryan Price's four in the first five runnings of the race. The fourth-placed horse was the reigning champion hurdler, Anzio, and the fifth, Salmon Spray, in receipt of 3lb from Iron Blue, went on to be champion four years later. Back on the flat, Iron Blue seemed to be up to his usual tricks when backed from 12-1 to 7-1 for the Queen's Prize, and refusing to battle close home. However, the following season he showed himself transformed by the move to Manton, winning twice at Ascot and twice at Newbury, earning a 17lb hike in the *Timeform* ratings and their description: "Very useful handicapper." At which point Todd started dreaming of the Champion Hurdle, but Iron Blue broke a leg at home on the gallops.

Sidney Banks's Blue Mountain was no more than average on the flat. He was five when Todd sent him hurdling. It would be hard to describe a season better planned, or more perfectly executed. He had two 'sighters' in strong novice hurdles, and ran second of 28 when well supported in the Newbury novice event that Iron Blue had won before him. Blue Mountain was then made second favourite in a division of the Gloucestershire Hurdle. They went lickety-spit, and Dick Broadway held onto him until after the second last. A line of horses who'd forced the pace weakened up the hill and Broadway took an opening on the rails to lead at the last and win, going away, by four lengths.

Blue Mountain was a one-hit wonder. Sidney Banks took him back to Bedfordshire to train from his farm, and he ran a dozen times over the next two winters without winning another race. Still, any National Hunt owner with a horse that wins just once would want it to be on a March afternoon below Cleeve Hill.

Nosey was one of the best staying hurdlers of his time. That came as a huge surprise to the two trainers who had him before George Todd, and to various senior jockeys. Their consensus view was that he didn't stay the minimum trip. On the flat, he failed even to win a seller, and after two seasons and various placed efforts over timber he was written off as a short runner. At which point, Jack King bought him and sent him to Manton. His first season was a set-back: he ran once, tore a tendon and had to be fired. A year went by before Todd worked another miracle. In a little over three weeks, Nosey won three handicap hurdles, twice for Terry Biddlecombe, once for John Worrall, over distances of 21 furlongs twice, and three miles. The following season he was laid out to perfection. There was a run-round at Newbury under top weight, and then his win at the Cheltenham Festival, in the Spa Hurdle, over 25 furlongs, by four lengths and eight.

He had more in hand than that, reckoned the *Sporting Chronicle*, who pointed out that, "By the flood of money which came for Nosey, his success will not have taken the Wizard of Manton by surprise." Nosey won again at Cheltenham a month later, giving weight in a handicap to 17 rivals. As a nine-year-old, he won the same race carrying 12st 12lb, giving 40lb to the runner-up and at least 30lb to everything else. Before that, he ran in the Champion Hurdle, by no means unfancied, but up against a mighty rival from the other side of Marlborough, Bob Turnell's Salmon Spray. The outcome paid for every local bookmaker's holiday: Salmon Spray fell and brought down Nosey.

Apart from that sort of unavoidable mishap, Todd was as deadly over hurdles as he was on the flat. The stable's jumps apprentice John Worrall became convinced one winter that Sea Leopard was being prepared to win first time out. He was doing all the horse's schooling, and then he saw it appear on the 'specials' list in the feed house. The other lads pooh-poohed: how often did George have debut winners?

But sure enough, when Worrall arrived in the paddock at Sandown Todd said, "You know the horse. Keep him out of trouble and take it up at the last," and he did. Afterwards Worrall ran into Billy Carter, who asked him, "Is your guv'nor pleased?" "Why?" "He should be: I put on £4,000 for him." Presumably, the professional backer Carter got the best available price – 5-1 – before Sea Leopard plunged to 9-4. That would certainly have pleased Todd, as £20,000 to £4,000 that afternoon equates to *£56,000* to win *£280,000* in our money. Job done: Sea Leopard never ran over timber again, and Todd passed him to Kenneth Mackenzie's wife Lelia, for whom he became a stalwart stayer on the flat.

One afternoon around Christmas, Todd was at Warwick when an outsider from a small yard won a maiden selling hurdle. George went to 540 guineas to buy Penharbour and passed him to Jack King. He ran four times on the flat and won once, but that wasn't why Todd remembered him so fondly. Three months after buying Penharbour, he ran him twice over hurdles in six days, the first time in another seller to have a real bet, and then in a handicap. He won both.

Penharbour was so fragile that he could barely walk on firm ground, let alone gallop. He won seven times: six when ridden by Terry Biddlecombe, favourite each time, and once for John Worrall. Todd's training career was replete with examples of his patching up old crocks, and managing and placing every animal to give it the best possible chances. However, one suspects that if he was asked, which among all his old favourites' campaigns gave him the greatest satisfaction, Penharbour would have an honoured place on the podium: just 12 runs, spread over eight years, and seven times a winner.

Among Todd's flat-race favourites, Shira was an out-and-out stayer who acted on any ground but was favoured by soft. He was usually bandaged. He started off as a two-year-old at around seven furlongs, making so little impression that the *Timeform* annual for 1962 assessed him as, 'Evidently of not much account.' The view was shared by his owner Norman Mackay. He eyed his horse's awful-looking knees at Warwick one afternoon, became despondent, and asked Todd if he thought anyone would give him £500 for the cripple?

Todd bought Shira on the spot, though he did later pass on a share to another of his owners. Shira was stepped up to 10 furlongs for his three runs as a three-year-old, all in selling handicaps: last of nine, ninth of 14, 20-1 each time. Then on heavy going at Lingfield in November with Scobie Breasley riding, he was heavily backed into favouritism to beat five rivals, and drew steadily away to win by four lengths.

As a five-year-old, Shira ran just once. He was put up in distance to two miles in a handicap at Lingfield, started surprisingly short in the betting, and won easily, despite firm ground. There was nothing in even this latest run to suggest that Shira was going to be raised 29lb in the *Timeform* ratings during the following season, or that he'd be desperately unlucky not to go through four races unbeaten. It was the culmination of a long-range plan by Todd. His horse had run only 10 times in four seasons, had won on extremes of going, and had only once raced over the distance that Todd was sure he needed. For good measure, he was at the bottom of the handicap. He went back to Lingfield in May and won as a well-backed favourite under a claimer. The same boy rode in the Ascot Stakes at the Royal meeting.

Fully five furlongs out, Shira was sent for home, and when the challenges arrived his young jockey looked weak in the finish. He was caught on the post and beaten a short head by the Geoff Lewis-ridden Tubalcain. The horse's next race was at Lingfield, and he made all and won easily under a more experienced apprentice, John Hayward. Shira returned to Ascot for the two miles six furlongs Brown Jack Stakes. It was a re-run of the Ascot Stakes. In their first meeting, Shira had received 15lb from Tubalcain. In the rematch, it was only 10lb, Shira having picked up a penalty at Lingfield. Tubalcain had a powerful case at the weights, and he was favourite to confirm the form.

It seemed déjà vu all over again when Hayward sent Shira for home, but this time the run was delayed until the entrance to the straight and there was a stronger rider in the saddle. Shira won by two-and-half lengths. His six-year-old season was even better. Once again, Todd kept him to four runs, with the Ascot Stakes and the Brown Jack Stakes the centrepieces. He brought off the double. At the Royal meeting, he faced Tubalcain again, the pair of them re-handicapped so that his old rival again seemed weighted to win, but the momentum was with Shira. For the first time he was held up by Hayward, who launched him down the centre of the course with only a furlong to go, and hit the front close home to win by a length. Shira's line was cast in calmer waters after that, but he never won again, though he was second in another Brown Jack as a nine-year-old.

Todd doted on two horses above all others in his pantheon: Bradfield and Caught Out. Bradfield didn't run as a two-year-old and was usually among the 'also rans' at three. As a four-year-old, he won twice from four starts, bought in after selling handicaps at Windsor and Brighton. The next year he won four from five, three of them in apprentices' handicaps. As a seven-year-old, he won twice at Ascot, in a two-mile handicap and a boys' race. He won again over the course the year after, beating another much-loved old stayer, Grey of Falloden. At nine, he won twice more, and was second three times. His end-of-season *Timeform* rating rose for the fifth consecutive year. Bradfield won one race in each of the following two seasons. He retired sound at 11, having, like Penharbour, won in seven of his eight seasons' racing. He ran exclusively in Todd's colours, and he gave winning rides to seven different apprentices, including Pat Eddery.

Bradfield and others of 'George's old platers' gave racegoers a pleasure that's usually confined to National Hunt enthusiasts: seeing an old friend running year after year, until its best distance is a given, its ground preference established, its attitude known to all. There might be a couple of seasons at the start when no one, including the owner, had the vaguest notion of the time of day, month or year. But once the catch was safely in the net, as when Terry Stringer steered Tarquinian home at Windsor, the muddy waters tended to clear.

Caught Out became a minor cult. Tommy Frost bought him as a yearling for 600 gns. He was a thorough nuisance, and soon gelded. He didn't win as a two-year-old, and during a busy three-year-old season, he won just once. Frost became frustrated with him and he suggested to Todd that they should sell the horse. Instead, Todd kept him in his own colours. Not even the greatest optimist could have imagined that five seasons later, Caught Out would be the subject of a profile headlined, 'Horse of the Year.' It appeared in the *Financial Times* under the by-line of Dare Wigan, racing correspondent of *Country Life*. It read in part:

> "Good wine improves with age, and so, it seems, do some horses. For example, if a panel of regular racegoers were invited to nominate a horse of the year 1961, I image that Caught Out, a nine-year-old gelding, would attract a goodly number of votes. Caught Out's first appearance on a racecourse was in the May Stakes for two-year-olds at Newmarket. Evidently something was thought of him, for he was backed from 10-1 to 5-1 in a large field. But he ran disappointingly, and the *Raceform* comment was limited to one word, 'small'.
>
> "As a three-year-old Caught Out ran six times, winning a modest handicap at Salisbury and being placed second twice. And in 1956, as a four-year-old, he took part in nine races, his only success being in [a selling handicap] at Windsor, after which he was bought in by G. Todd, his owner-trainer, for 500 guineas. The following year, Caught Out won three races to the total value of £790, and so would have at least earned his keep. And in 1958, he won the Charlton handicap at Goodwood, worth £1,204, when, after starting slowly, he came through in the final furlong and pulverised his opponents with an astonishing burst of speed. This ability to appear from nowhere at the end of a race was

> to become the hallmark of a remarkable, and seemingly ageless, performer. In 1959, for example, in which Caught Out only won one event, a handicap at Brighton, he was barely sighted until a furlong from the winning post, yet finished so fast that he was able to put three lengths between himself and the runner-up, to whom he was conceding nearly a stone.
>
> "[This season] after three 'pipe-openers,' the old gentleman turned up at Goodwood on July 27 and won the Drayton handicap by four lengths. It was a fantastic race. Two furlongs from home he was still at the back of the field, and then he suddenly appeared, corkscrewing his way through his astonished opponents.
>
> "In August, carrying a 10lb penalty, he won the Steve Donoghue apprentice handicap at Epsom comfortably by 1½ lengths, appearing late on the scene, as usual. And then, last Wednesday, when saddled with an additional 10lb penalty, he won [at] Salisbury, with Midsummer Night II, winner of last year's Cambridgeshire, two lengths behind him in third place. The manner of his victory suggested that he would not have been troubled to win with another 10lb under the saddle. Who could have guessed that a nine-year-old gelding with a comparatively undistinguished record spread over seven-and-a-half seasons would suddenly behave as though fitted with a small jet engine?"

The Sporting Life hailed Todd as, "A genius with aged and infirm horses." *Timeform* looked back at Caught Out's quick-fire treble and paid the horse and trainer this compliment:

> "At nine years of age Caught Out was better than ever, and he amassed more prize money in his eighth season than in all the previous seven put together. This was a remarkable achievement, and one that does his trainer great credit, for Caught Out began his racing career by running without much success in the most modest company, and even as a five-year-old nobody was sufficiently interested to bid for him after he had won a seller."

If just one horse were to be chosen to attest to Todd's genius, it would be Caught Out. Tommy Frost's son Tom says that with hindsight,

> "The key was to drop him out. At the beginning, George thought he'd be best suited to being ridden up with the pace. It was only when an inexperienced apprentice missed the break and got hopelessly left at the start that the penny dropped. Caught Out relaxed and coasted at the back, and then picked up his bit and came through the field, just as if he knew where the winning post was.
>
> "He went very well for Terry Stringer and the other boys. He came right about the third week in July every year and by the end of August, he was gone. He was a dear little horse, but Father got exasperated with him. He wasn't upset at all [when the horse started winning]. He and George were very close. It was just unfortunate that Caught Out didn't start winning decent races until he was six or seven!"

Todd had a particular conceit: when he sent in his entry each year to the publishers of *Horses in Training*, he didn't rank them alphabetically, or in strict order of age, or elevate his best horses to the top of the list. Instead, his standard-bearers were his beloved old handicappers. Caught Out led the Manton roster in *Horses in Training* for seven years in a row, including when the stable housed Todd's Group One winners. He was a youthful 16 when he last appeared in the annual. He was replaced at the head of the Manton horses by I Claudius and then Shira, and later by Bradfield. Caught Out didn't win the year after his famous hat trick, but he won one race as an 11-year-old and was second in the Steve Donoghue boys' race at Epsom. Then at 12, with what ranks alongside any of Todd's training feats, Caught Out brought off another treble, all in apprentice handicaps, all in August. During 15 years in training, he ran 84 times, winning 15 races and placing in a further 32.

In Dick Hern's words, if you have livestock you also have dead stock. George Todd loved his horses but, the likes of Caught Out and Bradfield apart, he was rarely sentimental about them. He preferred to have his horses put down at home, rather than see them go to an uncertain future.

Early in his career he gave a horse away to what he supposed was a good home, and was appalled to see it in a field, tail to the wind, miserable and hungry looking. He swore never to make the same mistake again. It was one of his assistants' tasks to hold his horses' heads while the vet shot them. Paul Cole found it harrowing: "I'd see the knacker's van turn up, then Todd would shout, 'Paul'." On occasion, the horse destroyed wasn't unsound or ageing. It was simply an animal that had shown Todd that not even he was going to win a race with: "They were beautiful, healthy animals. He always thought everybody else would maltreat them, that they could fall into bad hands. [Plus] there was a little bit of, 'Nobody's going to have this and do better with it'," says Cole.

Sometimes, it was a personal farewell. Graham Stephens and another lad were working behind a wall at the farm one day when Clever Joe was brought down. Unseen by Todd, they watched him cry as he cradled the horse's head: "We've had some great times together, old lad." they heard: "Now it's time for you to go." His assistants would take a bowl of carrots with them. One carrot, a second carrot, and the horses were shot at the third. So George's old boys went to Heaven's pastures as close to bliss as an arthritic old horse can be: with a mouthful of carrot.

Chapter 25

The good horses

The first of the 'best' list was Radha Sigtia's 1,850 gns yearling purchase, River Chanter, by Chanteur II out of a Fair Trial mare, River Test. Sigtia was something of a mystery to Todd's other owners. He's remembered in his native Bombay as a heavy and successful punter. To this day, he's commemorated by the Royal West India Turf Club's Radha Sigtia Trophy, a prized Class II handicap run every spring. He first came to prominence in Indian racing in the 1950s. Within a few years, he was spending more than half the year in England. He was a good judge of trainers; his horses were split between Todd and that super-shrewd Yorkshireman, Sam Hall. Of the two, he found Hall the most amenable: Todd made him nervous. There was a story that Sigtia made his fortune by cornering the Indian market in imported razor blades. But those whom he mentored in Bombay racing circles say that his only business was 'turf investor.'

River Chanter was a Todd rarity, an early two-year-old. He lined up at the Craven meeting against a field of mostly backward rivals, and was backed from 9-2 to 7-4, winning comfortably. He ran abysmally and was tailed off in the Coventry Stakes, before putting in a series of solid efforts that placed him a little behind the best of his age group, including a staying-on three lengths fourth in the Royal Lodge Stakes at Ascot. River Chanter finished the season in glory, despite having run seven times and seemingly fully exposed. First, he won a nursery at Ascot on very soft ground by four lengths, heavily eased. He landed a gamble under Scobie Breasley in a valuable stakes race at Hurst Park, and then returned to Newmarket for the Dewhurst. He was second favourite there to Aznip, who'd finished a length and a half in front of him in the Royal Lodge; the pair of them each gave 4lb to their six opponents.

Ridden this time by Joe Mercer, River Chanter made all and ran on gamely to hold off Aznip by a length. By any standards, he'd enjoyed a satisfactory first season, winning four races and *£114,950*. In the Free Handicap, he was rated 12lb below the best of 1961's two-year-olds, 1lb ahead of a colt of Dick Hern's, Hethersett.

The consensus view was that River Chanter was game and that he stayed a mile well, but was some way short of classic-winning material. That was how his three-year-old campaign worked out. He ran in the three-runner Brighton Derby Trial, beaten an easy five lengths by Hethersett. Nonetheless, he renewed rivalry with Hethersett in the Derby. Jimmy Lindley rode, and was told to keep River Chanter handy and make the best of his way home from the entrance to the straight. Lindley followed his instructions to the letter: he led early, was in a share of third place after a mile, led again soon after the entrance to the straight, and for a furlong or so looked as if he might stay there. Two furlongs out he was headed by the eventual winner, the Vincent O'Brien-trained Larkspur, and from that moment he back-pedalled, eventually finishing eighth.

Afterwards, Todd blamed himself both for running the horse at all, and for giving Lindley orders which ensured that if River Chanter had stamina limitations, they'd be shown up. But as it turned out, the tactics were a blessing: behind River Chanter as he freewheeled down the hill to Tattenham Corner, two outsiders clipped heels and fell. Five other horses were brought down, including the favourite Hethersett. The horse and his rider Harry Carr were both badly bruised. Mercifully, both fully recovered, and they won the St Leger easily. River Chanter's season went in the opposite direction: he ran in the best company: the Eclipse, the King George VI and the Gordon Stakes, without ever threatening the principals. In his four-year-old season, he seemed to have deteriorated by 21lb or more, and most of his runs were back at a mile.

Anyone with a memory, not even a long one, would know that a horse of Todd's could easily disappoint for a whole season, and then deliver a nasty surprise to any bookmaker who'd forgotten it. At five years, River Chanter won three 10-furlong handicaps in a row, at Epsom and twice at Sandown, ridden each time by Scobie Breasley, landing Sigtia *£75,000* in prize money, and twice a well-backed favourite. John Lawrence hailed his revival as 'a masterpiece': "With all his famous patient skill, George Todd has nursed River Chanter back." The colt retired to stud a redeemed, sound, game horse. No more than a good one, but George Todd's first winner of what's now a Group One race, and a pathfinder for the other, better horses who followed him. Sir Peter O'Sullevan says of Todd that, "It's rare for a man to handle selling platers and classic horses with the same sure hand." Having glimpsed the heights with River Chanter, Todd was much more careful with the other potential stars who passed through his hands. In the early months of 1961, he thought River Chanter was simply a precocious two-year-old. When the next good horse presented himself, there wasn't to be any repeat of River Chanter's 10-race first season.

In the yearling sales of 1961, Tommy Frost paid £1,800 for a French-bred son of Buisson Ardent. He was roan-coloured, and Todd took an instant dislike to him: "He's no bloody good, and I don't want any pink horse in my yard," he told Frost. The yearling went to Dick Perryman at Newmarket. It wasn't long before word came back to Manton that the colt was looking distinctly useful in its early breeze-ups. Todd conceded that he might, after all, think about training the colt. By then, the deadline for 1963's classic entries had passed. The horse turned out to be the best miler that Todd ever handled: Roan Rocket. In contrast to River Chanter's hectic two-year-old campaign, Roan Rocket ran only three times, the first of them when he was a 25-1 outsider, ridden by Vic Gardner to finish eight lengths sixth of 16 in a Salisbury maiden.

Gardner says, "I was told to keep him out of trouble. It was a busy, rough race. Lots of horses converged and got cut about. I managed to keep Roan Rocket out of it. I could just about have won on him, but I did what I was told, just gave him a nice ride. Afterwards, I got a present every time he won."

Despite his promising debut, it looked a big ask for Roan Rocket when he was upped in class for his next race, the Rous Memorial Stakes at Goodwood. He was backed from 10-1 to 7-1. Todd admitted to having £100 at the opening price, which was presumably the tip of the iceberg. But every gallops-watcher in Newmarket had been drooling over a newcomer of Noel Murless's, Peter Le Grand, who was made the red-hot favourite. Roan Rocket was held up by Breasley, challenged a furlong out and quickly went two lengths clear, winning impressively. Peter Le Grand finished third. Murless was aghast after the race, telling Todd that it was the best two-year-old he'd had for 10 years. Next time out, it won the Washington Singer Stakes. Roan Rocket finished his first season in the Somerville Tattersall Stakes at Newmarket. He went down to post looking tremendous and won in a common canter, Breasley again biding his time, letting Roan Rocket go when running down into the Dip, and again winning by two lengths, hard held. It was a success tinged with regret: on the one hand, it confirmed that he was a good horse and acted well at Newmarket: on the other, he didn't hold a 2,000 Guineas entry.

Like many a good colt with that omission in his curriculum vitae, one target stood out in his three-year-old campaign: the St James's Palace Stakes. Todd decided to give Roan Rocket one outing to get him spot-on for Royal Ascot: the Lockinge Stakes at Newbury. It was a wet spring. Tom Frost says, "I remember going to Manton a week before the race with father and George saying, 'He's not fit really. I'm not sure if I should run him. But he has to be got ready for Ascot'." Interrupted training or not, Roan Rocket had a dream prep race. His opponents were headed by The Creditor, a high-class filly who'd won four races the previous season; and Young Christopher, runner-up in the Irish 2,000 Guineas a fortnight earlier. The pair duly finished first and second, but back in a dead-heat for third, Breasley rode an eye-catcher on Roan Rocket.

The form book noted: 'Has done well; good steady headway final two furlongs; finished well; needed race.' What followed in the St James's Palace at Ascot was summed up by *Raceform* as a canter. *Timeform* called Roan Rocket's performance, 'scintillating.' But there was a shadow over the race. Breasley had ridden Roan Rocket to perfection in his two-year-old wins and in the Lockinge, never remotely knocking him about. However, Breasley was retained by Sir Gordon Richards, who had an intended runner himself in the St James's Palace: Port Merion, the easy winner of the Free Handicap.

With Breasley not available for Ascot, Tommy Frost told Todd, "Let's get Lester." A week before the race, Port Merion was injured. Frost's phone rang: it was Breasley, asking for the ride back on Roan Rocket. Sorry, Frost told him, we're committed to Lester. Scobie took it badly: "You can jock him off. He's always doing it to me." Breasley then went through the, 'I'll never ride for you again' routine. The longer the call went on, the more Frost stood his ground.

Breasley picked up a spare ride in the St James's Palace, but his humour can't have improved as Piggott cantered alongside him two furlongs from the winning post. Todd's instructions to Piggott in the paddock had been to, "Ride him like Petite Etoile." Some confidence: five years before, the

Noel Murless-trained filly had been unforgettable, winning all six of her races as a three-year-old, two classics among them. Lester used to unleash her brilliant speed as late as possible.

Tom Frost saw the St James's Palace from the Silver Ring: "As he rode past me, Lester was looking this way and that, wondering when to let him go." Roan Rocket's win promoted him to the position of the best three-year-old of the season. Behind him at Ascot were the second, fourth, fifth and sixth from the 2,000 Guineas. He beat the two lengths second in the Guineas, Faberge II, by six and a half lengths, and the four lengths Guineas fourth, Minor Portion, by seven lengths. Racing, like life, is littered with 'if only' stories. Tommy Frost was entitled to add another. If George Todd hadn't taken a dislike to his 'pink horse,' every reading of that season's mile form suggests that had he been entered and trained for it, Roan Rocket would've won the 2,000 Guineas.

Roan Rocket's only other run that season was in the Sussex Stakes at Goodwood. None of the three-year-olds that he brushed aside at Ascot bothered to re-oppose. The Guineas form was represented by the third from the race, Balustrade, and an also-ran, Derring-Do. Roan Rocket gave them both 2lb. He was odds-on. Piggott kept the ride. Tommy Frost took another telephone ear-bashing from Breasley, and when the Australian was rebuffed, he had a go at Todd as well, without success.

As before, Scobie managed to pick up a spare, on Derring-Do, but after flopping in the Guineas and again in the Lingfield Derby Trial, Derring-Do hardly looked likely to feature in the finish. Roan Rocket won all right, but it turned out to be a struggle. Held up as usual, he was produced two furlongs out by Piggott, led at the distance, but had to be shaken up to beat Derring-Do by half a length, with Balustrade close up in third.

The Sporting Life said there were, 'Long faces after £15,000 win,' to describe Todd's and Frost's reactions. That ignored the Krug being downed in the members' bar, but it did seem that Frost's colt had run about 10lb below his St James's Palace form. Frost was loud in praise of Piggott's ride. It took only half-an-hour for Breasley to get his revenge. He was riding a horse called Fine Bid for Todd in the next race, the Chesterfield Cup. Fine Bid's owner was terminally ill, and Todd wanted to train him a last winner at Goodwood. He got a puzzling ride from Breasley: glued to the rails, he had no room at all, switched outside with a furlong to go, and was beaten two lengths in third. The inside rail is a perilous place to be behind horses at Goodwood, and it could've been assumed that Scobie had just been unlucky, but it had all happened a few years before, on Sidney Banks's Double Red, who shared favouritism in the 14-furlongs Bentinck Stakes with a horse of the Queen's, Almeria.

There were only seven runners, and Todd had set the race up for Double Red with a pacemaker, who did his job for nine furlongs, where Almeria took over. In the straight, the race reduced to three: Almeria, Double Red and one other. It takes some doing to be boxed in when you're one of three, with the Sussex downs spread before you, but Scobie managed it that day. Watching on television in the hostel at Manton, one of the lads called out, 'Evens Double Red' and vacuumed up all the spare cash in the room. Perhaps it was the same lad to whom Scobie had confided, 'You have to keep something by for a rainy day.'

At Goodwood, Sidney Banks gritted his teeth and muttered, "That was one for Her Majesty." Todd turned to John Cherry and said, "We were put through the hoop there, John." The report in *The Sporting Life*: "Denied opening one furlong out, switched to outside," could have described what happened to Fine Bid in the Chesterfield seven years later. This time, there was no question. Breasley jumped off Fine Bid, snarled, "That'll bloody serve you right," and stalked into the weighing room.

Todd understood, more than most, that human beings are imperfect. John Hislop said that he, "Appreciated the difficulties and temptations, [and] tolerant of these, forgave easily. 'Poor little devil, he's been going bad and has got himself in with a funny lot,' he once remarked to me of a jockey who had palpably chopped him in a race, yet he often put him up afterwards."

Todd continued to give Breasley rides, but Tommy Frost didn't. Breasley was one of the best riders of his time, of any time. As a child, he used to play a game of catch-up along the pavements. He stalked passers-by towards lampposts until the last possible moment and then ran to catch and pass them, literally, on the post. He rode thousands of races the same way. That's a handy talent for a jockey riding for a gambling stable; it gives the handicapper no real measure of a winner's superiority.

Sir Peter O'Sullevan said, "Scobie used to scare the pants off George. Sure, George liked his horses to be ridden quietly, but perhaps not as quiet as Scobie made it. Not too close to silence. George might be haemorrhaging financially; Scobie would come in and tell him, 'He'll do better than that.' Or, 'I could've been third' – when George had had an each-way bet." It was worse for the lads at Sir Gordon Richards's yard when Breasley was the stable jockey. Time and again, they bet their boots on some blue-blooded and highly-tried debutant, and mostly they lost their money. Scobie would drop it out, running on nicely at the finish. As O'Sullevan said, Scobie was interested in the development of the horse. He did as little work-riding as possible, much preferring breakfast in bed, so he used the racecourse to find out things about a horse that most stable jockeys would have discovered from its work at home.

There was a view in the hostel at Manton and elsewhere that not much time had passed between Scobie's start in England in a tied cottage, and his being chauffeured around in a Rolls Royce, while owning large houses in London and Barbados. Certainly not enough time for the changed circumstances to be explained entirely by retainers and winning percentages. Some of it was jealousy. It isn't possible to ride over 3,200 winners, as Breasley did, without being 'busy' almost all the time, but Scobie first came to England after one of the stewards in Melbourne told him that he was a marked man because of suspicions about his betting.

Breasley's biographer Chris Poole relished a story of how when Scobie turned to training, he had a 100-1 winner of a Group race. Afterwards, a steward saw Breasley's wife May and said that he hoped Scobie had got the price? The unexpected reply was, "Nah, he hasn't had a bet since he stopped riding." Poole named the horse as Hittite Glory, winner of the 1975 Flying Childers at Doncaster. Over the years, the story was set in different races in different countries. May herself told it as a joke in a speech at a racing dinner, which suggests it was apocryphal, but the fact that it was told at all contains an element of 'no smoke without fire.'

Roan Rocket ran six times as a four-year-old, without improving on his record of three Group One wins. His seasonal debut was again in the Lockinge, and again it was little more than a public gallop, albeit a high-class one. Next, he stepped up for the first time to 10 furlongs in the Eclipse. Piggott had been claimed by Noel Murless to ride the warm favourite, Sweet Moss. The Queen's colt Canisbay was a rank outsider in a field of eight.

In Piggott's absence, Todd recruited another Australian jockey, Bill Williamson. Murless ran a pacemaker for the favourite, and it set a strong pace to the entrance of the Sandown straight. At that point, the script was torn up. Instead of Sweet Moss staying on, he dropped right out.

Canisbay took the lead. Williamson held on to Roan Rocket until a furlong out, tackled Canisbay, and nosed in front. In the last few yards, Canisbay, running against the rail, fought back to beat Roan Rocket by a short head. It wasn't a 'hats off' day. Roan Rocket had become a popular favourite, while Canisbay not only started at 20-1: his trainer Cecil Boyd-Rochfort hadn't had a winner for weeks and didn't bother to accompany his horse to Sandown. Canisbay passed the post in near-silence.

Williamson told Frost that, "I wish I'd ridden him before; I just came a little bit too soon." Roan Rocket was in front three strides before the post and three strides after. No one blamed 'Weary Willie,' but either Piggott or Breasley, supreme masters of timing, might have turned the short head in Roan Rocket's favour. On Canisbay's next outings, he was thrashed 15 lengths by Oncidium and then finished last in the Champion Stakes. He was palpably inferior to Roan Rocket.

The 'pink horse' went back to Goodwood for the Sussex Stakes to face a strong contingent of three-year-olds: the winners of the 2,000 Guineas, 1,000 Guineas and St James's Palace Stakes, plus a French colt, Grey Dawn, who was the previous season's top-rated European two-year-old, and for good measure the only horse ever to beat Sea Bird.

The overseas challenge was completed by an Irish raider, Paddy Prendergast's Carlemont, who'd started second favourite for the Irish 2,000 Guineas but finished fifteenth of 21. That didn't seem promising, but it was said that the colt had coughed. At Goodwood, Carlemont was massively backed against Roan Rocket. Todd and Frost had no way of knowing it, but their horse probably faced mission impossible. Carlemont had missed weeks of work because of injury. He was walking on the roads when a bullock poked its head though a hedge next to him and bellowed.

Prendergast said that his colt, "Took 10 minutes to fall and then you never saw such knees in your life." Once Carlemont recovered, he worked all over Prendergast's older horse Red Slipper, who began the year by defying 10st in the Irish Lincoln and ended it by carrying off the Prix de la Foret and the Prix du Moulin. Prendergast was serenely confident, with good reason.

Roan Rocket beat the classic winners and everything bar Carlemont, who won by three lengths. Having dropped from the clouds, the Irish colt never ran again. Roan Rocket had run his race, and he ran it again in the Hungerford Stakes under a typical Piggott ride, holding on to him until a hundred yards out and winning so imperiously that John Oaksey described Roan Rocket as, "Irresistible as a breaking wave." He went to stud a high-class horse, and might even have been a few pounds better than he showed on the racecourse, because he was persistently unsound. Most mornings he came out of his box lame and took a few minutes to walk it off. Before his narrow win in the Sussex Stakes, he sweated heavily over his loins, as if something was hurting. It wasn't until he'd retired that a vet discovered that Roan Rocket's fourth and fifth vertebrae were misplaced.

> "At approximately five o'clock on a Friday afternoon in June a burst of cheering, the like of which had not been heard since Brown Jack retired from the racing scene in 1934, broke out over the Ascot racecourse. Trelawny, having made most of the running in the Queen Alexandra Stakes, held a decisive lead over Grey of Falloden passing the two-furlong pole, and he looked assured of victory. With every stride the roar increased in volume, and when he passed the post three lengths ahead of his rival, hats were flung into the air, and spectators made a concerted rush to the unsaddling enclosure to greet this great stayer."

The quote is from the essay on Trelawny in *Racehorses of 1963*. The word 'great' was noteworthy. The *Timeform* founder Phil Bull abhorred the word's overuse. A 1972 essay on Brigadier Gerard noted that, 'It is important [to] realise that when we use the word *great* we do not do so thoughtlessly. In the past thirty years fewer than a dozen horses have merited the description *great* in these pages." So there stands Trelawny in the most exalted company. In the eyes of the racing public, Trelawny was the horse that Todd would be associated with above all others.

As *Timeform* concluded, Trelawny was, "A wonderful example of his trainer's skill and patience with long-distance horses." Trelawny was home-bred by Sir John Astor, by the Astor family's 1948 St Leger winner Black Tarquin out of their 10-furlong winner Indian Night. Trelawny was sent with the other yearlings from the Astor's stud to be trained by Jack Colling at West Ilsley. He had just one run at the back end of his two-year-old season, and then Colling persuaded Sir John to have Trelawny cut. He was very big and rather fractious, and Colling hoped to calm him down. Colling liked a modest bet, and famously pleaded to be given, 'A stable full of geldings and I'll break the bookmakers.'

The operation had the desired effect: Trelawny became much more amenable, and won three minor 12- and 13-furlong races the following season. That a horse with so much stamina in his pedigree could win over middle distances as a three-year-old was encouraging, but not sufficiently so for Sir John, who raced to breed. Trelawny was sent to the December sales, and sold to Mrs Stella Carver for 2,500 guineas. She took the horse away from Colling and sent it to Syd Mercer at Lambourn.

The new trainer helped to maintain Trelawny's steady progress. After stepping up to two miles for the first time and winning a Birmingham handicap, Trelawny carried a 6lb penalty in the Chester Cup. The tight turns of the Roodee weren't likely to favour the long-striding Trelawny, and he was soon well behind. He made up ground hand over fist as the field turned into the straight, and poked his head in front, right on the line. It was clear that no distance would be too far for him. He was then third in the two-and-a-half mile Ascot Stakes before running miserably in the Northumberland Plate. It was a useful lesson: the horse hated travelling. He fretted and sweated all the time he was in a strange box, and if he stayed away from his own stable, he wouldn't eat. The answer was to get him to the races and back on the same day.

Trelawny's final run for Syd Mercer was in the Goodwood Stakes, and it was nearly his last. He was injured, and the racecourse vet thought he should be put down on the spot. The horse's connections decided to make every effort to save him, and Trelawny was taken back to Mercer's yard, where it was found that he'd broken a cannon bone. The leg was plastered. After three anxious weeks, Trelawny was able to put some weight on it, and from then on, he made a routine recovery. At the end of that season, Syd Mercer retired. For a couple of months, the horse remained at the yard with Mercer's young successor, Peter Walwyn, but Mrs Carver decided to play safe and send the horse back to Jack Colling.

As a five-year-old Trelawny ran eight times, showing that he was completely sound, and he ran two excellent races. The first was back at Chester, for the Cup and the cheese, where he was again flying at the finish, but this time failed by the minimum distance to get up. There was a solid form line through one of his opponents, Doctor F – second behind Trelawny in his first Cup, and now fourth – which suggested that Trelawny had improved by around 10lb from the previous season. Afterwards he disappointed in the Ascot Stakes, but bounced back in the Brown Jack Stakes in July, winning in a fast time by 10 lengths.

At the unsaddling, a disagreement that had been simmering between Colling and the owner was made all too public. Mrs Carver had been a top event rider, and a successful point-to-point jockey. She thought this gave her the credentials to challenge Jack Colling about her horse's riding arrangements. Stella Carver greeted Trelawny and his jockey Joe Mercer by nominating a race at Longchamp as Trelawny's next target. Colling ignored that. She continued brightly, "I've just talked to Lester, and he says he can ride him." "At least wait until I've got the saddle off," hissed Colling. The owner-trainer relationship limped on for the remainder of the season. Finally, Mrs Carver had her way, and Mercer was jocked off in favour of Piggott for a minor handicap at Windsor.

The sequel was inevitable. Jack Colling thought so highly of Joe Mercer that he first retained him as his stable jockey while Mercer was still an apprentice. When Colling retired, he encouraged Major Holliday's private trainer Dick Hern to take over Hodcott House. Holliday called the move, "Worse than stealing my butler." Colling also recommended Mercer to Hern as his stable jockey. That long-standing partnership led to Brigadier Gerard and countless other big-race winners.

Mercer was recognised as one of the most stylish jockeys of his time. Stella Carver couldn't see it. Colling trained only for people he liked or respected. He told her, "Joe Mercer is my jockey and I wouldn't put anyone else up for anything. You'll have to take your horse elsewhere." Carver's husband had the awkward task of going to Colling to ask, "What do you propose?" "George Todd is the best trainer of stayers in the country," Jack told him. So, as a six-year-old, Trelawny went to Manton and to the ranks of the greats. Todd's friend Colling had improved Trelawny by 10lb or so in a season: Todd himself would increase his rating by another 20lb over the next three seasons.

Chapter 26

Trelawny

Trelawny took a detour on his way to Manton. The Carvers were keen jumping owners; their steeplechaser ESB won the 1956 Grand National when Devon Loch jumped the obstacle that never was. The Carvers decided that Trelawny should go hurdling. George Todd wouldn't hear of it, so the Carvers sent Trelawny to ESB's trainer Fred Rimell for the 1961-62 winter. He ran and was placed four times, including at Cheltenham in a division of the Gloucestershire Hurdle. He was miles back for most of the race, scythed through the field to lead up the run-in, but was caught close home by an outsider.

His fourth outing was in the Coronation Hurdle at Liverpool. The flat, sharp course wasn't likely to suit Trelawny, and sure enough, he didn't get into contention until too late, and found another long shot had got first run on him.

Todd and the flat racing season were calling for Trelawny, and he was transferred to Manton to be trained for the Chester Cup, where he followed his previous first and second placings by finishing third. He was at the back of the field until four furlongs from the finish, and then passed horse after horse from the turn in, eventually beaten half a length and 10 lengths. The winner was Golden Fire, whose trainer Doug Marks arrived at the course asking, "Where do they hand over the cheque?" Trelawny's next outing was in the Ascot Stakes. The horse had settled in well at Manton; his lad John Flatt remembers him as 'a saint' in his box and in his work.

The Ascot Stakes had been a frustrating race for Todd. In a 12-year period, he had no less than eight horses finish second or third. Trelawny settled the score in spectacular fashion. He was set to carry 9st 8lb. Only once before had that kind of burden been defied in the race, when

Ravensbury won under 9st 9lb in 1895. Trelawny had worked so well after the Chester Cup that Todd openly told all and sundry that he thought it would win. For good measure, he advised an each-way saver on his second string in the race, Fortwyn.

The pick of the opposition seemed to be Golden Fire, only 7lb worse off for his win over Trelawny at Chester. Golden Fire was close to the lead as they turned for home. Behind him, Breasley had kept Trelawny much closer to the pace than usual.

As the bell rang, Trelawny took a clear lead and ran on strongly to win unchallenged by four lengths from the fast-finishing Fortwyn. It was a thoroughly popular win, not least because of a public gamble on Trelawny. Quintin Gilbey wrote in the *Sporting Chronicle*, "There has never been a greater trainer of stayers in my time than George Todd, who performed the most remarkable feat of his career when [saddling] first and second in the Ascot Stakes."

Trelawny came out like a fresh horse the next morning, and Todd decided to go for the long-distance race double in the Queen Alexandra Stakes on the last day of the meeting. His four rivals included the first two from the previous year's race, Moss Bank and Agreement. Trelawny was close in the slipstream of Moss Bank as he cut out the running. On the home turn, Breasley pulled him out, woke him up, and beat Agreement by a comfortable length and a half.

Horse and rider enjoyed a warm reception as they came back. The Ascot Stakes and Queen Alexandra double wasn't a great rarity, but it was 25 years since it'd last been achieved, and then by another Manton horse, Joe Lawson's Valerian. Trelawny's next run was in the Goodwood Cup, and here for the first time he met top stayers: the Ascot Gold Cup first and second, Balto and Sagacity.

The Queen's jockey Harry Carr gave Sagacity a wonderful ride, forcing the pace on every downhill gradient, slowing on the uphill stretches, and eventually making all. The slow, quick, slow tempo seemed to baffle Balto's French jockey, who gave himself too much to do in the closing stages. It was left to Trelawny to mount the only serious challenge to Sagacity. He drew alongside the leader two furlongs out, but was outstayed close home. The pair met again in the Doncaster Cup, and ran much the same race against each other, but were disappointing in third and fourth.

Derby hopes: Joe Lawson's Kingsway, Way In and Merchant Navy finished first, third and seventh in the 1943 2,000 Guineas. Pictured returning from morning work before the Derby, the trio made no impression at Epsom

Joe Lawson at home: he liked to remember a winner with a whisky and soda, but ulcers dictated that much of the time, he was confined to milk.

Below, the loft of a piggery near the stable yard was consecrated as a small chapel in the 1920s. The lads prayed for winners while the pigs grunted below.

Sir Alfred Munnings' 1936 painting, *Lord Astor's Horses*, shows Joe Lawson on his hack with (left to right) Traffic Light, Rhodes Scholar and Early School, respectively that year's best staying filly; the St James's Palace Stakes and Eclipse winner; and the Coventry Stakes winner.

Below, Crossways in East Ilsley was George Todd's first yard. His wife ran a post office to help pay the bills.

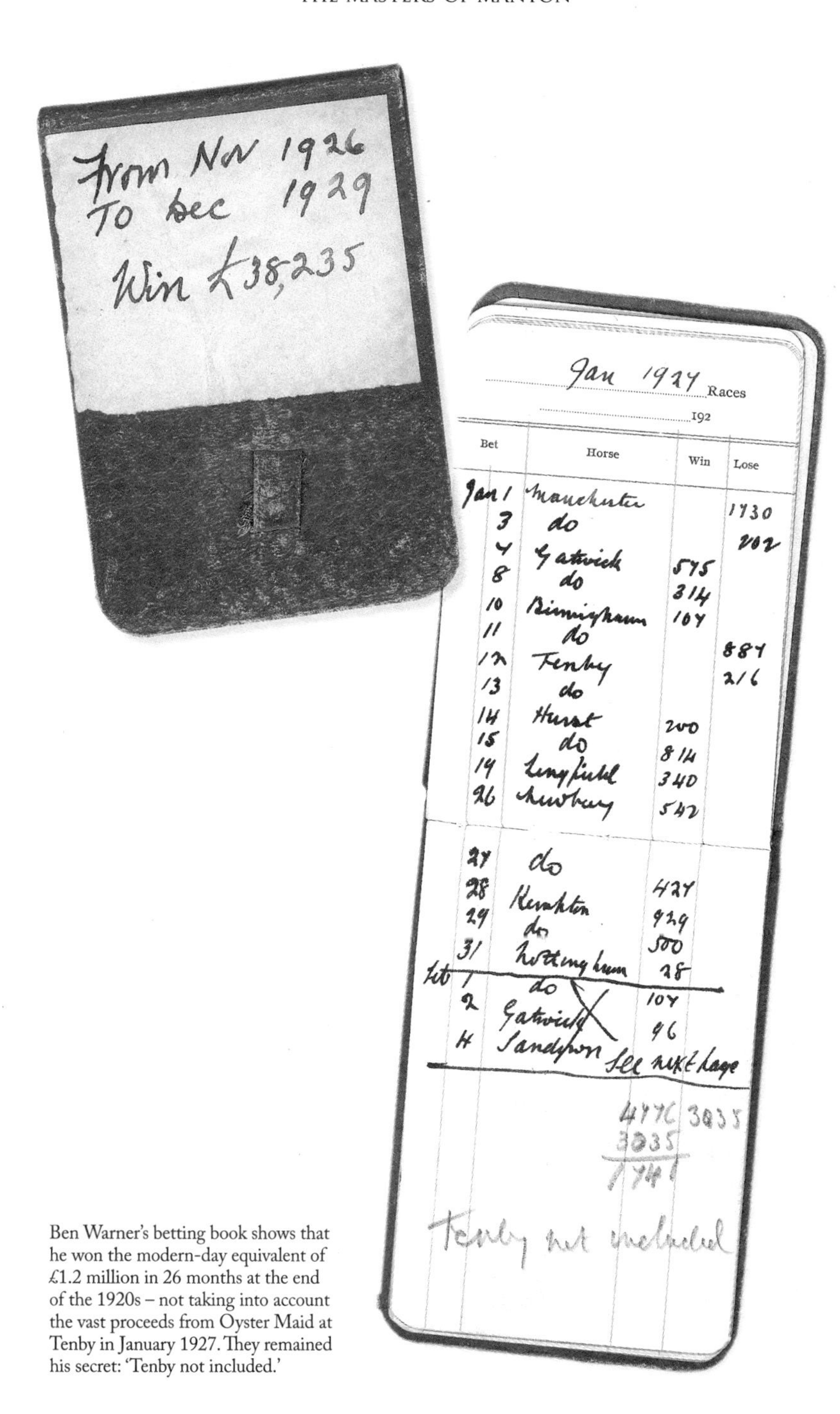

From Nov 1926
To Dec 1929
Win £38,235

Jan 1927 Races
192

Bet	Horse	Win	Lose
Jan 1	Manchester		1730
3	do		702
4	Gatwick	575	
8	do	314	
10	Birmingham	107	
11	do		884
12	Tenby		216
13	do		
14	Hurst	200	
15	do	814	
17	Lingfield	340	
26	Newbury	542	
27	do		
28	Kempton	427	
29	do	929	
31	Nottingham	500	
Feb 1	do	28	
2	Gatwick	107	
4	Sandown	96	

see next page

4776 3035
3035
1741

Tenby not included

Ben Warner's betting book shows that he won the modern-day equivalent of £1.2 million in 26 months at the end of the 1920s – not taking into account the vast proceeds from Oyster Maid at Tenby in January 1927. They remained his secret: 'Tenby not included.'

Contentment: Ben Warner in celebratory mood with his commission agents, Ted Mason (left) and Tommy Westhead. Warner and Westhead both put on bets for George Todd.

Below, Crowded Roodeye: Chester's all-time record crowd saw George Todd's Retsel easily land a gamble in the 1946 Chester Cup.

Incorporating "The Sportsman," "Bell's Life in London," and "The Sporting Telegraph"

No. 22,207 (128th Year) LONDON: MONDAY, MARCH 20, 1950 Price Threepence

Nickalls and Aubrey Ren- combine to bring you the of the Lincolnshire Handi- in which the success of matic has made some of the s Double books look a little Dramatic has been ied with many fancied d National candidates, and all-over this evening at the ria Club will see the un- ng of heavy commitments.

DRAMATIC LANDED MAJOR LINCOLN GAMBLE

Roger Bannister, Oxford miler, smashed his own Inter-Varsity record with 4min 14.2sec at the White City. New figures were also set up in pole vault, by A. J. Burger, Oxford Rhodes Scholar, with 12ft. (Page Three.) At Murrayfield on Saturday, Scotland beat her traditional rivals in the Calcutta Cup match, the issue being in doubt up to five minutes of "no-side." See Page Two.

The Lincolnshire Handicap runners after the field had gone two furlongs. The winner is in the second row, on the left. He was still behind the leaders after a further two furlongs, but Gordon then brought him out, and he struck the front from Hatchik, Tir-na-Nog, Gold-borough, and Fair Judgement. The Park Lodge horse failed to get in an effective challenge, and Dramatic ran on strongly to win comfortably by three lengths.

The finish, with Gordon looking round confident that he had made the best of his way home to land the Manton gamble from last year's winner Fair Judgement.

Imperial Cup Double

MEYRICK GOOD

ever-popular Imperial Cup d the races confined to riders attracted a tre- us crowd at the concluding of the Grand Military g at Sandown on Saturday. n the previous day, there ome excellent "shows" of anship among the soldiers part in the Past and Pre- and the Grand Military 's' Chases.

senior steward for the s races is General Sir d McCreery, who rode the s of the Grand Military Cup in 1923 and 1928 on Darling and Dash o' White. was present on each occa-

ne has been a member of andown Park Club longer Major Ernest Gaylord, who e that he joined back as 1898. In act the chairman him that the im an honorary life

MASTER BIDA

were treated to a or the Imperial Cu a little disappointin aster Bidar was no

—Now For Liverpool

CARD on the Grand National will be called over at the Victoria Club, London, at 3.30 p.m. this evening.

Mr J. V. Rank has engaged Glen Kelly to ride Shagreen. C. O'Connor will have the mount on Contradiction.

Captain Darby Rogers runs Susie Le Alba in the Knowsley Plate and hopes to send Safety Pin and Saldfitude to Liverpool.

A. Breasley, Australian jockey who has been engaged to ride for Mr Rank this season, will have his first mount in England at the meeting. He rides all the stable's runners, which are—Thursday: Ocean Plate—Promotion; Friday: Jock Scot, Decorum; Saturday: Highland Division, Encounter.

Masked Light, favourite for the Two Thousand Guineas, is to run in the Union Jack Stakes over a mile on Wednesday. Only if the going is heavy will he not meet the engagement. D. Smith, if not required for Lord Derby's second in the race, will ride Masked Light.

Fuller third in the Lincolnshire Handicap may run in the Lanca- shire Hurdle next Saturday.

TRIUMPH OF VETERINARY SCIENCE

Real Racehorse For

Geoffrey Brooke's

ntinued on Page Seven

Barnes Park ... respectively 31, 32, and 34.

Vanity: Todd's wife thought he spent too long sprucing himself up for this photograph of French Design and the apprentice Vic Gardner. French Design was a Cesarewitch and Goodwood Stakes winner. Not long after, he won a second Goodwood Stakes.

Below, Abroad: owner Radha Sigtia, jockey Frankie Durr, Sodium and the horse's lad Terry Lewis after Sodium's 1966 Irish Derby win. The Curragh was 'abroad,' so Todd stayed at home.

Opposite, The coup: The Gordon Richards-ridden Dramatic paid for Manton when winning the 1950 Lincoln. George Todd is at the top right in the photograph; owner Ted Saunders (dark overcoat) is walking behind his colt; Cyril Higham and Wally Mills (carrying the horse rug) lead in Dramatic.

The last of the old-fashioned trainers: George Todd was Master from 1946 to 1973. 'He was patience personified, had a brilliant knack with unsound horses, and he knew when they should be backed.'

Todd's Army: some Manton apprentices in the early 1950s. From left: Johnny Frampton, Hughie McDowell, Graham Stephens, paid lad Danny Sullivan, Peter Stanley, Bobby Betts, Wally Carter, David Churchley, Dramatic's lad Cyril Higham, and Malcolm Hall.

John Cherry was George Todd's last head lad. Todd's retirement plan envisaged Sir Gordon Richards taking the main yard at Manton, and Cherry training from the 24-box Astor yard. Audrey Todd vetoed the project, to her own great cost.

Trelawny then had his first proper rest for 18 months, Todd refusing to let him go hurdling. Next year, Trelawny made his fourth appearance in the Chester Cup, running on late as usual, but beaten a long way in fifth. The stage was set for a return to Royal Ascot. It was a huge ask for Trelawny: he was set to carry 10st in a field of 22 in soft going. No horse had ever carried that weight in the race, still less won under it. The next horse in the handicap received 8lb, the other 20 got from 19lb to 42lb. The chief reporter of *The Sporting Life*, Tom Nickalls, summed up the outcome: "Trelawny under 10 stone had a ton in hand." Breasley saved ground on the rails all through the race, not far off the leaders, until he pulled Trelawny out to challenge in the straight. In front of him was a stable-companion, Sea Leopard, who with an apprentice's allowance was carrying just 6st 7lb. Sea Leopard had made most of the running, and wasn't stopping, but as the crowd saw that Trelawny was going appreciably better than anything else, a roar went up. The sudden noise may have been the reason for Trelawny jinking right for a stride or two and tightening up two of his rivals.

Breasley quickly straightened out Trelawny, and he cut down Sea Leopard to win by three-quarters of a length with another length and a half to the main victim of the interference, Lost Property. There was tremendous cheering as Trelawny was led into the unsaddling enclosure. It was hushed when the public address system broadcast that the stewards had objected to the first three finishers. It was a confusing announcement. By no stretch of the imagination could Sea Leopard be under scrutiny: he'd made most of the running. There was no enquiry; none of the jockeys or trainers were called in. 'Objected to the first three' meant only that the stewards were looking at the patrol film. Having done so, they over-ruled their own objection, and to general delight, the all clear was given. If Lost Property had finished second instead of third, his position with Trelawny might well have been reversed. But the Ascot crowd had the result that they wanted, and the best horse won.

After the race Todd was asked, would he be running Trelawny again in the Queen Alexandra? No, he said: "He's done a wonderful thing. I wouldn't be keen to risk breaking his heart by tackling fresh horses again so soon." Mrs Carver disagreed: she was adamant that her horse should attempt the 'double double'. Not for the first time, Todd turned to Jack Colling. He told his friend, "I don't want the old boy to run. He knows what he's in for and he's sweated up a lot." "Wait until you see him come out in the morning," cautioned Colling: "Don't lose your temper like me and lose the best stayer in the country. You'll never get another like him." In the event, Trelawny was bouncing on the Friday. Another public gamble made him a hot favourite. The only other to be backed was a promising four-year-old, Grey of Falloden, who'd finished a long way ahead of Trelawny in the Chester Cup.

Todd was so confident of Trelawny's reformed style of running that he suggested to Breasley that if no one else set a reasonable pace, he should force it himself. Scobie duly took Trelawny into the lead after five furlongs, and stayed there for a mile. An outsider shot past and several lengths clear, but Breasley ignored it. When the leader caved in half a mile out, Trelawny moved to the front again, and a great wave of cheering broke out from the stands as he led Grey of Falloden into the straight. The younger horse was staying on strongly, yet in the last two furlongs Trelawny drew away from him, with Breasley looking round. There was pandemonium as he passed the post.

Breasley said that Trelawny was the greatest stayer he'd ever ridden. Todd, ecstatic, said Trelawny would've made the Gold Cup, "A proper gallop – and he'd have trotted in." That claim could never have been put to the test, because at the time geldings weren't eligible to run in the Ascot showpiece. However, Trelawny had covered the full Gold Cup trip in the Ascot Stakes on the Tuesday in a time seven seconds faster than Twilight Alley did when winning the Cup two days later, and Trelawny carried 14lb more. Furthermore, the ground had dried during the meeting. The *Sporting Chronicle* assessed the going as a tenth of a second faster per furlong for the Gold Cup, thereby adding a couple of seconds to Trelawny's appreciably better time than Twilight Alley's.

In 1962, he became the seventh horse in 90 years to win the Royal meeting's two long-distance races that were open to geldings. A year later he became, and remains, the only horse to do it again, and under a record weight in the Ascot Stakes. He, Todd and Breasley deserved all the acclamation. The literary side of Fleet Street quoted from *The Song of the Western Men:*

And shall Trelawny live?
And shall Trelawny die?
There's twenty thousand Cornishmen
Shall know the reason why!

It was the wrong Trelawny. The horse was named after a minor nineteenth century author, while the poem's subject was a bishop who objected to James II's plan to restore Catholicism. And for all the poetic posturing, the bishop had a fair trial, was acquitted and walked free. But the quotes struck the right notes of heroism and defiance. The *Bloodstock Breeders Review* called him, "The most popular horse in training." The respected handicapper TE Watson wrote that, "His second Ascot Stakes win rates Trelawny as great a stayer as we have seen since the War."

After Ascot, Trelawny went again to the Goodwood Cup, and faced three opponents. The former Grand Prix de Paris and Gold Cup winner Balto was back for more and there was a three-year-old, Raise You Ten, who'd run second in the Dante Stakes. Trelawny was odds on and made all, beating Raise You Ten by six lengths, conceding 18lb, hard held. Balto was beaten 17 lengths, providing another link to that year's Gold Cup, in which Balto was beaten only seven lengths. Trelawny came back to another great reception.

No one could've foreseen it, but that was his last flat-race success. After his usual prep race the following year he was again set to hump 10st in the Ascot Stakes, with several of his regular victims in opposition. Everything was set fair for another triumph, but there was a jockey change. Breasley was claimed to ride in the race for Sir Gordon Richards.

In his place was Ron Hutchinson, and Hutch fluffed his lines: the form book's summary was: "Well behind 2 miles. Headway final three furlongs. Too much to do." While Trelawny was meeting traffic problems on the last bend, a flyweight of Dick Hern's had made first run.

At the line, Trelawny was two lengths in arrears, conceding the winner 40lb. Back in fourth was Sea Leopard, which made Hutch's misjudgement all the more agonising. In 1963, Trelawny had given Sea Leopard 49lb and beaten him three quarters of a length; now he gave him 47lb and beat him four and a half lengths. Had he been ridden more handily, he must have completed his hat trick in the race. Still, there was the Queen Alexandra waiting to compensate.

A deluge caused Thursday's card to be abandoned, but when Friday's declarations were published, Trelawny had frightened off all opposition. It was to be a walkover: all he had to do was carry Scobie past the winning post. He was denied the consolation. The downpour continued, and the Friday and Saturday cards were lost.

Trelawny returned to Ascot in July for the Brown Jack Stakes. The going was hard. As post time approached, Todd grew more and more anxious. He told Peter O'Sullevan, "I hate to risk him on this ground. I'm sure he won't like it." He went off to confer with Stella Carver, but in the crowds, he couldn't find her. When they did speak, it was past the deadline for withdrawals, so Trelawny took his chance. Even by his standards he faced a daunting task, carrying 10st again, with the next of his 10 rivals on 7st 11lb. He simply couldn't let himself down on the going and went down by four lengths to his younger half-brother, Gurkha. They lowered the course record by over four seconds.

Trelawny paid a heavy price; he was lame behind as he was led away. He'd jarred ligaments and split a pastern. The post-race thoughts were to retire him, but thanks to the horse's own easy temperament and the repair work of Todd and Bob Shanahan, the old horse was gradually returned to full soundness. After his prodigious weight-carrying efforts in the Ascot and Queen Alexandra Stakes, *Timeform* had rated him 1lb higher in *Racehorses of 1964* than in the 1963 annual, reflecting his marginal improvement over Sea Leopard.

As an eight-year-old, his *Timeform* rating of 128 was his highest ever. A year later, it was replaced by a question mark. It would have been better if he'd been retired in his pomp. He made a belated seasonal debut in the Queen Alexandra, where he finished last, beaten over 30 lengths by Grey Of Falloden. Even allowing for improvement by the younger horse, who made up into a top stayer, it was a shattering decline from the same race two years earlier.

Nothing in the rest of the summer was any better. The Carvers then decided to relaunch Trelawny as a hurdler. That was the last straw for Todd: "If you're that greedy, I won't train him," he said, and for good measure told them to take away another horse they had with him.

Back with Fred Rimell, Trelawny delighted racegoers by racking up a quick hat trick the following March, ridden each time by Terry Biddlecombe. On Gold Cup day at Cheltenham, he won the Spa Hurdle easily, and at Liverpool he won the Coronation Hurdle. In the following National Hunt season, he deteriorated suddenly, as he'd done on the flat. He was asked to race seven times, still under huge weights, and managed only one placing, finally running in moderate races at minor tracks, to no obvious purpose.

His owners even wanted their now 11-year-old to be schooled over fences. He'd never been an entirely natural hurdler, falling once and making the occasional bad mistake, and Rimell persuaded the Carvers that chasing was an option too far. Trelawny died only two years into his overdue retirement. Of all horses, he deserved a headstone in a quiet place, but he was fed to hounds like a fallen farm animal.

Chapter 27

England's horse

As Trelawny's light dimmed, a new star arrived, and like many another, he was sent to Manton because of Todd's reputation for handling an unsound or difficult horse. It was a three-year-old colt of whom great things had been expected, only for him to flop horribly in the Derby: Lord Howard de Walden's bay colt Oncidium.

For a few weeks in the spring of 1964, Oncidium was England's horse. To an unwelcome degree, the big prizes of the post-war years disappeared off to France and Ireland. In the 1950s, it was Marcel Boussac's horses. In the early 1960s, the dominant figure in English racing was the Irish genius Paddy Prendergast, who was champion trainer from 1964 to 1966. When Oncidium lined up for the Derby, he was bidding to break a sequence of seven classics without a home-trained winner. He was by the St Leger and King George VI winner Alcide out of Malcolmia, who only raced three times, winning a one-mile stakes race at Epsom. She was trained at Newmarket by Jack Waugh, and he took charge of her son 10 years later.

Oncidium had a light two-year-old campaign, placing once from three starts. His second run as a three-year-old revealed his talent. He trounced 13 opponents in Sandown's 10-furlong Royal Stakes on heavy going; 10 of the 13 held Derby entries. Six lengths second was Indiana, who soon after paid Oncidium a compliment by easily winning the Chester Vase from Con Brio, who promptly won the Brighton Derby Trial. Oncidium was ridden at Sandown by Eph Smith, who'd won the Stewards' Cup on Dramatic for Todd 16 years earlier. Smith rode again when Oncidium lined up for the Lingfield Derby Trial.

On paper, the race lived up to the promise of its title. The 16 runners included most of the English-trained horses with any chance at Epsom. Indiana reopposed, and Con Brio provided a line to the Brighton trial.

Considering how well his Sandown win had worked out, Oncidium was a generous 11-2. A few minutes later, ante-post punters were queuing up to take 8-1 for the Derby. Oncidium turned the Lingfield trial into a procession, never out of the first two, and winning by five lengths. Indiana's deficit was eight lengths, up from six at Sandown, so the form seemed rock-solid. Oncidium stood out as England's best hope for keeping the Blue Riband at home. He faced a mighty obstacle: the Irish colt Santa Claus, winter favourite for Epsom and then a facile winner of the Irish 2,000 Guineas. But Oncidium's Sandown and Lingfield performances suggested that England too had a star.

At Newmarket, Jack Waugh and his team weren't quite as confident as the racing press and public. George Duffield, who was apprenticed to Waugh, remembers that the colt, "Had his own ideas some mornings - lots of ability, but a bit cranky, plenty of mental complications. [Waugh's head lad] Jack Button used to ride him; he was a fantastic horseman. Some days he rode him like a hack, out of the string, playing around, letting him do his own thing." After the Lingfield trial, Waugh wasn't entirely happy: "He thought Oncidium had a harder race than he would've liked. That wouldn't have suited the horse mentally. It wouldn't take a lot to persuade him not to put his best foot forward," says Duffield.

On Derby day, Oncidium looked magnificent in the paddock, and started second favourite behind Santa Claus. He was drawn right on the inside, which left Eph Smith to bustle him up to take a good early position. He got to the lead by the top of the hill, and as the field turned for home, his nose-banded head was in front. His pedigree and his style of running at Lingfield suggested that all he would do was stay, but when Smith pressed the accelerator, the gauge read empty.

Seven horses passed him in the straight, most gallingly Indiana. At the post, the Scobie Breasley-ridden Santa Claus came late to beat Indiana by a length. If Oncidium had reproduced either of his earlier runs against Indiana, he would've been the easy Derby winner. Smith was criticised in some quarters, but it was hard to see what he did wrong. Afterwards he said that Oncidium, "Was dropping his bit all the time and not taking any interest at all. He constantly hung his head away from the rails [and] just went along in a listless fashion."

Smith was so upset that he devoted a chapter of his short memoirs to a diatribe against Oncidium: "A pig of a horse." "The only thing you could do was try to forget him and hope never to get another like him."

On the Saturday after the Derby, Noel Murless was on Newmarket Heath when to his surprise he saw Oncidium in strong work. It wasn't a training routine that he associated with a colt that had run in a classic four days before. Murless told Howard de Walden: 'They're galloping the guts out of your horse.'

Murless put forward George Todd as the right man to sort out a problem, and isolated Manton as the ideal stable. Murless would've loved to train at Manton himself. One evening after he and George and their wives had dined with Gordon Richards at Beckhampton, the men sat down to play cards. To Audrey's alarm, Murless announced that, "We'll play for Manton." The night was long and well refreshed. The only certain winner was Murless's housekeeper. She found some big white fivers that had been lost down the sides of the chairs, like feathers from a duvet, but at least there were no title deeds to Manton.

Howard de Walden could never fathom Todd. As his quip about the 'Iron Curtain horse' implied, he wasn't kept over-informed about his horse's progress. Todd kept his counsel, but below the still surface, there was a lot of vigorous paddling going on. Few horses at Manton ever received as much attention as Oncidium. His training regime for many weeks comprised long solo walks across the downs, ridden by John Cherry. Oncidium had arrived at Manton with his own lad from Jack Waugh's yard. Todd called Cherry over and said, "I think we'd better send the boy home, John. If it doesn't work out with the horse, I don't want him phoning everyone. I'd rather he went, and we do it our way. Will you look after the horse?" 'Of course,' Cherry said, and rates Oncidium the best horse he rode in his 25 years at Manton: "But I pulled up to have a chat with the gallops man. He walked up behind us, and the horse just took off with me. He was that stoked up. Otherwise we didn't have many problems with him."

The tailor-made routine for Oncidium was typical of Todd's approach to each horse as an individual. Sidney Banks decided to have a bit of fun with one of his own horses, Santaway. Over several years at Manton, Santaway won a race or two every year, including the Banks's 'silver wedding day stakes.'

Banks thought he'd campaign the veteran from home. After a frustrating few weeks, he called Todd: "How the hell did you train the old bugger,

George? I can't get him to go on my gallop." "Hmmm. When we wanted him to do some work, we sent him off on his own with a lad," replied Todd: "We told the boy to make his way, by hook or by crook, to the far end of the downs and then come back as quick as he could. Sometimes they were gone all morning. That's how I trained him." So Santaway, mighty pleased with himself for defying his lad, as he thought, would return to his stable at top speed, galloping himself to fitness.

After dark one winter evening, a young apprentice, David Hunt, had a message that Bob Shanahan wanted to see him. At the time Hunt was the yard's clandestine 'runner' for the local bookie, so he expected the worst. He needn't have worried. "Put your coat on," Shanahan told him: "You're riding out. I'm going to lead you down to the gallops. Go up at a good pace and the guv'nor will be waiting at the top with a torch." "They brought this horse out, I galloped it in the moonlight and when I pulled up Todd was there. When I came back to the yard, Bob was waiting. He took the lead out of the saddle, weighed me, and said, 'I'll unsaddle. You can go along now. Don't mention this to a soul'." Alas, the secret gallop didn't pay off: the horse ran over hurdles the next day and finished only third.

Oncidium's first race for Manton was the St Leger. Eph Smith again took the ride, and the horse looked tremendous in the paddock and on the way to post. He was a big mover in the market, but seemed to run lifelessly, staying on late into fifth, 10 lengths behind, again, Indiana. There was an excuse: a stray dog had rushed out among the horses on the turn for home, and Oncidium had been forced to check. After the race, de Walden asked Todd if he thought it was worth keeping Oncidium in training? "I would if he was mine. But perhaps you need the money?" This to the owner of 100 acres of central London. Oncidium had one more run as a three-year-old, ridden by Breasley and stepped up to two miles for the Jockey Club Cup. The opposition wasn't as testing as the company the horse had been keeping, and he won easily.

As a four-year-old, Oncidium made his debut in a typically competitive Coronation Cup at Epsom. That hadn't been the plan. The colt's first target was the John Porter Stakes, but he was coughing for weeks either side of the race, which in his absence was won by Staff Ingham's Soderini, who went on to take the Hardwicke Stakes. Todd had only three clear weeks with Oncidium to prepare him for Epsom, and two days before the race there was a scare when he struck into his near hind. He was bandaged at Epsom, but not for the first time he attracted significant support. The 10 runners included Soderini and the winners of the previous season's English and Irish St Legers, the Oaks and the Prix Vermeille, as well as the third-placed horses from the Derby, St Leger and Grand Prix de Paris. Oncidium laughed at them. Breasley held on to him until well into the straight, and a furlong out he had a brief tussle with Soderini before going away to win, ears pricked, by a comfortable length and a half, with a further five lengths to the third. That evening Todd gave John Cherry a present of £100, "For all you've done with the horse." "Please thank Lord Howard," said the delighted Cherry. "He doesn't know yet," replied Todd.

Oncidium's former rider Eph Smith watched the Coronation Cup with horror: "Everyone started to say how Mr Todd had worked wonders with [Oncidium], how it took a good jockey to ride him and what a wonderful horse he was. Well, on that showing he was, and it began to look rather bad for Jack Waugh and myself."

Oncidium was back on a pedestal. "French challengers routed in Coronation Cup," crowed *The Sporting Life*: "Oncidium looks a good thing for the Ascot Gold Cup." On the morning of the race, its front page headline was, "Oncidium for England!"

Providence was tempted. Oncidium was sent off the even money favourite and ran a stinker. Had there been betting exchanges, the 'lay' columns would have filled up before the Gold Cup field had gone six furlongs. Passing the crowds and at the turn away from the stands, Oncidium was a depressing sight, pulling hard and repeatedly changing his legs. At the final bend, Breasley still had his mount more or less in contention, but when he picked up his whip, the horse hung badly and found nothing. He finished fourth, beaten over 18 lengths, including eight lengths behind the third horse, Autre Prince, whom he'd thrashed in the Coronation Cup.

The papers had a field day with Oncidium's mulish display, but at Manton they had a more sinister explanation: they were sure he'd been doped. There was even a suspect, a lad who'd come to the yard with a draft of horses. He seemed to do a lot of poking around, and had stayed long enough to find out that the yard's loft had an access point from outside, and that there was a trapdoor in the ceiling close to where Oncidium was stabled. But in the absence of any proof, there was nothing for Todd to do but press on with Oncidium and retrieve what he could from the rest of the season. The horse ran mostly honourably. His third to Meadow Court and Soderini in the King George VI was the nearest he came to repeating the level of his Coronation Cup win, and taking the consistent Soderini as a yardstick, it was about 5lb inferior.

His last race was in that best of all renewals of the Prix de l'Arc de Triomphe, when Sea Bird beat a top-class field by six lengths and five. Oncidium almost didn't run at all: he failed a starting stalls test in Paris. Howard de Walden only found out when he opened his newspaper. He pulled some strings and his horse was allowed another try.

When he took it up with Todd, he was told, "Oh, they use those things there. Oncidium has never seen one." It wasn't a great surprise when he started slowly and finished far back. There was a happy ending for England's horse. De Walden sold him as a stallion to New Zealand for £60,000 (*£735,000*).

He paid for himself many times over. He died prematurely after injuring himself, but in six years, he was twice champion sire of Australia and New Zealand. His final covering season was, 'the most spectacular by a single stallion in the history of Australian breeding' up to that time. His stock's prize money in Australia in 1974-1975 more than doubled the previous record.

It wasn't long after the Arc that Todd and some of his owners were at the Houghton sales. Todd was in a foul mood. He'd been playing poker for most of the night, unprofitably, and he was hung over. He had orders for three yearlings. Various lots that he'd earlier marked down as interesting were led out without him lifting a finger. Eventually he made three successful bids. He sat down with Kenneth Mackenzie and Bob Capon to divide them up.

The first pick went to Mackenzie. It grew to be a sweet-natured horse, but useless. The second choice, Capon's Dawn Attack, was so slow that it finished up as his farm hack. The third – "Who's left?" asked Todd - went to Radha Sigtia. The colt was Sodium, who was to win the St Leger and the Irish Derby. He was by the shock Derby winner Psidium out of a maiden, Gambade. She was bought out of the Aga Khan's dispersal sale by Major Ned O'Kelly of the Kilcarn Stud near Navan. The Major was admirably candid to call Gambade, "As slow as an old man in boots," but it probably didn't help her colt's sale price. He was knocked down to Todd for 3,500 gns [*£49,000*].

During Sodium's three-year-old season, Todd also had a filly called Parthian Glance. She was never entered for the Oaks, but she won the Ribblesdale, the Yorkshire Oaks and the Park Hill, so that in 1966 Todd had a classic-winning colt and arguably the best staying filly.

Two years earlier, he had the best three-year-old miler, Roan Rocket and the best stayer, Trelawny. In between, Oncidium was the equal highest-rated older horse of 1965. It must have been bittersweet for Todd. The decades fiddling around with selling platers to survive, and then he was into his seventieth year before Fortune sent the Group horses his way.

Sodium's first two runs were reminiscent of some of those platers of the past. He wasn't remotely busy. The apprentice Glyn Foster rode him in the Donnington Castle Stakes. The form book noted, "Strong, workmanlike, scope, late headway, never nearer." Glyn Foster's account is more direct: "I could've won 15 bloomin' lengths if I'd been trying."

Sodium's next outing, again at Newbury with Glyn Foster, came under, "Never troubled leaders," but his final runs as a two-year-old oozed promise. He was second in the Royal Lodge Stakes, with Black Prince II in fourth; and then fourth in the Observer Gold Cup at Doncaster, beaten three lengths by Jack Jarvis's Pretendre. The form of these two races was closely reproduced the following season. Sodium was odds-on to win a muddling Brighton Derby trial, while Black Prince II was winning the other trial, at Lingfield, from Charlottown, trained by Gordon Smyth. Charlottown was unlucky, as he'd been left with 15 lengths to make up in the short Lingfield straight.

After a delay at Epsom for Charlottown to be re-shod in the paddock, the result seemed to sort out the pecking order. Charlottown won by a neck from Pretendre; five lengths back came Black Prince II; Sodium was another two lengths away in fourth. The four were well clear of the remainder. When he was saddled, Sodium had been shivering, frothing at the mouth and lashing out. He was sweating and uneasy in the paddock.

The stewards gave Todd permission to withdraw the colt if he wanted. With misgivings, he opted to let Sodium take his chance. His jockey Frankie Durr had him up with the leaders throughout. He stayed on up the straight, but was readily left behind by the front three. Durr reported that Sodium had choked and gurgled during the race. Todd ordered a private dope test.

It was negative, but two unrelated physical problems came to light.

A piece of straw from the racecourse stables was found to be lodged in the horse's windpipe; and not long after, he developed an abscess in a foot, which might have been causing discomfort at the time of the race.

Five weeks later, Sodium took on Charlottown again in the Irish Derby. Twenty-three went to post, but the race appeared to concern only a handful, with the Irish 2,000 Guineas winner Paveh the best of the home team. The two English colts were both held up for the first half of the race. Sodium had an uninterrupted passage through the tiring horses around him, and took on Paveh just over a furlong out. He settled the issue quickly, and although Charlottown charged through in the last half-furlong, Sodium was always holding him, and won by a length.

Charlottown had to switch outside and came a little wider than Sodium had done, but Peter O'Sullevan wasn't alone in arguing that Sodium won cleverly, and had a length or two in hand at the post. The Sweeps Derby was a huge, high-prestige prize. But it was 'abroad'.

Howard de Walden was one of many who heard from Todd, "I never travel. I went abroad once to a place called Passchendale, didn't like it, have never been [away] again." Radha Sigtia was left to go to the Curragh himself. After his colt's win, he said rather unpatriotically that he wouldn't take Sodium back to stud duties in India: "[He'd] be much too valuable to stand in the East." Kenneth Mackenzie was also at the Curragh. After Sodium's win, he searched for a phone, at length finding one in the home of one of the Curragh trainers. He dialled Manton. Audrey Todd answered. No, George wasn't available, and he wouldn't be back for an hour. As Sodium was winning the Irish Derby, Todd was alone on his downs, walking the dogs.

Sodium ran for another big prize a fortnight later: the King George VI at Ascot. He was favourite to beat a small field that included the previous year's Prix Vermeille winner, Aunt Edith, trained by Noel Murless and ridden by Lester Piggott, who made a decisive move on the turn in, taking two lengths out of his pursuers. Sodium mounted a sustained challenge and clawed back the deficit to half a length, but Aunt Edith wouldn't be passed. She was the first filly to win the King George. Lester had the ride in Sodium's next race, the Oxfordshire Stakes at Newbury, an intended warm-up for the St Leger. Charlottown re-opposed, to Todd's delight. When told a couple of days before the race that Charlottown might not run, he said, 'There won't be a bet if he doesn't.' Sodium was odds-on but ran a stinker, finishing third of four, beaten 13 lengths. Again, Todd called for a dope test, and again it showed nothing, but Sodium was sick after the race with kidney trouble. It was only a little over three weeks before the St Leger.

It wasn't until the last few days that Todd managed to get some serious work into Sodium. Charlottown was a warm favourite at 11-10, the Derby second Pretendre was 3-1 and Sodium 7-1. Among the supporting cast were Black Prince II and an improving handicapper, David Jack, winner of the Magnet Cup. Piggott rode David Jack, and Frankie Durr was re-united with Sodium.

Black Prince II set out to make the running, and was still at the head of affairs when David Jack passed him two furlongs out. Charlottown at once joined him, and the two were head to head until well inside the last furlong. Just as Charlottown won that battle, Durr produced Sodium with a long, raking run up the favourite's outside. They came close together, and Charlottown fought dourly, but at the post, Sodium was a head to the good.

The stewards held two enquiries. One was into possible interference between Sodium and Charlottown; it was quickly resolved. The other was into the disparity between Sodium's form at Newbury and at Doncaster. That too had a happy outcome; Todd told the racing press that, "The stewards were very nice and accepted that horses are not machines. I told [them] that Sodium had kidney trouble soon after [Newbury] and at one time, I thought he might not have been able to run [today]. The St Leger is the one race I thought he would win as a three-year-old."

Sodium was rated the best horse in the three-year-old Free Handicap, and the best of his age by *Timeform*, in each case 1lb ahead of Charlottown. The two colts probably hit on a lucky year. There was an outbreak of swamp fever[1] in France, resulting in a ban on their runners in England and Ireland. When European middle-distance form came together in the Arc, French horses filled the first seven places. In eighth was Aunt Edith, who'd beaten Sodium at Ascot.

At Manton, Audrey Todd fretted. She pictured George at Doncaster, flushed with success, tipping £5 notes to every stranger who wished him well or offered him a drink. She phoned the weighing room and asked to speak to him. He ignored the message. She had a call put out on the

[1] equine anaemia

public address system. He muttered, "I know what she wants," and went back to his champagne. A party gathered that evening in the Ailesbury Hotel in Marlborough. When anyone arrived from Doncaster, Audrey buttonholed them: "How much money has George given away?"

Chapter 28

'My small bet'

One April morning in George Todd's early years at Manton, a crocodile of archaeology enthusiasts wound its way across the downs. They were looking for the Manton Long Barrow, a 4,000-year-old burial mound. They found a muddy scar in a field where the mound had been. John Claydon, who was Todd's farm bailiff at the time, was confronted by a furious 'professor type': "I said, you'd better go to the yard to see Mr Todd." The meeting between Todd and the professor didn't go well. "It was very brave of him to take George on," chuckles Claydon: "Ignorance is bliss." No one was allowed anywhere near the yard without Todd's say-so, and he chose not to understand what the professor wanted: "That's a [wheel] barrow over there. Count it and go. I don't want to see you here again."

The next arrival was a reporter from the *Daily Mail*. "The only barrows at Manton are here in the yard," barked Todd: "And they're full of horseshit." Audrey tried to be diplomatic. The paper quoted her saying, "My husband is most upset. He has told the Ministry of Works he will do everything he can to put the matter right." There wasn't much that Todd or anyone else could repair. Todd had rented some land to his backer, Jack King. With a view to improving the land, King had bulldozed what he took to be a large, stony bramble patch: "I've seen plenty of graveyards but none looking like that." His excavations turned up some impressive stones. They were blown to smithereens. "We had great big bangs up there for a week," recalls Claydon. A local MP asked a question in the House of Commons, but fortunately for Todd and King, the time limit for action under the ancient monuments law had passed.

Todd had infinite patience where horses were concerned, but the shortest of fuses when anyone interfered with the conduct of his business. First in line were any punters who dared step into the market before his own money was down. Racecourse stewards also featured high on his list of irritants. For years, George used the racecourse as a schooling ground. Countless races served as the overtures and first acts of his carefully plotted equine dramas.

The occasional steward noted that every now and then, betting fireworks would point with uncanny accuracy to a sudden improvement in the form of a Todd-trained horse. On those days, Todd had prepared his explanations, and prepared his jockeys, too. Much was suspected, but nothing proved, until the arrival of the patrol camera. Todd then took a new tack. One of the senior stewards' secretaries of the time remembered with horror that, "Calling George in was the most terrifying thing. He always seemed to have his licence ready. He'd throw it on the table and accuse us: 'This horse is a dog and if you gentlemen can't see that, you can have my licence back now'." Invariably, the stewards finished up by begging him to take it back. And though the camera forced him to moderate his tactics, he could handle that as well.

One day at Windsor when Bradfield drifted in the betting and was spotted ambling round at the back, finishing seventh of eight, the stewards invited George to have a look at the film. Todd folded his arms and glared back over their heads, while the film played silently across his chest. It's a moot point as to who was angrier, Todd or the stewards. They put out a statement saying that they,

> "Enquired into the riding of [John] Hayward on Bradfield. They heard evidence from both stewards' secretaries, G Todd the trainer, and Hayward, and also viewed the camera patrol film. They informed Todd and Hayward that the riding and running of the gelding gave grounds for the gravest suspicion."

He never had another runner at Windsor. In his defence, he trained numerous cast-offs and crocks and animals bought out of sellers, and they weren't likely to be models of consistency. Indeed, he came closest to serious trouble with a horse for whom the word 'ungenuine' could've been invented. It was a hurdler called Jive, who came out of a Sandown seller. George had a fancied runner in the race, Baldachino. He was the worst, most temperamental horse that Tommy Frost ever owned, but this was supposed to be his day. Todd was dismayed when Jive, ridden by Lester Piggott and trained by his father Keith, beat Frost's horse comfortably. He decided to buy Jive at the auction.

He said later that he got the impression that Piggott senior seemed quite pleased to let the horse go, and that when he got Jive back to Manton, the horse showed, "A very nasty temperament, an enlarged joint and bad feet." Tom Frost, who rode out on Jive, remembers, "A horrid little horse." Jive barely stood training, but Todd persisted, and in due course a familiar sequence unfolded. Jive was unquoted in the betting and beaten more than 20 lengths in a Kempton seller. Then he ran in another selling hurdle at Sandown, where he was tailed off at one stage before rocketing home, only a few lengths behind the winner.

A month later, he was back at Sandown, heavily backed to 15-8 favourite. In the early stages of the race, he dropped out and was offered at 4-1 in running. No sooner had Todd taken that price than Jive picked up his bit, scythed through the field to lead approaching the last hurdle, and went away to win as he pleased. Jive had improved by 10 to 12lb from the previous race, and the stewards asked Todd to tell them why. He said that Jive was a rogue and had run well for a new jockey, John Worrall, the boy who'd been riding work on him at home.

The explanation was accepted by the Sandown stewards, but not by one *Sporting Life* reader, who wrote a sarcastic letter to the paper. He pointed out that Jive had run five races for Todd; four times weak in the betting and unplaced, then well supported and winning.

> "Does (Jive) have some means of communicating his running plans to his connections? If so, what means of communication does he adopt?"

This had the same affect on Todd as a mayfly on a trout. He wrote, *"Letter-writing is not one of my hobbies and I don't enjoy it."* He continued at some length, the gist of his reply being that Jive was a thief. The paper headlined his letter, *"My small bet on Jive – by George Todd."* Perhaps not ideal. The Epsom trainer Jack Reardon defended George with a blast at the 'trash' *The Sporting Life* was publishing.

Reardon wasn't the best witness for the defence. He seldom trained more than half a dozen horses, but he bet on a scale similar to Todd himself. One day in the 1950s when a plot went astray he said mournfully, "It could have been worse. I only had £5,000 on it."

The replies from Todd and Reardon gave the original writer the chance for some more heavy irony. In a second letter he asked, if Jive was such a rogue and villain, why had Todd bothered to buy him in after the Sandown win? The timing was awful. Three days later, Jive ran under a penalty, again ridden by Worrall, and was notably weak in the betting. He tailed off, and this time he stayed tailed off. Todd was on holiday, so the stewards interviewed Worrall and the travelling head lad, Wally Mills. They weren't satisfied with what they heard and they referred the running of Jive to Portman Square. It looked bad for Todd. The regulars in The Bear in Marlborough ran a book on the 'George Todd licence stakes.' It was odds on the trainer spending a while on the easy list. He and John Worrall attended an hour-long hearing at the Jockey Club. To some surprise, they were exonerated.

After the enquiry, Todd said that, "The stewards were well satisfied with the horse's running and accepted all the evidence." He was much more careful after Jive, but privately he continued to hold stewards in low regard. He used to say that most punters would do better to acquire a knowledge of race-riding, study the stewards at each meeting, and confine their betting to the outcomes of objections.

Chapter 29

The last of the old-time trainers

Todd was a mass of contradictions. He was a former Hunt employee who didn't approve of field sports. He bought a large estate but took no interest at all in its farming side. At first, he left it to Jack King, then hired John Claydon as bailiff; and then a farm partner, Harry Johnson, to whom he delegated with evident relief. Claydon noticed that when *The Archers* was first broadcast, George paid it the closest attention: "I was expected to do most of the things the Archers did. He seemed to get all his farming ideas straight from Philip Archer."

Todd was a stickler for detail, yet notoriously unpunctual. He spent his life around horses and the yard, yet had a passion for ballroom dancing, and was vain to a fault. Lester Piggott once reported to Noel Murless that, "Mr Todd's gone a bit funny." Piggott had been staying at the Metropole in Brighton for a Goodwood meeting, and had seen George having a manicure and taking dancing lessons. The picture of Sidney Banks's French Design on page 249 is a record of Todd's self-regard as well as his genius for long-range planning. He'd spent what seemed to Audrey an eternity fussing around with his suit and his pose. As the photographer worked, a window opened and she called out, "Vanity, thy name is Man."

French Design's partner in the photograph, Vic Gardner, had never sat on the horse before. One day he was told to smarten up and fetch Banks's colours. French Design was steadily building a claim for a place among Todd's top stayers. He was a seven-year-old who'd won at least one race in five consecutive seasons, and had already run in the Cesarewitch four times, finishing sixth in 1951, second in 1952 and winning for Doug Smith in 1954. French Design had also won the 1952 Goodwood Stakes. Despite extravagant tail-swishing under pressure, he was thoroughly game and genuine.

After the photograph, French Design made his 1955 reappearance in the Goodwood Stakes, ridden by Gardner, repeated his win of three years earlier, and was made favourite for the Cesarewitch from the first betting show. He injured himself in his final gallop a few days before the race, and never ran again.

Racehorses of 1955 thought, "[He] would have stood an excellent chance of being the first horse to win the Cesarewitch twice. Eight years old, and having his first outing since the previous October, he paid a remarkable tribute to the skill of his trainer by winning the Goodwood Stakes for the second time, a feat which had not been accomplished for more than a hundred years."

French Design's Cesarewitch win seems to have put Todd's connections and their punters to sleep. He had another runner in the race, King's Love, who was advanced to strong favouritism following what seemed to be a full-dress trial on the old long-distance gallop at Manton. Various horses jumped in and dropped out, and at the finish, King's Love had a four-length call over French Design.

Sidney Banks was always irritated by Todd's secretiveness, and he was upset by French Design's weakness in the ante-post betting. Had he been privy to the Todd family grapevine, Banks wouldn't have had a care in the world. If your father is a pork butcher in a small town and you're one of eight children, you have no money, so Todd tried to help his siblings as best he could.

When he was financially secure, that included buying a house for his unmarried brother and sister. Before then, he had something to give them: what the ancients called the philosopher's stone - a way to make gold. When he had a good thing and his own money was on, he let his family know. There are Todd great-nephews and nieces who remember today that their parents put the pocket money on French Design.

George's sister Ida attracted attention in Horncastle because she seemed always to leave the local bookmaker clutching winnings. People notice such things. Ida took to visiting the bookie by side streets and back alleys, to avoid seeing anyone she knew. She lived to 102. Some time in her 80s, the roundabout walk became too much, and she wrote down her bets for a neighbour to take to the bookie: not at all what George would've wanted.

The assessment of Todd's character that was widely quoted after his death was John Hislop's description: 'cool and fearless.' He was hardly cool: there was his quick temper, and also his acute superstition. At one time, he had a hurdler for Kenneth Mackenzie: "George liked buying horses but then he didn't always like the ones he'd bought. He decided he didn't care for this one."

Todd sent the horse to run at a remote, minor course. A senior jockey had been booked. When Mackenzie arrived, his horse was there, the travelling lad was there. The jockey was waiting. He wanted to know, "Where's Mr Todd? What are my instructions?" But there was no sign of George. He'd set off from Manton and seen a single magpie.

"This'll never do," he told his driver; "We're going home." They were almost back at the yard when Todd changed his mind. When he spilled out of the car at the racecourse, his horse was already on its way to post. All Todd had time to say to Mackenzie was, "Get as much on this as you can." The horse won by a short head. After the race, Todd asked Mackenzie, had he got a couple of hundred pounds to give to the jockey, who, despite the present, was furious. And although the horse had won, George told Mackenzie that he didn't want it, and another trainer would have to be found.

Todd's unpunctuality meant that, whether he was driving himself or being driven, it was usually at breakneck speed. The result was that he met lots of policemen. One day when his driver was on holiday, he hared off to Newbury to back another of his hurdlers. He was pulled over on the A4. Out came the notebooks. Todd, exasperated, told the officers that he had to get to the races to saddle a horse, and he was running late. They began the ritual questions.

Todd interrupted: "The horse is called No Restrictions. It will win. I suggest you find a bookie." Within the hour, No Restrictions had trounced a big field by five lengths and more. It started at the rewarding odds of 100-8. Not surprisingly, that was one brush with the law which didn't result in a summons.

Over his lifetime, Todd was triumphantly ahead of the bookmakers, but the winning peaks had deep troughs between them. He lost money mug-punting on other trainers' horses, and in the last decade of his training career he had some rocky years. The clearest sign that he was moving down a gear or two came the year after Sodium's classic win. After the seasons of Trelawny, Roan Rocket and Oncidium, most trainers would be welcoming new owners. Todd halved his string from almost 50 in 1965 to just 25 two years later. He'd already talked to some of his friends about retirement. If he was having a bad betting run, it cheered him up to talk about how much money Manton was worth. He told the journalist Tom Nickalls that in 1963 he'd turned down an offer of £250,000 [*£3.44 million*] for the yard. He complained of his betting that, "I must be getting old. Whenever I have a little bit extra on now, they seem to get beat." The Beckhampton trainer Jeremy Tree made an opportunistic, low offer for Manton for one of his owners. George asked Jack Colling what he thought: "Don't be mad, George. You have that much on one of your selling platers. In fact, you have that much on other people's platers!"

After all the years of financing Manton and his champagne lifestyle by successful betting, Todd didn't enjoy handing back his winnings. Another factor in his decision to wind down was the rapidly changing world outside Manton's walls. It was harder to find good lads, and impossible to impose the discipline that was integral to his training routines. Philip Larkin wrote that:

> "Sexual intercourse began
> In nineteen sixty-three…
> Between the end of the Chatterley ban
> And the Beatles' first LP"

The liberating effect of the birth control pill, the death of censorship and a new, irreverent pop culture all played a part in the vast change in young people's lives and opportunities in the early 1960s. The slow emergence of the country from post-war austerity, into prosperity at every level of society, created opportunity and choice. Standing to attention at evening stables and being shouted at wasn't high on the list of a 1960s teenager's aspirations.

As might be expected, Todd's negotiations to sell Manton didn't always run smoothly. The owner-breeder Arnold Weinstock expressed his interest. He went down to Manton, was shown round, and settled down to discuss a price. Audrey Todd brought in tea. Weinstock, oblivious, continued to talk terms. At one point, he signed a blank cheque and offered it, as Captain Machell had done to Alec Taylor in the same room a hundred years before. After Weinstock had left, Todd told friends, 'I'm not going to sell Manton to some chap who doesn't stand up when my wife comes into the room.' Paul Cole had an owner with over £1 million earmarked for

Manton. Cole was a little anxious about how Todd might view a former pupil-assistant as his successor, so he took to the skies and gave his owner an aerial tour by helicopter.

Then Sir Gordon Richards, who'd been leasing a yard at nearby Ogbourne, suggested what seemed the perfect hand-over of the reins. He would lease the main yard and the gallops; John Cherry would take the 24-box Astor yard. Todd was delighted with the plan. Sir Gordon would bring a powerful roster of new owners to Manton. Cherry would have his chance to train. He'd been invited to join an up-and-coming younger trainer as travelling head lad. It would give him more time on the racecourse, to meet prospective future owners. Todd twisted Cherry's arm: "If you go, I won't be able to carry on without you," but also made a promise: "When I pack it up, I'll get you a yard and you'll have horses to train."

Sir Gordon's proposal went as far as draft contracts. He was due at Manton one Sunday morning to complete the formalities. The day before, Audrey vetoed the arrangement. She'd been George's 'back office' for over 40 years. Perhaps she just felt like putting her spoke into the wheel, or perhaps it was her revenge for his occasional wanderings. The outcome was a disappointment for Sir Gordon, crushing for John Cherry and finally, a financial disaster for Audrey herself.

The last big winners that Todd trained were Fair World in the 1971 Dante Stakes, Lord Nelson in the 1972 King Edward VII Stakes, and Picture Boy in the 1971 Hunt Cup. Picture Boy was a 720 gns Newmarket yearling purchase. Todd thought him the best-looking colt at the sale, but it was a dark night and nobody seemed to want him. He was offered to Kenneth Mackenzie, Todd saying that he'd keep a share because he liked the horse so much. Picture Boy ran twice when backward as a two-year-old. The following season he ran promisingly in a one-mile maiden, and was qualified for handicaps. His next start, at Kempton under Glyn Foster, was noted as, "late headway; never nearer." Then Todd suggested to Mackenzie, "Be at Newmarket on Saturday. He's sure to win." He went, and Picture Boy duly won. It was the day that George Duffield fiddled with his boots in the paddock, to send a signal. Picture Boy was backed from 6-1 to 9-2.

Earlier in the afternoon, old Blazing Scent landed an 11-2 to 9-4 gamble in an apprentice handicap. "We had quite a party," recalls Mackenzie. As a four- and five-year-old, Picture Boy went without a win, but was placed in a number of well-contested handicaps. He jarred himself badly in Kempton's Jubilee on firm ground early in May. It was thought unlikely that he'd race again, so Mackenzie sent him back to Newmarket to be sold as a potential stallion. When the catalogue appeared, Picture Boy was described as a gelding. As Todd joked, that put off quite a few prospective buyers. So back went Picture Boy into training. Restored to soundness, he continued in the same vein as before: a hat trick of close thirds in high-profile handicaps. There was nothing 'dark' about the horse. He'd been campaigned openly for three years without getting his head in front, or his handicap mark lowered. So Mackenzie was surprised to be told by Todd, a week before Royal Ascot, "The horse is very well and he's ready, but I haven't got a jockey. Unless you can find one, he won't run."

Mackenzie heard a good word for Jock Wilson: "I phoned and told George, 'I've found you a jockey.' It was one of his tetchy days. He said, 'Good God. Couldn't you have got anybody better?'" When they went to the paddock, the instructions to Wilson were, "Don't hold him up. Let the horse decide." Mackenzie said that he'd like to know if Picture Boy had a chance. Todd told him, "Come with me to see them going down to the start and then I'll tell you." After he'd watched Picture Boy stride out on the heavy ground, Todd turned to Mackenzie: "The horse is going to win - unless your rider messes it up." Mackenzie hurried off to the Ring with £500.

He did well, averaging 15-1 to his money, against a starting price of 11-1, and Jock Wilson did equally well, riding Picture Boy prominently until racing into the lead two furlongs out, and keeping him right up to his work to win easily by four lengths. Mackenzie split his *£70,000* winnings with Todd, and picked up *£42,000* in prize money. After the race, a group of Japanese breeders offered *£280,000* for Picture Boy. Todd asked to keep the horse for a few months more, to win one of the handicaps that always eluded him, the Jubilee. He was in training for that race when he broke a leg.

Kenneth Mackenzie and his wife Lelia were among a group of owners and fellow trainers whom Todd was especially close to. George was a creature of habit. Having decided that he'd never go abroad again, he discovered Torquay and its Imperial Hotel. He was delighted to prance around a tea dance without any curious jockey seeing him, he was served a plain grilled Dover sole most evenings, and for many years he and Audrey stayed in the same suite of rooms for a few weeks every winter.

A scarcely changing cast of their friends would join them: Jack and Sue Colling, Dez and Mollie Baring, the Mackenzies, farmer Jack King, the Johnson Houghtons, latterly Arthur and Lydia Hurlstone, who made a fortune from selling a toiletries business. When Ben Warner was alive, the Todds would walk over to one of his hotels for dinner. During the summer months, there was a similar unvarying routine. If he was racing anywhere handy, then George headed off after the last race to the French Horn at Sonning, where the usual suspects would gather round him. At Manton on Sundays, he served up champagne cocktails to his owners.

At the end of his life, George made an overdue peace with the racing press. Here again, there was a contradiction. During all the years of struggles, non-triers and gambles, Todd was phobic about journalists. His horses' wellbeing, their plans and the stable's news were his business and his alone. Yet visitors like Nigel Baring, sitting down to breakfast after riding work, saw Todd avidly scouring the papers for a mention of Manton, exclaiming, "Here, look what they're saying about us!" Over time, there were journalists who broke through Todd's carapace. Peter O'Sullevan would win Todd round over a glass of champagne at the races, be invited back to Manton for a second or third, and hear that some aged warrior was definitely now retired. "Come on, George, you don't mean that. He loves his racing. Surely there's another day for him?" and a story would be teased out.

Collectively, though, Todd saw the press as a barely tolerable nuisance. Never more so than at Lingfield when his good stayer Sea Leopard won an apprentices' staying race. George had thousands on Sea Leopard. The horse won. At the unsaddling, the pack descended on George. What was the plan? Would Sea Leopard run in the Cesarewitch? Meanwhile, the apprentice, buckling under a lead-laden saddle, staggered into the wooden shack that was the Lingfield weighing room. It had a design flaw: the jockey's room was reached before the scales. The boy turned the wrong way. The race and the bet were lost.

Todd blew his top and blamed the hacks. But they'd always respected him, and they acknowledged the ending of a great training career, and an era passing with him. The Horserace Writers Association gave him a Derby award for lifetime achievement at a luncheon in 1972. George and Sir Gordon Richards both spoke at the event. Between them, they brought the house down, looking younger if possible than the day, 22 years earlier, when they'd combined to bring off the monster gamble on Dramatic. But George found out soon afterwards that cancer had him in its grip. Not long before his death, he asked John Cherry to drive him up for the last time to look over the downs. He collapsed, so thin that he could have fallen out of his jacket.

Bradfield and Caught Out had their heads over the gate of a paddock to greet him. In his will, he made sure that they were given the same considerate end as all the others before.

> *"It is my wish that under no circumstances should any aged horse belonging to me be sold but my usual custom be observed with regard to having such horse humanely put down by my stable veterinary surgeon on the premises."*

In his final months, Manton changed hands. From all the would-be buyers, Todd took a liking to a young trainer, George Peter-Hoblyn. The sale price was agreed at £1.25 million [*£10.86 million*]. Peter-Hoblyn was short - to be exact, a million and a quarter short - but he had a backer, the financier John Bloomfield, who signed the cheque.

Todd went to die in his familiar rooms at the Imperial Hotel in Torquay, reluctant to see even his old friends. His estate was valued at £722,334 [*£5.74 million*], an astounding sum considering that he began life without any inheritance, his first job paying £7 a year. Every penny that he had came from shrewd betting on the horses that he trained, over a period of 45 years. He gave a lot back.

If he sold Manton for £1.25 million and then had almost half a million less in his estate not long afterwards, it suggests that some large accounts had been settled in between. Rumours spoke of him owing tens of thousands to the bookmakers. He evidently paid them all, and looked after his surviving brothers and sisters too.

Then, as if in a nightmare, estate duty took almost everything else. Audrey was left with around £10,500 [*£83,500*]. Had Manton been rented to Sir Gordon Richards, remaining in Audrey's ownership, George's estate would have been taxed as agricultural land, at 55 per cent. A nasty bite, to be sure, but Audrey would have received upwards of £320,000 [*£2.19 million*], with the benefit of several years for her to make further tax plans. Because the estate was entirely in cash, it attracted the highest possible tax rate. The Todds had successful businessmen among their owners.

How they failed to ask for, or perhaps act on, their advice is beyond understanding. Jack King's son Percy, as staunch a supporter of Todd as his father had been, openly questioned the lunacy of selling Manton when George was dying.

John Cherry worked for Todd for a quarter of a century, from picking weeds on his first morning to head lad, and then the unfulfilled hope of a chance to train at Manton himself. He took Todd's ashes onto the downs and scattered them by a neolithic standing stone on the Barton gallops.

At George Todd's death, Manton had been home to four trainers in just over 100 years: Old Alec for the first 24, Young Alec for the next 33, Joe Lawson for 19 years, Todd for 27 more. The light shone down by that century by classic winners and leaderboards doesn't favour Todd. The Taylors and Lawson headed endless lists of leading trainer and leading prize-money earner. The horses they stabled included champion after champion. Todd only appeared in the Top 10 trainers' list once, when he was the fourth-placed trainer in Sodium's year. He never trained more than 30 winners in a season. Yet, arguably, he achieved as much as the trio of giants who went before him.

There was a continuum: the trainer George Taylor had a son Tom, who begat Old Alec, who built Manton; then his son Young Alec, then the trusted right-hand man, Joe Lawson. George Todd had no racing pedigree or connections. He didn't have a penny to his name until he was well into his 30s. He defied Joe Lawson's gloomy prediction that he would, 'Never be able to manage Manton.' He paid his way there for 27 years and accumulated a substantial fortune. He was hard, but he made a point of never asking his lads to do something that he couldn't do himself.

Christmas Day at Manton was a work day like any other, so Todd would without fail ride out, although, to exercise the dogs and inspect the gallops, he preferred to walk on any other day. When Todd trained and backed a winner, the lads all shared in it. When they made an individual contribution, they had a personal reward. And if Todd repeatedly used the racecourse for rehearsals while a gamble was being incubated, then so did many others of his time. He was simply better at it than the rest, and for far longer. When the scrutiny of the camera patrol became too intense, he turned his talent to training Group race winners.

Quentin Gilbey, who for many years was the doyen of the racing press room, wrote in the *Sporting Chronicle*:

> "I have often pondered as to whether more honour is due to the big men like the Taylors and Joe Lawson [who] trained the very best horses and made the very best use of them, or whether the supreme achievement on the part of a trainer is to win races year in and year out with horses of humble origin. [George Todd rose] to fame and fortune the hard way, for no owners had sent him expensive and fashionably bred yearlings to train.
>
> "[His] success has been achieved with cheap purchases and other people's cast-offs, many of whom were none too sound and required the most skilful and patient handling if they were to pay their way."

Gilbey was writing, not after Roan Rocket or Sodium, but years earlier, when Todd had won a race with some moderate animal that another trainer had rejected. That's how Todd would have wanted it. He trained horses that interested him, for owners whom he got along with, proper people. He had a decided view on most things, and it didn't involve touting for new owners or expanding his string or chasing awards. He was happiest nursing Penharbour's terrible legs to his annual hurdles win and bringing the teenager Caught Out back for another high summer surprise.

After Sodium provided his only English classic winner, the press at Doncaster asked him, was this the best day of his life? "Well," he told them, "I was mighty pleased the day the hospital boat brought me back from France."

The *Bloodstock Breeders Review* called him a trainer who fully deserved the adjective 'great':

> "The fact that he succeeded in keeping his charges happy was proved time after time, for [Todd] became synonymous with an ability to maintain form in, and even improve, ageing horses. When most trainers were ready to cast out useful animals, on the supposition that their best days were past, Todd would be beginning to take an interest in them. He was patience personified, had a brilliant knack with unsound horses and he knew when they should be backed.
>
> "Todd managed not only to maintain Manton at its glorious peak… He did it all with a small string, steadfastly refusing offers of horses as he believed that each animal was entitled to individual attention and that a large team involved a reduction in standards… He was the last of the old-time trainers and no man ever commanded higher respect from the other senior members of his profession".

When George Peter-Hoblyn was welcomed to Manton, the yardman gave him a bunch of keys. It opened every door that he could see, except one, next to the feed house. Another key was found. It was Todd's wine store. Inside, most of the racks had collapsed, but there was one still filled with the dimpled bases of champagne bottles. For a moment, Peter-Hoblyn thought that several Christmas days had arrived together. But the bottles were empty, every one.

The classic winners

Alec Taylor		
1851	Derby	Teddington
1851	1,000 Guineas	Aphrodite
1860	St Leger	St Albans
1868	2,000 Guineas	Moslem
1873	2,000 Guineas	Gang Forward
1875	St Leger	Craig Millar
1878	Derby	Sefton
1880	2,000 Guineas	Petronel
1881	1,000 Guineas	Thebais
1881	Oaks	Thebais
1887	1,000 Guineas	Rêve d'Or
1887	Oaks	Rêve d'Or

Job Marson	Sir Joseph Hawley John Stanley
Job Marson	Sir Joseph Hawley
Luke Snowden	Lord Ailesbury
Thos Chaloner	WS Stirling Crawfurd
Thos Chaloner	WS Stirling Crawfurd
Thos Chaloner	WS Stirling Crawfurd
Harry Constable	WS Stirling Crawfurd
George Fordham	Duke of Beaufort
George Fordham	WS Stirling Crawfurd
George Fordham	WS Stirling Crawfurd
Charles Wood	Duke of Beaufort
Charles Wood	Duke of Beaufort

'Young' Alec Taylor

1905	St Leger	Challacombe
1909	St Leger	Bayardo
1910	Derby	Lemberg
1910	Oaks	Rosedrop
1914	2,000 Guineas	Kennymore
1917	2,000 Guineas	Gay Crusader
1917	Derby	Gay Crusader
1917	Oaks	Sunny Jane
1917	St Leger	Gay Crusader
1918	2,000 Guineas	Gainsborough
1918	Derby	Gainsborough
1918	Oaks	My Dear
1918	St Leger	Gainsborough
1919	Oaks	Bayuda
1921	2,000 Guineas	Craig an Eran
1921	Oaks	Love In Idleness
1922	Oaks	Pogrom
1925	1,000 Guineas	Saucy Sue
1925	Oaks	Saucy Sue
1926	Oaks	Short Story
1927	St Leger	Book Law

Otto Madden	Washington Singer
Danny Maher	Alfred W Cox
Danny Maher	Alfred W Cox
Charles Trigg	Sir William Bass
George Stern	Sir John Thursby
Steve Donoghue	Alfred W Cox
Steve Donoghue	Alfred W Cox
Otto Madden	Lord Astor
Steve Donoghue	Alfred W Cox
Joe Childs	Lady James Douglas
Joe Childs	Lady James Douglas
Steve Donoghue	Alfred W Cox
Joe Childs	Lady James Douglas
Joe Childs	Lady James Douglas
Jack Brennan	Lord Astor
Joe Childs	Joseph Watson
Ted Gardner	Lord Astor
Frank Bullock	Lord Astor
Frank Bullock	Lord Astor
Bobby Jones	Lord Astor
Henri Jelliss	Lord Astor

Joe Lawson

1929	Oaks	Pennycomequick
1932	2,000 Guineas	Orwell
1936	2,000 Guineas	Pay Up
1937	1,000 Guineas	Exhibitionnist
1937	Oaks	Exhibitionnist
1939	1,000 Guineas	Galatea II
1939	Oaks	Galatea II
1941	1,000 Guineas	Dancing Time
1943	2,000 Guineas	Kingsway
1945	2,000 Guineas	Court Martial

George Todd

1966	St Leger	Sodium

Henri Jelliss	Lord Astor
Bobby Jones	Washington Singer
Robert Dick	Lord Astor
Steve Donoghue	Sir Victor Sassoon
Steve Donoghue	Sir Victor Sassoon
Bobby Jones	Robert S Clark
Bobby Jones	Robert S Clark
Richard Perryman	Lord Glanely
Sam Wragg	AE Saunders
Cliff Richards	Lord Astor

Frankie Durr	Radha Sigtia

Acknowledgements

A book that spans a hundred years and a large cast of characters may bear a single author's name on its cover, but in truth it's the product of the goodwill, help and memories of many. The late Robert Sangster's purchase of Manton ensured it continued as a training yard. My first thanks go to his son Ben Sangster for giving me frequent access to the estate during my research.

The mystery of how 'Fairie' Cox came to own a share in a silver mine was cleared up by Narelle Crux, former archivist at BHP. I'm grateful to Bruce Deane, Edward Mahony and Michael Watt for background on Tattersalls' 20-year ownership of the yard in 'Young' Alec Taylor's time. Roy Brennan recalled the riding career of his father Jack, who between the wars was successively apprentice, work rider, and retained jockey. Susan Colling told me about her late husband Jack's many links to Manton. Fergie Sutherland gave me his recollections of Joe Lawson, whom he succeeded at Newmarket's Carlburg yard. Other past and present trainers who helped me include George Peter Hoblyn, who took over Manton in 1974; Clive Brittain; Peter Walwyn; Mercy Rimell, for her recall of Trelawny; Julie Cecil, for stories about her father Noel Murless' friendship with George Todd; and especially Paul Cole and Patrick Haslam, who successively filled the daunting role of Todd's pupil-assistant.

The editors of the *Horncastle News*, *Marlborough Gazette* and *Newmarket Journal* kindly published my letters asking for their readers' help. George Todd's early days have been filled in by family members June Smith, Mike Taylor and Brian Todd, and the Todds' Horncastle neighbour Susan Fox.

Among the senior jockeys who rode for and against Manton, Terry Biddlecombe, George Duffield, Jimmy Lindley, Joe Mercer and Lester Piggott have all helped.

George Todd's owners Betty Garton [née Cooke] and Kenneth Mackenzie were generous with their time. Among Todd's former owners, Dez Baring is brought to these pages by his sons Peter and Nigel and his daughter Anne Dalgety; Tommy Frost by his son Tom; and Sidney Banks by his son Michael. Thanks to them all for their stories, and in Tom Frost's case for his father's scrapbook, and for his comments on the Todd chapters.

Many of the apprentices and paid lads who served in 'Todd's Army' talked to me. If a complete portrait of Todd emerges in these pages, it's thanks to Derek 'Dickie' Bates, Dick Broadway, Eric Campbell, Ron Cartwright, David Churchley, John Flatt, John Friar, Glyn Foster, Vic Gardner, Malcolm Hall, David Hunt, Bill McCluskey, Margaret Shanahan, Graham Stephens, Terry Stringer, Albert Tucker and John Worrall.

John Cherry was Todd's last head lad, and the first person that I interviewed for this book. He put me in touch with many of his friends and contemporaries at Manton. The day that he showed me round the old yard and the gallops was a highlight. But for a calamitous decision of Audrey Todd's, Cherry himself would have trained from Manton.

Thanks to John Claydon and Harry Johnson, respectively Todd's bailiff and farm partner, and Richard Brickell for his introductions; Tim Cox for giving me access to the wonderful resource of The Cox Library; James Hill for patiently finding numerous contacts; James Lambie, the chronicler of *The Sporting Life,* for sources that I might never have found for myself; Major Srinivas Nargolkar, the former keeper of the Indian Stud book, for his profile of Radha Sigtia; Sir Peter O'Sullevan for his assessments of Todd, and of Todd's sometimes strained relationship with Scobie Breasley; and Dr Terry Rogers for searching the Marlborough College archives.

John Bloomfield, who bought Manton from George Todd, compiled some entertaining notes on the yard's early history, in particular its skirmishes with the Marlborough touts. George Windsor-Clive found those notes for me. The turf historian and writer Michael Tanner generously shared some of his own research on the Taylors.

My thanks to Anthony de Freitas for his analysis of Alec Taylor's will. He, and Alan Chester and Philip Malcolm, kindly read the final draft of the book. If any mistakes remain, they're mine alone.

Finally, my wife Heather has put up with my absences, silences, highs and lows, scattered papers and all-invading piles of books. Her continued tolerance, good humour and support made it possible.

Bibliography

Astley, Sir John Dugdale *Fifty Years of my Life* [1894]

Bird, TH *Admiral Rous and the English Turf* [1939]
Bloodstock Breeders' Review [from 1912]
Breasley, Scobie and Poole, Christopher *Scobie, A Lifetime in Racing* [1984]
Browne, Capt TH *A History of the English Turf* [1931]
Bull, Phil *The Best Horses of* [1943 to 1947]

Chetwynd, Sir George *Racing Reminiscences* [1891]
Childs, Joe *My Racing Reminiscences* [1952]
Colling, Susan *Jack of His Own Trade* [1993]

Dalgety, Anne *Moll and Dez* [2001]
Day, William *Turf Celebrities I have known* [1891]
De Walden, Lord Howard *Earls Have Peacocks* [1992]
Dixon, Henry Hall [The Druid] *Scott and Sebright* [1862]
Donoghue, Stephen, *Just My Story* [1927]

Fairfax-Blakeborough, Jack *Turf Who's Who* [1932]
Fairfax-Blakeborough, Jack *Paddock Personalities* [1935]
Felstead S Theodore *Racing Romance* [1949]

Galtrey, Sidney *The Horse and the War* [1918]
Galtrey, Sidney *Memoirs of a Racing Journalist* [1934]
Godwin, John *Tom Coulthwaite, Wizard of the Turf* [1993]

Hamlyn, Geoffrey Hamlyn *My Sixty Years in the Ring* [1994]
Hislop, John *Hardly a Jockey* [1993]
Humphris, EM *The Life of Fred Archer* [1923]

Lambton, Hon George *Men and Horses I have Known* [1924]
Lawrence, Richard *The Rise and Fall of Tenby Races* [2003]

Marsh, Richard *A Trainer to two Kings* [1925]
Mortimer, Roger; Onslow, Richard and Willett, Peter:
Biographical Encyclopaedia of British Flat Racing [1978]
Munnings, Sir Alfred *The Second Burst* [1951]

Onslow, Richard *Captain Mac-Hell* [1999]
Orchard, Vincent *Tattersalls* [1953]

Paget, Guy *The History of the Althorp and Pytchley Hunt* [1937]
Pearce, Edward [editor] *The Diaries of Charles Greville* [2005]
Pope, Michael *All Such Fun* [1992]
Porter, John *Kingsclere* [1896]

Ramsden, Caroline *Ladies in Racing* [1973]
Richards, Sir Gordon *My Story* [1955]

Sievier, Robert Standish *The Autobiography* [1906]
Smith, Eph *Riding To Win* [1968]

Tanner, Michael *Pretty Polly* [1987]
Tanner, Michael *Teleprompter and Co* [1986]
'Thormanby' *Kings of the Turf* [1898]
Timeform, *Racehorses of* [from 1948]

Watson, Alfred ET *Galicia, Her Forbears and her Offspring* [1915]
Welcome, John *Fred Archer* [1967]
Welcome, John *Neck or Nothing* [1970]
Weston, Tommy *My Racing Life* [1952]
Willett, Peter *The Story of Tattersalls* [1987]
Willett, Peter *Dick Hern* [2000]
Wright, Howard *Bull* [1995]

Index